REVISIONING MISSION:

THE

FUTURE

OF

CATHOLIC
HIGHER
EDUCATION

JOHN RICHARD WILCOX, PH.D.

WITH

JENNIFER ANNE LINDHOLM, PH.D.
AND SUZANNE DALE WILCOX, ED.D.

The Oxherding illustrations are reprinted by permission of Tuttle Publishing, copyright 1957, 1985, from *Zen Flesh Zen Bones*, compiled by Paul Reps and Nyogen Senzaki. The Ten Oxherding illustrations are drawn by Tomichiro Tokuriki.

Lines from *Riding the Ox Home*, by John Daido Loori and Kazuki Tanahashi, are reprinted by permission of Shambala Publications, copyright 2002.

ISBN: 1478194251

ISBN-13: 9781478194255

Library of Congress Control Number: 2012921553
CreateSpace Independent Publishing Platform
North Charleston, South Carolina

This work is dedicated to
Brother Thomas Scanlan, FSC, PhD,
President Emeritus, Manhattan College,
and
Dr. Brennan O'Donnell, President, Manhattan College,
without whose support this book would not have been written,
and to
Dr. Michael Galligan-Stierle, President and CEO,
and the members of the Association of Catholic Colleges and Universities,
for whom this book has been written.

CONTENTS

FOREWORD

A key element in strengthening and preserving mission in Catholic higher education is a faculty that embraces and embodies the institution's mission. *Revisioning Mission* aspires to elucidate a comprehensive way in which Catholic culture can be robust, dynamic, and persistent in a college or university setting. Dr. John Wilcox's book provides Catholic higher education faculty and administrators with another significant tool to accomplish the complex task of incarnating *Ex corde Ecclesiae*'s claim that for a Catholic university to be "both a university and Catholic, it must be both a community of scholars representing various branches of human knowledge, and an academic institution in which Catholicism is vitally present and operative" (ECE, para. 14). In this work, Dr. Wilcox has provided a clearly written and practical methodology for implementing and cultivating a Mission Community. And, in so doing, he confronts the tendency in academic culture today that often promotes the fragmentation of work and spirit.

Building upon his first book, *Enhancing Religious Identity: Best Practices from Catholic Campuses* (coedited with Irene King), as well as on the work of other scholars in the field such as Philip Gleason, Melanie Morey and John Piderit, and John Haughey, Dr. Wilcox recognizes that Catholic identity is disingenuous unless truth-seeking, whole-making, and ethos are integrated across the campus. The Mission Community is one response to the call to create such integration.

Revisioning Mission sets out to educate new faculty through a series of continuing education opportunities, including the option to join a Mission Community. The innovative concept of the Mission Community speaks to the desire within us to find unity between our spiritual selves and our professional and academic lives and, in the process, sustains the larger mission and culture of the university. Dr. Wilcox acknowledges the special responsibility each member of the university community has to be a living exemplar of such unity, which is more easily achieved together in a Mission Community.

I applaud Dr. Wilcox's presentation of concrete mission integration options that will enhance the academic and faith-based worldview essential at Catholic higher education institutions. This text provides rich and abundant options for the mission and ministry team, and the academic dean, to consider as they facilitate the development of new faculty hires. Ultimately, Catholic colleges and universities offer to their students and society a unique and transformative way of proceeding, one that is grounded in values, virtues, and transcendence. Dr. Wilcox gives the Catholic higher education community a practical mechanism that will provide a living endowment for future generations.

Michael Galligan-Stierle, Ph.D.
President and CEO
Association of Catholic Colleges and Universities

PREFACE

Over the past twenty-five years, I have become increasingly concerned about the future of Catholic higher education. I have concluded that the most critical challenge is the transfer of leadership from the founding religious congregation to lay people. Such a transfer is already taking place at many Catholic universities. * However, lay leaders must see themselves, as the De La Salle Christian Brothers would say, working "together and in association" with the founding congregation.

Some institutions have Sponsorship Covenants, which are moral agreements between the board of trustees and the congregation intended to ensure the future of Catholic culture and the religious heritage of the founders. While a covenant is an important first step, there is a long road to be traveled not only in preserving the fruits of the past, but also in nurturing a robust and dynamic Catholic institution as it moves through the twenty-first century. I have often asked what is required now in order to render the future less obscure and uncertain. There are two requirements that I believe are essential: education of the mind and formation of the heart.

Education of the mind addresses the lack of knowledge and understanding that is prevalent at all levels of Catholic higher education. The administration, faculty, and staff of Catholic universities are ethnically and racially diverse men and women, representing the full range of human belief, from secular humanism to the most devout faith in established religion. Their perceptions of

Catholicism and Catholic education are a function of their journey through life, beginning with place of birth, upbringing, and education, and encompassing political and religious conviction. They are affiliated by choice or by circumstance with a worldwide religious enterprise and the mission of the Catholic Church embodied in the culture and heritage of their workplace. The vision and mission of their particular institution are not well understood and prevent all too many administrators, faculty, and staff from merging their personal commitment to teaching and learning with the goals of Catholic education in their university.

Formation of the heart encourages thinking deeply and living contemplatively. In this light, the university invites each affiliated person to begin a journey of education and understanding which, it is hoped, will lead to an embrace of the university's vision and mission, internalization of its values, and a commitment to participate in leading the Catholic university into the future with its culture and heritage flourishing. Of course, the mystery of each life's journey precludes the assumption that all will accept this challenge in identical ways, or uniformly follow the road I lay out here. Some will be excellent educators in their disciplines, but not particularly interested in the "more" of the university. Others will integrate aspects of the Catholic intellectual life, especially social justice thought, into the curriculum. Another group will identify their work with their life and see it as a calling or a ministry, while still others will go even further and assume a leadership role in Catholic education. It is my hope that the universities are populated by individuals who see themselves as on a personal journey, not just working at a job, and who will therefore assume the different roles described in *Revisioning Mission.*

This book has been written primarily to explain the central tenets of the Catholic university to new hires, but it is also a resource for all who work in Catholic universities. I believe that even many longtime administrators, faculty, and staff have had few opportunities to ask the many questions that have arisen in their minds, or to engage in conversations in which those questions can be answered with knowledge and insight.

Catholic institutions are distinctive and value-laden. When a professor signs her or his contract, the rights and responsibilities of the educator and the university are clearly spelled out. The agreement is a legal document. But there is another dimension to the agreement, one that goes beyond what is legally binding. Each new hire, whether an administrator, professor, or staff member, is implicitly invited to support the vision and mission of this distinctive educational institution.

My deepest wish is to make this invitation explicit. My goal is to see a structure arise—a Mission Community—composed of lay people working in concert with the founding congregation in common commitment to Catholic higher education. If the congregation has been the historical living endowment, this new entity, the Mission Community, will be the new living endowment. This revisioning of mission as a partnership is the first step in securing the future of Catholic higher education.

Acknowledgments

Fostering the continuity and growth of Catholic higher education has been my passion over the last twenty-five years of my calling to the role of Catholic educator. My career has brought me the simple joy of being able to put deeply held convictions into print and the consolation of knowing many administrators, faculty, and staff, both at Manhattan College and at other Catholic institutions, who share my passion. Most of all, it has brought me the satisfaction of having created a legacy that may contribute to the sustainability of the Catholic universities in the United States. That has been my greatest reward, but there would be no legacy and no reward without the presence of a community of like-minded persons who have helped me at every stage of the work.

First and foremost, I thank my wife, Dr. Suzanne Dale Wilcox, a spiritual director, who wrote the essay on adult spirituality, read many drafts of the book, and provided moral support throughout the months that it took to finish the book. I am still amazed at the extensive reading and reflection that Suzanne brought to her essay. Her work kept me going when I frequently found writing a challenge.

Dr. Jennifer Lindholm, director of the Spirituality in Higher Education project at the University of California, Los Angeles, contributed the essay on Catholic university students. Jennifer brought the expertise developed from her seven-year-long study of student and faculty spirituality to bear on her synopsis of the inner life of students who enter Catholic undergraduate programs, and of the spiritual life of their professors. Her encouragement also supported me in finishing the book.

Brother Thomas Scanlan, FSC, president emeritus of Manhattan College, and Brennan O'Donnell, president of Manhattan College, generously provided me with the time needed to complete the book. Without their support, this book would have taken far longer to write. I am also grateful to the many participants in the annual meetings of the Association of Catholic Colleges and Universities, especially the mission officers, and to the mission officers of the six Lasallian colleges and universities in the United States. Over the years, their support has contributed greatly to the development of this book.

Daniel S. Mulhall, my editor, consistently kept me on track and frequently raised that essential question: "Does this sentence, paragraph, or essay really express what you think or believe?" The additional editorial assistance of Emily DeHuff, James Gelarden, Mary Beth Baker, Caity Jones, and Kristen Holt-Browning has brought further clarity to the work. A special word of thanks to Katharina Riehle for the cover design. Charity Njau, graduate assistant in the Office of Mission at Manhattan College, went above and beyond her responsibilities, helping especially with footnote and bibliographical formatting.

Among the individuals to whom I am grateful for their support and feedback on the various essays are Miguel Campos, FSC, Dominic Colonna, Kristen Cuppek, Richard Emmerson, Michael

Galligan-Stierle, Lydia Gray, Lois Harr, Michael James, Thomas Johnson, FSC, William Mann, FSC, Frederick Mueller, FSC, Raymond Ricci, Gerard Rummery, FSC, the late Luke Salm, FSC, Sean Sammon, FMS, Andrew Scotnicki, Lorraine Sloma-Williams, Amy Surak, Carole Swain, Richard Tristano, James Wallace, FSC, and Alan Weyland.

Finally, I owe a special debt of gratitude to Michael Galligan-Stierle, president and CEO of the Association of Catholic Colleges and Universities, for writing the foreword to this book, and to John Haughey, SJ (senior fellow at the Woodstock Theological Center, Georgetown University), and Peter Steinfels (co-director of the Fordham Center on Religion and Culture) for crafting their insightful comments. Last, but not least, I am deeply grateful to Ronald Pasquariello, schoolmate, confrere, colleague, and a dear friend for more years than either of us would like to see in print. His careful reading of the text has been a special blessing for me.

The fact that I am in debt to these editors, colleagues, and friends does not mean that the reader can lay blame for any errors at their feet. If any are found, they are mine alone. Finally, if I have forgotten to mention by name a friend or a colleague who assisted me, please accept my apologies for the oversight, together with the warm appreciation that you know my heart remembers even when my mind forgets.

John R. Wilcox, Ph.D.
Professor Emeritus, Religious Studies, and Director, Center for Lasallian Studies

Manhattan College

Bronx, New York
February 13, 2012 (the thirtieth anniversary of the martyrdom of Brother James Miller, FSC, Guatemala, 1982)

PART ONE

STRUCTURE AND CONTENT OF THE PROGRAM: A HOW-TO-MANUAL

Overview of Part One

While most of this book consists of content essays corresponding to the various sessions which constitute the program, the book also functions as a "how-to-do-it" manual. Part One focuses on the "how to" aspect by providing guidelines for the startup of Revisioning Mission and by structuring a seven-session program for new faculty.

The intent, of course, is not to limit the Revisioning Mission (RM) program to one year or solely to new faculty. This book has been written with the whole university community as its ultimate audience, although the orientation session of the program is addressed to new faculty hires. Not only are they an important focus at a Catholic university, but primarily addressing only one specific group provides a more coherent focus for the book.

Although it is targeted mainly to those responsible for developing and leading the program, presidents and other members of the senior administration will also find Part One beneficial. For the Revisioning Mission program to be successful, it needs the full support and commitment of the administration at the highest level. They need to understand the preparation and financial investment that are required for an excellent program. Excellence

1

will generate an enthusiastic response from new hires, which will lead in turn to their participation in the Mission Community (MC), one of the goals of the orientation and of the program as a whole.

The following sections present an overview of the purpose and content of the program, a précis of the orientation, and of each of the six sessions during the academic year. The next section details the process that will bring the RM program to life. The remaining sections address practical concerns as well as philosophical dimensions that will enrich the entire program during the course of the year.

Overview of the Revisioning Mission Program

Purpose of the Program

Revisioning Mission is a faculty development initiative for new hires that seeks to create a culture of hospitality, a sense of comfort and belonging, and an environment of respect and listening in which responses to questions are provided quickly and the resolution of problems is achieved promptly. The program conveys a message about the type of community a Catholic university seeks to create. RM will be conducted over the course of seven sessions, with new faculty participating in an orientation session before the start of the academic year and in three two-hour discussion sessions in both the fall and spring semesters. These discussions are usually followed by a reception to help build a sense of community among participants. RM is neither a means of indoctrinating nor of proselytizing.

The program has two goals. The first is to educate new faculty with regard to the life and mission of a Catholic university. The university has a moral obligation to explain these points in some detail to newly hired professors. Much of the confusion faculty feel about the institution stems from a knowledge vacuum, because many hires are not well-informed Catholics or are of another or no religious persuasion. No one can expect these individuals to feel at home in an environment about which they know very little. Moreover, an invitation to join the Mission Community will fall on deaf ears if there is ignorance about the university's position as a Catholic institution as transmitted by the founding congregation.

The second goal is to develop a Mission Community composed of new hires who respond, along with other faculty, administrators, and staff, to an invitation to join those already committed to preserving and enhancing the Catholic culture and religious heritage of the founding congregation, as the university continues its journey through the twenty-first century.

A Mission Community is not only a vision to which the university should aspire; it is an action plan to engage new hires now, not at some distant time in the future. Essay Six in Part Two addresses this topic in detail. Here I provide only a brief explanation of what an MC is and why it is important.

Mission Communities are made up of members of the faculty, administration, and staff who have become immersed in the knowledge and the spirit of the university and its mission. As a result, the MC becomes a dynamic "living endowment" of the founding congregation and lay partners attracted by and freely committed to the university's place in Catholic higher education. It is a group that people join voluntarily, and it is made up of individuals from the diverse divisions within the university. Members need not be Catholic, but they should understand and support the Catholic culture and congregational heritage of the university.

Outline of Program Content and Goals

Orientation prior to first day of class: "The Faculty Learning Community: New Hires and Beyond."

Learnings: a culture of care and respect, need for community, development of networks, mentors, balancing professional and private life.

Session One: "The Catholic Culture of the University: A Work in Progress."

Learnings: distinctiveness, diversity, worldview, history, Catholic church/university, and cultural characteristics.

Session Two: "Students at Catholic Universities: Their Spiritual Development."

Learnings: profile, attitudes, values, aspirations, spirituality of students and faculty.

Session Three: "The Spiritual Journey: Wayfaring at the University." *Learnings*: universality of the quest, search for meaning and purpose, transcendence.

Session Four: "The Catholic Intellectual Life: A Worldview for the Curriculum."

Learnings: the worldview of CIL and examples from literature, philosophy, science, and other fields.

Session Five: "The Religious Heritage of the Founding Congregation: A Living Endowment."

Learnings: the founding story, values, history, mission, commonalities with lay people, case study.

Session Six: "The Mission Community: A New Living Endowment."

Learnings: importance of congregational and lay leadership, Mission Community open to all, the spiritual journey reconceived.

Overview of Orientation

Goals of the Orientation Session

The goals of the "Faculty Learning Community" orientation session are twofold: first, to welcome and support the faculty from the time they sign a contract, especially when they begin to adjust to their position on campus; and second, to create a faculty learning community (FLC) in which new hires feel comfortable and develop a comprehensive knowledge base about the university.

The essay on faculty learning communities in Part Two, "Faculty Learning Communities: New Hires and Beyond," will present a more detailed picture of the FLC. As we shall see, a faculty learning community presents a secular template or framework for engaging new faculty. The FLC model will be the framework for each of the RM sessions. The learning community will be the appropriate venue for a discussion of the larger culture in which it gathers and will facilitate acclimation into that culture.

You will note that I have described the FLC as a "secular" template, and I have done so intentionally. It would be inappropriate to call it a Mission Community or a "Dominican," "Franciscan," or "Mercy" learning community. A religious congregation's appellation would clearly send the wrong message at the beginning of a faculty member's journey through a first-year program.

Faculty learning communities are "cohort-based learning communities" that are created to "address the teaching, learning, and developmental needs of an important cohort of faculty or staff that has been particularly affected by the isolation, fragmentation, stress, neglect, or chilly climate in the academy" (Cox, 2008, p. 7). The faculty member's first year on a new campus is usually one of moving in, settling down, and meeting colleagues. In this context, the work of developing syllabi and teaching can be overwhelming, even with support from the chair and the department. Meeting on a regular basis with colleagues during the first year provides a setting in which to discuss the challenges and opportunities facing the new hire. The camaraderie and learning that such a supportive program offers will ease some of the burdens of the first year. An FLC provides an opportunity for faculty to share their experiences, have their questions answered, develop networking, enrich pedagogy, discuss research with one another and with senior faculty, and speak with administrators. The year should result in the development of an individual strategic plan leading to tenure. The FLC also provides the foundation upon which community and leadership will develop. In addition, the new hires will begin to develop a network among themselves and with the senior faculty who are participating in RM in their role as mentors.

Preparing for the Faculty Learning Community on Campus

Introducing an FLC on any campus is very frequently an experiment in interdepartmental collaboration and faculty collegiality that is only now on the radar of many public, private, Catholic, and other religiously affiliated universities. This challenge is further complicated because the proposed year-long Revisioning Mission program, if it is be effective, requires the participation of all newly hired faculty.

A Catholic university has a moral obligation to introduce all new faculty members into the culture, spirituality, intellectual life, the religious heritage of the founding congregation, and the aspirations of Catholic higher education. Directly related to this obligation is my conviction that participation should be a mandatory condition of hire. The program will provide a shared knowledge base among a diverse group of new hires who have a need to know and a right to know how and why Catholic universities are different from secular public and private institutions.

Time spent on development of the FLC is critical to the success of this initiative at Catholic universities. The Miami University of Ohio FLC program offers the following caveat: "Communities do not appeal to everyone." (Cox, M. D., 2009). This sobering aspect of academe and the culture of American individualism must be taken into account in the planning and presentation of an orientation that is a condition of hire. At the same time, we must keep in mind a yearning for community on the part of Generation X hires. The tension between individualism and the thirst for community must be addressed. I believe that making the first-year program mandatory and other mission-related programs invitational resolves the tension to some degree.

This caution is especially important in the context of Catholic university life, about which there are already preconceptions, caricatures, and erroneous convictions. Furthermore, a number of administrators and tenured faculty will, without doubt, have misgivings about the program and may undermine its credibility among the newly hired. Transparency is also critical to retention because the administration and faculty are the background music (or noise) that will enhance (or weaken) acceptance on the part of the newly hired.

Finally, there is a great deal at stake in proposing the FLC as the organizing principle in the education of new hires or any other sector of the university. "FLCs can profoundly affect campus culture and may represent a major institutional change. Thus, the institution's approach to managing change in general must be taken into account when considering whether and how to establish an FLC on campus" (Shulman, G. M., Cox, M., & Richlin, L. 2004, 42)

According to Shulman, et al., (2004), important questions must be addressed before establishing an FLC. First, will there be a strategy for helping the campus community, particularly those at the levers of power, see the value of a program that educates new faculty about the foundation of the mission: the Catholic culture and religious heritage of the founding congregation? Will the university's administration give the support needed for the program to succeed? "Establishing an FLC program is like moving a string. If you push the string it may move but will likely bunch up. The 'pull through' process involves leading people by permitting them to have influence from the beginning. . . . Thus, the challenge for campus leaders is to devise an implementation strategy that pulls people toward voluntary Faculty Learning Community acceptance." (p. 44-45). Without clear, positive support for the initiative by administrators and other campus leaders, Shulman, et al. recommend putting the project on hold.

They also note that, while one person may direct the program, an implementation team will be necessary because of the need for mentoring new faculty, addressing logistical issues, and recruiting speakers. "A strategically appointed FLC implementation team has significant advantages over an individual or a weak committee that lacks the time or credibility to convince others" (p. 43). Such a team should consist of individuals who have sufficiently high position, power, diverse viewpoints, informal influence and power, and are experienced leaders.

Another key question is, what vision guides learning in this faculty community? "An effective vision will make it abundantly clear what the purpose of the FLC is and provide guidance for making it part of the campus culture" (Shulman et al., p. 43). The vision in this case is an outcome of an ongoing transformation: the future of Catholic higher education is now primarily in the hands of lay people working collaboratively with the founding religious community.

Here is an example of a vision statement that promotes RM:

> *An Informed Intellect and a Committed Heart*
> The graduates of [this Catholic university] acquire intellectual expertise in the liberal arts and a chosen major, as well as achieve affective commitment to the common good, the global community, personal integrity, and openness to all religious traditions, particularly Catholicism. As the same time, the Catholic culture and the heritage of the founding religious congregation provide the worldview, but always in dialogue with other worldviews, whereby the university gives meaning to reality, which in turn gives rise to the institution's values ("those aspects of university life that are highly prized and acted upon") and principles (norms or criteria for action), all of which are the foundation of the Vision and accomplished as the Mission.
> (John R. Wilcox)

Another important question to be addressed is, how will the FLC be communicated to the university community? Good planning will lead to effective communication. There are three "visions" that require both planning and excellence in order to communicate effectively: First, the university's vision, as in the above example. Second, the vision for RM: "New hires and others committed to the future of the Catholic university." Third, the vision for the

FLC: "A cohort of new hires mutually supportive of one another and who are developing as professors in a university characterized by a culture of respectfulness, attentiveness, and assistance."

At the end of the process leading to the approval of the FLC, everyone on campus should know and understand the university's vision and that of Revisioning Mission, see the importance of learning communities, and be eager to begin the conversations. Furthermore, "dialogue about the FLC is more persuasive than a monologue, so it is important to engage the key stakeholders in two-way conversations in order to build widespread commitment to the program" (Shulman, et al., p. 43-44).

How will the program leaders demonstrate quickly that the project is workable and beneficial to the new hires and to the university? In other words, does the program respond in a timely manner to the fundamental concerns and perennial needs of new faculty? Linking each person to a mentor and giving careful attention to both pedagogical and scholarly concerns should also create a positive regard for the program. The FLC will have something that other faculty and administrators at the university do not usually have: an interdisciplinary, interschool, intentional community that has a great deal in common in terms of needs and aspirations, along with the expected goodwill and support of the larger university community.

The Catholic university affirms the dignity and respect owed the individual—not as an isolated person, but within the community. These are foundational principles that these learning communities build upon from the outset. Respect and community demand that the most immediate concerns of new hires be addressed promptly. With that task taken to heart, the other critical issues of RM can assume their place of importance.

We respond best when we have a transcendent goal, as in the university's vision statement; a clear road map with destinations and intended results, as in RM; and markers to establish yearly benchmarks for and measurements of the progress being made, as in formative and summative assessments of outcomes. The most meaningful immediate results will "trickle down" to the department level as participants discuss the learning community with their colleagues and demonstrate by their example the value of these communities. It will be difficult to dismiss the initiative if there is continual, near-term, positive feedback.

Hospitality and Preparedness for Excellence in Programming

Hospitality, which is discussed below, requires that time be set aside at the beginning of the orientation to help resolve outstanding problems. Doing so conveys an important message about the university and allows the participants to focus on the orientation itself. Needless to say, cell phones and social media should not interfere with the session.

To ensure excellence, one more general guideline is in order. I would strongly suggest that the RM team read over the appropriate essay several days before this and subsequent meetings. There may be topics, issues, or questions that should be thought about and engaged with before the sessions. For instance, invite an expert on Catholic social teaching to participate, at the appropriate time, in the discussion on Catholicism and social justice. If there is one in the FLC, so much the better.

The FLC provides a context and format for ensuring that each meeting will also enhance community among new faculty hires. While developing community itself is the most important outcome of the first session, there are several topics in the essay on this subject in Part Two, Core Themes for the Sessions, that will help faculty understand the relationship between community and Catholic higher education. FLCs are tools for enhancing teaching, research, and curricular innovation as well as a multitude of other university projects or programs. They are used across the spectrum of American universities. However, we shall see that FLCs have an affinity with Catholic education in particular, because community is at the heart of Catholic social teaching and intellectual life more generally. Having said that, I want to reiterate that they are not "Catholic organizations" intent on bringing new hires around to a particular religious point of view.

As indicated above, the RM team will find the essay essential for structuring the FLC. There are assuredly resources in place on campus. The vast majority of Catholic institutions have mission officers and mission committees, a campus ministry team, and many administrators, faculty, staff, and students committed to the continuity of a vibrant Catholic university. I will use my own institution as an example. Manhattan College has a Vice President for Mission, a Director of Lasallian Studies, the Lasallian Education Committee, and the local community of Christian Brothers. As a result, there is also a cadre of graduates from several educational programs sponsored by the De La Salle Christian Brothers on the international, regional, and district levels, as well as "alumni" of Collegium, a summer colloquy on the Catholic intellectual life. Manhattan College's resources are replicated at other institutions as well.

Questions for discussion are included in or follow the essays in Part Two. Please choose the ones that will be most helpful to the group. Others may arise from the dynamics of a particular set of participants. I believe it is better to have too many possible questions than to have too few or none. Use them at your discretion. The following questions and suggestions may be helpful to the RM team as the members discuss the FLC session:

- Does the team have a common understanding of what constitutes an FLC and why it provides an important structure for the following sessions, especially the last one on the Mission Community?
- Review the university mission and vision statement, strategic plan, and the most recent self-study and accreditation report. The team should have a précis of each of these documents and should be prepared to integrate them into each session, especially into the first one on the FLC.
- Each team member should map out the next three years by developing a personal strategic plan. The team will then ask the new hires to do this exercise in

the first session. Reflection such as this will help the participants focus on the challenges and opportunities they face. The purpose of the exercise is similar to one of the goals in writing across the curriculum: "writing to learn." The personal strategic plan is an exercise in learning more about one's self and developing a sense of the immediate future. It is not meant to be a polished essay as in "writing to communicate."

Supporting Faculty Learning Communities for the Long Term

The faculty learning community provides a structure for RM over the course of the year. As a framework for faculty collaboration in research and problem solving, it has been utilized on a number of campuses, public and private secular institutions as well as religiously affiliated ones. As we have already seen, an FLC enhances the culture of a Catholic university because of the emphasis on community and the common good. The goal of RM is for the learning community to evolve into the Mission Community and for the latter to make use of many valuable aspects of an FLC.

However, once introduced on campus, an FLC can become a useful framework for committees of the university, problem-solving groups, collaborative research, and student learning. To identify group activities, committees, or the classroom as learning community conveys the image of equality—a "flat hierarchy,"[1] where mutuality and collaboration transform competition and individualism. In an FLC, a social network transforms the hub and spokes of typical meetings into a roundtable discussion where everyone has a dignified place and role. Eye contact replaces the view of a jacket, ears, and hairline in front of the student in class or faculty in large meetings. Opinions elicit respect because an FLC is not about one person having the right answer as opposed to a host of wrong answers. "Wrong!" is transformed into weaving a tapestry of oral contributions put forward by members without fear of being corrected or labeled. The freedom and level of comfort generated by sharing of insights demonstrates a high regard for each participant and creates insightful solutions to often complex challenges.

I can think of no more fitting tool to use in all areas of higher education.

Practically speaking, as RM evolves over the years, the leadership team should enlist internal or external FLC experts to bring the experience to a high level of excellence. At the same time, RM should engage academic leaders in the FLC experience with the goal of spreading the initiative beyond the new-hires program. Enlisting the support of learning centers on campus will also be an important strategy for activating FLCs in a number of projects throughout the university. Meeting with the principal investigators on research projects and presenting the FLC as an important methodology that enhances collaboration will also move the concept into an important area of the university. Finally, what at first seemed to be an instrumental activity—the FLC—has evolved in this program into an integral part of the Mission Community and then as an icon signifying fundamental characteristics of a Catholic educational endeavor: communities of learners transformed into responsible citizens committed to the common good.

Overview of the Six Sessions

Session One. The Catholic Culture of the University: A Work in Progress

Among the issues that tend to loom large for new faculty are adjusting to the culture of the university and understanding contemporary students. RM is designed so that the focus of the first session of the academic year will be on understanding the Catholic culture of the university and how the new hires fit within it. The contemporary student at Catholic universities will be addressed in Session Two.

The topic of the university's Catholic culture is of great importance because it goes to the heart of how the new hire (and the community as a whole) processes what he or she sees, hears, and reads about Catholic education and this university in particular. New hires bring preconceptions about the culture they have entered, and they find themselves immersed in a campus and classroom culture quite distinct from that of secular graduate programs or academic work in a secular university they may have attended.

Our shaping of the world around us is based on the complex processing of accumulated experiences in a variety of settings: gender, family life, religion, education, friends, career, relational commitments, life-changing events, and, at times, trauma. The irony is that as a result of this constant processing, we are not even aware of how these experiences shape our perception of everything around us. Continuing a journal during the session on Catholic culture will be a fruitful experience for the group, to the extent that participants are comfortable sharing their thoughts. The journal will also be valuable in each of the subsequent sessions and will present many opportunities for reflection on the first year at a Catholic university. (Who knows, perhaps there is a book in the making on the road to tenure.)

The shock of recognition rarely occurs unless there is an event, a person, or a competing culture, any of which can lead to the relativizing of much of what was always taken for granted. It is challenging enough to become an educator in the university. Doing so in a distinctively Catholic university, within the context of both the oldest university system and the oldest religious institution in Western civilization, is even more of a challenge.

Furthermore, the Catholic university has a moral obligation to explain itself as fully as possible. The reasons for the obligation are important. While it is a "right-to-know" issue, there also are more transcendent motives, such as hospitality to the stranger and support of the first-year professor's teaching. Hospitality and support will lead the new hire toward the conviction that he or she is cared about by the university. As a result of the program, the participant will gain contextual knowledge and deeper self-confidence. All of these strategies and characteristics are ultimately for the human flourishing of the students as well as the university community, but there is also a more fundamental motive for these strategies and characteristics. Simply put, in a Catholic university culture, God is the horizon toward which creation is moving. As a result, the Catholic culture of the university merits serious consideration early on in a revisioning-mission process.

The Catholic worldview serves as a heuristic for probing Catholic university culture. Likewise, we will probe the meaning of cultural analysis in order to fully appreciate Catholic culture. From that standpoint we will discuss the dramatic changes that have taken place in the Church and in higher education, which is a reflection of, but distinct from, the Church itself.

Moreover, Catholic university culture is organically connected to the Catholic Church. Who is welcome in this Catholic culture? Is it meant to embrace a multiethnic, multireligious, and nonreligious faculty, staff, and administration? Is this culture nondiscriminatory concerning sexual orientation? These are among the questions to be addressed. Other issues of importance to university culture are the global reach of Catholicism and the rise of Catholic evangelicalism. A commitment to the poor is not simply a dimension of the global reach of the Church. A "fundamental option for the poor" characterizes Catholic social teaching and has had a great impact on Catholic higher education in terms of curriculum and student life. The culture and values of the university reflect a concern for the common good. As a result, Catholic higher education is countercultural to American individualism. The resulting cultural tension will also be investigated.

Because of its countercultural stance, feeling at ease in a Catholic institution may be a challenge for faculty coming from secular private or public undergraduate and/or graduate programs. Yet for hires with little or no background in Catholic education, their appointment may have the elements of a liminal experience, a crossing into a new and unfamiliar world.[2] Many will be entering what is for them the uncharted domain of an educational community that traces its roots to the beginnings of higher education in Western Europe in the monasteries and to the first degree-granting university founded in 1088 at Bologna and the second at Paris in 1150. Hopefully, the themes of this year will put new faculty on a path leading to new insights and a fuller understanding of Catholic culture and education. In addition, teaching is experienced as a vocation by new hires at various times in their career; this, too, will be discussed during the program.

Session Two. Students at Catholic Universities: Their Spiritual Development

How much do faculty members know about, and how well do they understand, the students they teach? Are they well read in the literature of student life and development, and do they understand the culture that forms their students? Catholic universities that regard the individual student as a creature of God should have a thorough understanding of the emotional, spiritual, social, moral, and intellectual development of their students. Through RM, faculty will develop a high degree of sensitivity to students and their world.

During this session, the FLC will discuss Essay Two, "Students at Catholic Universities: Their Spiritual Development." The book on which the essay is based, *Cultivating the Spirit: How College Can Enhance Students' Inner Lives* (2010), by Alexander W. Astin, Helen S. Astin, and Jennifer A. Lindholm, is a valuable resource for all faculty interested in student spirituality. The book itself is a synthesis of two wide-ranging surveys: "Spirituality in Higher Education: A National Study of College Students' Search for Meaning and Purpose," and the 2007 CSBV Longitudinal Follow-up Survey questionnaire.[3] In the academic year 2004–2005, the Higher Education Research Institute of UCLA (HERI) surveyed more than 65,000 faculty at 511 institutions nationwide. The faculty project resulted in a report: "Spirituality and the Professoriate: A National Study of Faculty Beliefs, Attitudes, and Behaviors."[4]

Session Three. The Spiritual Journey: Wayfaring at the University

This session will utilize the HERI study on the professoriate. The challenge addressed in this discussion is how the individual faculty member shares his or her own spiritual journey with students and assists them with their spiritual quest. The session investigates the phenomenon of religion and spirituality as they are distinguished from each other in the twenty-first century.

How do faculty perceive either of these categories? One's religious life or spirituality is located in the cognitive and affective realms, and they are important considerations for the interior and professional lives of the professoriate. However, it is a student concern as well, although it is very often a taboo subject among the faculty and to some extent among the students. The students are on as much of a journey in life as are the faculty. How do members of the faculty address the topics personally and with their students? How does each group understand religion and spirituality?

Participants in RM may find it helpful during the program to reflect on and devote part of their journal to spirituality. Such writing will prove an invaluable reflection aid as the program progresses. A "spirituality journal" is a place to write about one's experiences, contemplate their meaning, and interpret their importance on one's journey. As an academician, the new hire "professes" in any and all fields to the transcendent value of knowledge, truth, the heritage of civilizations, creative thinking about the present, and aspirations for a better future. Because the journal addresses deeply personal concerns about meaning and purpose in life, new hires may find it very valuable in their acclimation to the university. This optimism is based on the positive findings of the Higher Education Research Institute (UCLA) study on the spirituality of the professoriate, to be discussed further on in this session.

Essay Three, "The Spiritual Journey," provides a framework for understanding the spiritual search and will be a resource throughout RM. It is the soul of Revisioning Mission; without coming to terms with each person's spiritual journey, whether theistic or secular, it will be a challenge to fully understand a religiously grounded place of work. This essay, as well as suggested readings and spiritual practices, will engage participants in reflection on their own life journeys. The spiritual practices and soul presence of adults on the university campus may well hold great promise for the future transformation of its culture. Integrative learning, contemplative practice, collaborative teaching—all rest on a foundation that takes for granted the presence of professionals who live reflectively, who know themselves, and who see their contribution with the clarity of a vocational call.

Among the questions to be discussed are: How intrusive would it be to offer spiritual and soul-provocative opportunities on the campus? What would be the cumulative result of such practices, if freely chosen? This essay reviews the literature on adult spirituality and then uses a Buddhist allegory, the Ox-Herding Story, to outline some useful reading and practices in the spiritual realm. Given time to reflect on their own spiritual journey, new hires will be encouraged to share their quests with one another during a meeting framed by reflective music and poetry.

Session Four. The Catholic Intellectual Life: A Worldview for the Curriculum

The faculty learning community is bound together by a covenant of values. Among these values are a belief in the pursuit of learning, in the collective wisdom of the ages, and in critical assessment of ideas, as well as in the transformation and creation of knowledge through research and teaching. An appreciation of this covenant of values lays the groundwork for a study of the Catholic intellectual life in the fourth session.

Catholicism remains the historical foundation of Western intellectual life. Because of its role in the past and in the present, RM will review its history, highlighting examples of its role in virtually all dimensions of life in Europe until the Reformation, and continuing after that in the Catholic countries of Europe while still having an influence in the reformed countries.

As the participants will see, the Catholic intellectual heritage is a library of religious literature such as commentaries on the Hebrew and Christian scriptures, the lives of the saints, theological texts, and philosophical systems, as well as literary, artistic, musical, and architectural masterpieces. These elements are one part of the Catholic patrimony, spanning two thousand years and shared in varying degrees with other Christians, Jews, and Muslims. It is a heritage that is at one and the same time burnished with age, malleable through the centuries, and vitally alive as it shapes contemporary Catholic thought, especially social justice theory and practice. Catholic intellectual life is vibrant and dynamic.

Participants will also read contemporary literary works by authors such as Flannery O'Connor, Graham Greene, and Walker Percy, philosophical and theological texts by Charles Taylor, Alasdair MacIntrye, and Henri Nouwen, poetry by Thomas Merton, Mary Oliver, and Gerard Manley Hopkins, and will view films such as *Babette's Feast* or *As It Is in Heaven*, among other examples of interpreting life and the world around us.

The Catholic intellectual life, like Catholic culture, is informed by an epistemology—it suggests a certain way of imagining, thinking about, understanding, and interpreting the world. This epistemology emerges from the belief that since God created all that exists, and since that which God created is good, creation itself reflects the glory of God and bodies forth the divine presence. This theologically grounded epistemology is the result of an analogical imagination, the great sacramental principle that gives rise to the Catholic worldview, the interpretative lens or driving force of the Catholic intellectual life.[5] As Anne M. Clifford (2008) notes: "Thus, Catholicism provides visible reminders of the true possibilities of life and invites the raising of our spirits through the visual arts, architecture, music, poetry, and the stories of those who have lived bravely and deeply" (p. 368).

Mark Massa (2008) reflects on the centrality of this epistemology: "'The analogical imagination' [is] embraced by Catholicism—centered on a *sacramental* worldview that celebrates the material world as good, and a *mediated* understanding of God that is suspicious of religious individualism and untrammeled freedom" (p. 26). A Catholic imagination is nurtured by community, communal piety, and the claims of the heritage. Understanding the worldview or epistemology responsible for the diverse manifestations of the intellectual life sheds light on the framework within which it developed and continues to grow. As a result of this study, the FLC will have a better understanding of the Catholic intellectual life and will be prepared to bring that understanding to the classroom.

Session Five. The Religious Heritage of the Founding Congregation: A Living Endowment

One of the most tangible means of understanding the religious heritage of the founding congregation is by inviting religious members working at your university, and members of the congregation's leadership team, to participate in this fifth session. Doing so will bring a richness to the conversation that might otherwise be lacking. Their presence will give substance to the essay by making the historical connection between the community and your institution a living connection. The congregational participants will also be able to compare and contrast the evolution of their own group with the case study in the chapter.

Unless they have come to know members of the founding congregation, many new hires are puzzled by this group, which may no longer even be visible on campus. Yet these religious created an institution that is clearly different from secular universities and distinctive among other Catholic universities. Pioneering men or women, often a century or more ago, created a curriculum and campus life with value-added dimensions difficult to duplicate. The values originated in the story of their own founding as a religious congregation and the mission these groups took on. One cannot speak of these values, however, without adding the values of Catholicism in which the religious congregation was nourished.

In this session, a case study of the De La Salle Christian Brothers helps new hires understand the origins of the Catholic culture and the epistemology or worldview of these brothers, and from this study, to gain a better understanding of the congregation that gave life to their institution. With their founder, Saint John Baptist de La Salle, "together and by association," the De La Salle Christian Brothers responded to a dire need in the urban areas of seventeenth-century France: the Christian education of young boys—the children of the poor and the working poor, who were "far from salvation in this world and the next." Today, in the twenty-first century, that religious heritage has evolved to include seventy-one institutions of higher education including technical schools and universities, the majority of which are in Asia, Africa, Mexico, Central America, and South America. They bring to their endeavors a profound sense of individual dignity bestowed by God, the Creator, on each student, especially the most vulnerable, while providing skills for economic security, a sense of responsibility for the common good, and a Catholic vision of the human pilgrimage.

I use this congregation as a case study because the Brothers exemplify the religious heritage propelling Catholic universities, distinct though each is from the other. To narrate the history and heritage of several groups would go far beyond the scope of this text. The Christian Brothers provide a foil with which to understand the founding congregation on your own campus and to investigate the research already completed by these religious as a result of Vatican II. That fruitful undertaking will do for your RM group what it has done for many of the 79,000 men and women lay partners around the world who have studied the life, pedagogy, and spirituality of De La Salle and of the Brothers. I doubt that the RM group will have any difficulty locating congregational resources on campus or on the Internet.

The story of "origins" should be well received by new hires. In fact, this module may prove a turning point in the perception they have of Catholic higher education, and this for reasons that will be appealing to many, if not most, academics. Origins of the congregation may reveal a critical distance from the contemporary social context in which the founder lived, insight into Church polity and politics in the founding era, and, in most cases, a passionate concern by the founder and first followers for social justice on behalf of the most vulnerable, marginalized members of society. These are compelling introductions to the Catholic culture and religious heritage of the university. Culture and heritage in this case cannot be bifurcated. One does not exist without the other: a Dominican, Jesuit, Lasallian, or Mercy university cannot exist with integrity except within the context of Roman Catholicism.

Session Six. The Mission Community: A New Living Endowment

In this, the last session of the year, the faculty will be asked to assess the state of Catholic higher education based on their own experience as a faculty member and as a participant in RM. Does distinctiveness characterize this university? Is there a unique foundation providing continuity into the future? In brief, is there an enduring, value-added dimension that can be articulated, taught, acculturated, and, most importantly, assessed? [6] These questions will be part of a discussion between the leadership of the founding congregation, the administrators, and the RM faculty. As background for this discussion, the group will study the relationship between founding religious communities and their lay associates, partners, or colleagues, not all of whom are Catholic.

At the conclusion of the sixth session, the new hires will be invited to join the Mission Community. The Mission Community is composed of those who have committed themselves to preserving and enhancing the Catholic culture of the university and the religious heritage of the founding congregation. Those who become a part of the Mission Community will be called upon to carry the Catholic culture and religious heritage of the university into the future. The Mission Community will have a role in ensuring that the identity, culture, and charism of the university's founders remain influential and prevalent long after those founders no longer have a physical presence on campus. A full description of the Mission Community and its importance to the university is presented in Essay Six.

The essays in Part Two of *Revisioning Mission* provide background material explaining the theme of each session, with questions for discussion throughout, and suggested readings at the conclusion of each essay. Individual program directors will most likely wish to supplement the suggestions with other helpful material directly related to their university's mission and congregational heritage, and to the contemporary understanding of the university's distinctive charism (Ford, 2006, p 41). There is also nothing preventing a university from developing a Mission Community for students, especially with the number of service learning programs that are already thriving and can serve as a foundation for such a community.

Process

A Note on Preparation

To reiterate a point made earlier: Introduction of an innovative program such as this one depends on a significant amount of preparation. Advocates for its adoption will need to sound out individuals who control the "levers of power" in the institution. There are those appointed to do so, such as the president, the cabinet, academic deans, and those in other decanal roles, all of whom possess manifest power. There are also those without appointment who informally control levers of power because of seniority, status, or committee membership. They possess latent power and may, at times, have more influence than do those who are appointed.

In most discussions about a program such as this, openness to and communication with (or the lack thereof) all sectors will have an important impact on the proposed program. It helps if the Mission Group (see Step 1 below) knows the culture and has access to the designated leaders. This point cannot be emphasized enough. Well-attuned advocates will be able to sense the opportunities and challenges that both official and unofficial leaders perceive in the program. One-on-one conversations convey a sense of the project's importance to conversation partners. It may actually take a number of conversations with the same individuals to reach the tipping point leading to the next step. Having the support of a senior administrator goes a long way in moving this initiative forward.

The Phases

Phase One: Crucial First Steps

The following suggestions for developing the program are intended to save you time as you begin. If they are not applicable in your situation, ignore them. It is better to have a tentative path to follow and not need it, than to have no path at all and wander aimlessly and become discouraged. Program buy-in is also critical and, as experienced university administrators and faculty know well, the successful introduction of an innovative program such as this one depends on a significant amount of preparation.

Step 1: Convince administration of need for RM program.

In the steps discussed here, I am presuming the existence of a group of administrators, faculty, and staff who have joined together to ensure the future of their Catholic institution. Given the number of mission offices already established, this is not a far-fetched assumption. I will call these "concerned citizens" the Mission Group (not to be confused with the Mission Community described above). Although calling a meeting of an existing MG will be easy, constituting a Mission Group where none exists will be more challenging and will take more time. If you are an administrator, early buy-in by key faculty members is of crucial importance.

The first step is for the existing Mission Group (MG) to meet with the president and provost, the vice presidents of enrollment management and human resources, and the mission officer to make the case for a program designed to prepare and retain new hires. The meeting's desired outcome is for the president and senior administrators to support the proposal. It is also vital that the president agrees to fund exploratory work by the MG as an ad hoc committee. If there is no existing MG, then the mission officer should bring together a group of interested administrators, faculty, and staff and meet as above.

Be clear at this meeting that RM will not take on all retention responsibilities. The latter is also a concern of the provost, academic deans, department chairs, and directors of faculty development. I mention this to alert the RM program director to this broader university group that also has retention concerns, with the intent of encouraging linkage and mutual support wherever possible.

Step 2: Educate the Mission Group.

Once the group convenes and discusses the proposed program, the following three suggestions may help its deliberations:

1. Read and discuss *RM* and other recommended readings.

The MG committee should begin by reading *Revisioning Mission* and gaining a command of the program content as set forth in this book. Seek out an individual on the committee or at the university who will lead the group in discussion of those books, chapters, or articles suggested in each essay. This will be a procedure to follow throughout the program.

Recommended Additional Readings

The following works will clarify and reinforce the value of a group working on the RM project:

- Roth, Mark. (2011). Groups produce collective intelligence, study says. *Pittsburgh Post-Gazette.* Retrieved from http://www.post-gazette.com/pg/11010/1116833-115.stm.
- Surowiecki, James. (2004). *The wisdom of crowds.* New York: Anchor Books. Surowiecki presents convincing argument for working in groups. "The simplest way to get reliably good answers is just to ask the group each time" (p. 5). Surowiecki's book is not a panacea for decision-making; however, his words should remind RM advocates how important a committee is in determining "reliably good answers." Since the program is not a book club, the easiest path may be to have a person familiar with his argument, as well as with the readings below, summarize the main points in Surowiecki's text and that of others who provide helpful insights into the project. If there is an expert on these authors who is not yet involved in the project, do not hesitate to invite that individual to speak about the books described below. Doing so may win a convert.
- Gladwell, Malcolm. (2000). *The tipping point.* Boston: Little, Brown. *The Tipping Point* will also stir the committee's imagination. Gladwell's argument—"How Little Things Can Make a Big Difference"—will help the group see, through concrete examples, how significant

change can be brought about. For instance, Gladwell asks and answers the question, "Who are the 'Connectors, Mavens, and Salesmen' in your line of work?"

- Heath, Chip, and Heath, Dan. (2007). *Made to stick: Why some ideas survive and others die.* New York: Random House. Likewise, Chip Heath and Dan Heath offer guidelines for making an innovative program such as RM a success.

2. Gather data and organize a plan of action.

The mission officer or chair of the MG should prepare an initial SWOC analysis (strengths, weaknesses, opportunities, challenges) concerning the feasibility of an RM program on campus. Sending it to the MG prior to the first meeting will provide the group with a basis for discussion and plan of action. Your goal is an ongoing SWOC analysis by the group.

3. Convene focus groups and revise the SWOC as needed.

Prior to all meetings, distribute an agenda with the goals for the meeting clearly stated, along with the most recent one-page draft description of the project and a second page with the most current summary of the SWOC analysis. Ask for input from the MG concerning the agenda and goals prior to each meeting.

Next, solicit focus-group leaders and secretaries from MG. Recruit experts in training group leaders and set up training sessions to insure quality. Finally, develop the agenda for your focus groups, framing the questions for discussion in such a way that they can be easily compared across group notes.

Conduct focus-group meetings with faculty from the several divisions across campus to enhance the knowledge base for refining SWOC and for continuing or delaying the project. Balancing randomly chosen groups with targeted groups from specific categories of organizations or committees is important.

As a general rule throughout planning and execution of the program, always include members of the founding religious congregation. From the beginning of RM, communicate this practice to the congregational leadership and seek their support.

Focus Group Suggestions

- *Request a meeting with governing bodies* such as the president and cabinet, congregational leadership, student-life division, academic deans, university senate, faculty and staff councils, and other groups sui generis to your university.
- *Gather focus groups* from each sector, but also develop random groups from among administrators, staff, and faculty, devoting more time to faculty by meeting with several random faculty groups.
- *Ask to meet with the student government leaders* by obtaining a place on their regular meeting schedule, thereby assuring an audience. Student government is usually a stable organization even though the membership changes virtually every year. Student input is extremely valuable but student groups invariably change each year. Tapping into other student organizations will also facilitate conversation and publicize the Catholic culture and religious heritage of the founding congregation, as well as make the students aware of the Revisioning Mission initiative.
- *The office of campus ministry* keeps track of the spiritual and/or religious pulse of the student body. The staff should be enlisted in evaluating student perceptions of the Catholic culture and religious heritage. Their findings may be a catalyst for increasing ministry buy-in or by conveying a convincing sense of urgency regarding RM. The campus ministry director would be an obvious committee invitee.
- *The role of student participation* depends very much on the local situation and previous experience with student involvement on committees. However, seek out the students whose insights about the university are valuable, but who are not part of the manifest student network. They are known by other students, yet they are largely invisible to administrators and faculty. The one group that may know them well is the staff in the

student-life division. In that division there are personnel in residence life, commuter affairs, student activities, and counseling. Consultation with representatives from the university newspaper staff and other organizations, the membership of which includes other "movers and shakers" on campus, will be highly valuable in obtaining a variety of perspectives.

▪ *Alumni support will be important for the success of this effort.* The alumni office is in regular contact with those who know the university from the students' side of the classroom. Working with representatives of the alumni society, especially recent graduates, presents an opportunity for gathering rich insights. Involvement of this office as well as the college relations office will transform alumni complaints about deficiencies in Catholic culture and the religious heritage into accolades for what is guaranteed to be a critical university initiative.

▪ *Input from the board of trustees is essential.* One effective way of obtaining their input is to meet with board committees responsible for mission, Catholic culture, sponsorship relations with the founding congregation, and strategic planning. Usually board-committee chairs report to the full board. Disseminating the program to the full board will lead to insights from a broad group of leaders in the public and private sectors. Their buy-in will add to the social capital the committee is garnering. Involvement may also lead to education sessions on mission with the board itself.

▪ *Participation by the students, alumni, and board* in exploring the RM initiative may produce unforeseen results, such as a desire to be part of the Mission Community or to form parallel organizations.

Now that you have some familiarity with RM and have conducted several focus-group meetings, use the initial SWOC as a baseline. Building on the original SWOC analysis and subsequent ones, develop a new analysis based on the notes from the focus-group interviews and feedback from the MG. Presuming that strengths and opportunities outweigh the weaknesses and challenges, continue moving forward.

In balancing the positives and negatives, you will need to give greater weight to some than to others. For instance, having a new president and/or senior administration favorable to the initiative may weigh more heavily than if the administrators have been in these positions for a decade or more. And the existence of a faculty unionizing movement may be a greater challenge than faculty anxiety about the future of a Catholic university.

The Mission Group should regularly assess the outcomes of the focus groups. Waiting until all focus groups are concluded presents a daunting challenge in terms of synthesizing the results. Doing so regularly does not obviate the need for a final synthesis based on the interim ones.

Step 3: Have the institution name an RM program director.

For Revisioning Mission to work effectively, it needs a director, that is, a person appointed by the president or provost to oversee that its many pieces work together coherently. The director normally should be a senior administrator or a member of the tenured faculty in order to have the authority and clout to implement the program effectively. If a lesser-ranked administrator or faculty member is chosen, he or she must be clearly supported by a higher-ranking person. The director must also have financial and personnel resources, as well as the time necessary to carry the project forward. Ideally, there should be codirectors, one a lay person and the other from the religious congregation.

Phase Two: Buy-In

Step 4: Secure the support of administration and faculty.

The support of senior administrators is essential to the program's success. Keep this group informed and up to date on the new-hires initiative. Regularly ask for their comments and criticisms. Solicit a commitment from them to support the program.

Buy-in from key faculty members very early in the process is also a critical need for program success. While the social capital of faculty already committed to the RM vision is indispensable, individual meetings with "movers and shakers" who are on the fringe, outside the circle of supporters, or suspicious of all things Catholic are equally important to moving the project forward. Personal conversation with these leaders and respectful responses to their questions will invite more challenging questions and may even correct misunderstandings or dispel the image of a covert group seeking to drag the university back to a supposed "golden age" of Catholic higher education. Given the diversity within any university, there are certainly no guarantees of preventing ill will, but overcoming the resistance to a perceived "other" is frequently accomplished by warm, respectful conversation.

To reiterate, the success of this program requires the active knowledge and support of administrators and faculty, along with that of other decision-makers and persons with informal access to the levers of power. You should be aware of who, among administrators and faculty, has the ability to influence important policy decisions or initiatives. Obtaining buy-in from them is crucial.

Step 5: Secure the support of governing bodies.

In almost all cases, Catholic universities implementing RM would not need program approval by campus governing bodies such as a faculty council, university senate, or board of trustees. Consulting these groups and soliciting their support, however, has important benefits. Each group should know, in some depth, the goals of the program and the theme of each session. The program embodied in this book also has applicability across the campus. Because of widespread discussion and publicity, all divisions of the university will know about RM. The individual essays used as background reading for each session will be of interest to the community and will give a deeper insight into Catholicism and the founding congregation. Such widespread use, especially in group discussions, will bring the entire enterprise to a "tipping point" where RM becomes integrated into the university culture.

Seeking the approval of the board of trustees has similar important benefits. Full knowledge of the program promotes confidence that the university takes seriously its culture and heritage, thereby maintaining its educational mission and relationship with the Catholic Church and the founding congregation. Most important of all, their detailed knowledge of RM is a "teaching moment" from which may develop a desire to learn more about the topics covered in the program. Board involvement with the program could then lead to educational programs for the trustees themselves, and, as a result, strengthen the university's place in American Catholic education and in the larger universe of the Catholic Church.

It is my belief that RM will increase the determination of the university to move into the future as a Catholic institution—but in solidarity with all sectors, especially the academic division and its new hires. Support from such groups will facilitate long-term development of RM and foster broader use of the faculty learning communities among the departments and schools of the university. Most important, developing a culture of "revisioning mission" will create an environment in which it will be more likely to retain new hires after the one-year program ends.

Step 6: Gather program resources.

Every university has unique resources that can be drawn upon to make RM successful. Some key groups that should be included in the planning conversation as early as possible are:

1. Grants Office. You will gain goodwill if you have a funding proposal in the works to support RM, although the project should not depend on such a proposal. Bring the grants office into the project early on, because its staff will have important insights to bring to your work, and it will also make their work easier in developing proposals. Outside funding, in almost all cases, smooths the wheels of progress.

2. Public Relations Office. Meet with the public relations officer about the program as soon as possible. The PR office can help you develop a name for the Revisioning Mission initiative. The

name or acronym can be used in funding the project and helping to grow broad recognition for it, so that it becomes part of the *lingua franca* on campus. Organizing an "RM naming contest" among new hires, the marketing club, or perhaps even the entire campus by means of the student newspaper, email, Twitter, Facebook, and other forms of communication and social media will create curiosity, interest, and buy-in. A prize for the winning name or acronym always helps.

3. Campus "Go-To" People. Every campus has individuals who know virtually everyone and his or her talents. Tap these "connectors, mavens, and salespeople" (Gladwell, 2000, pp. 30-88) to help identify the talents of individuals who will be crucial to the success of RM. I am thinking particularly of potential Web site designers, webmasters, other IT experts, and the "invisible" supporters of Catholic education, among others.

Phase Three: Implementation

Step 7: Create the RM Implementation Team.

At this time a major transformation is about to take place. You are now ready to create the team of faculty and administrators who will be charged, along with the director or codirectors, with implementing RM on a daily basis. While this team could simply be the organizing committee in a new form, it is best if the implementation team includes new and diverse membership as well. The following are suggested steps for organizing this team:

- In order to keep the project front and center on campus and to make it work effectively, develop an implementation committee. The committee should be a multiethnic and multireligious group with representation of men and women, administrators, faculty, staff, and members of the founding congregation.

- Presuming the prior existence of a Mission Group, several members will more than likely become the core of the RM Team, but the director will also have to keep the project at a high level of visibility. This strategy will make it easier to attract other committee members. Having met with many individuals and groups over the preceding weeks, chances are that you will hear the same names repeated when discussing the committee makeup. If these individuals do not volunteer, by all means take the initiative and approach them personally.

- A letter of invitation to join the RM team should be extended from the president and the chief academic officer of the university community. The chair of the MG should draft the letter. Following the program explanation, indicate the openness of the invitation. A letter from senior administrators indicates their commitment to the program. Furthermore, a letter from the president and the chief academic officer to the university community formally announcing the program, as well as an invitation to join the RM team, will receive broad attention and support.

- Sending a campus-wide invitation to join the permanent RM team creates transparency and deflates suspicion. There will always be the "usual suspects" who will join, but other volunteers often stun the organizers because they are "sleepers" who are deeply concerned about the university's future but who usually do not say much in public.

- Faculty convocations are important venues for the president or provost to announce the program. An oral presentation conveys the importance of this initiative and allows for verbal nuances that will make RM inviting.

Step 8: Coordinate communication and community support.

Good communication is another key to a successful program. One of the tasks of the new team will be to put together a communication strategy and to develop the means to carry it out. The following are suggestions for creating that strategy through a communication campaign:

- Keeping the president, the congregational leadership, the provost, deans, and the faculty abreast of developments will reinforce support, or in the case of skeptics, may cause some changes of heart. Being enthusiastic and creating a sense of movement increases curiosity, interest, and credibility while also encouraging important formal and informal conversations in many areas: in the cabinet, with the executive committee of the trustees, at quarterly board meetings, as well as at congregational leadership meetings and province-wide assemblies.
- The student newspaper, other publications, campus email, and the university Web site facilitate frequent and widespread communications as well. An RM Web site with regular updating will also spread the word and keep other universities aware of the program. Creating the Web site should be one of the first tasks of the committee.
- Recruit colleagues and students proficient in the use of social media (e.g. the internal university Web site, blogs, Facebook, Twitter, and YouTube) to create interest and support for RM.
- Ask the president to send a congratulatory thank-you letter to those who have volunteered for the ad hoc MG and the RM team. Publicize the latter committee's purpose and its members to the university community. Include comments by the president and provost.

Effective Communication: Catalyst for a Powerful Program

With the assistance of the provost, academic deans, and tenured faculty, RM will create an environment that encourages collaboration on curriculum, research, scholarship, and grant writing. Faculty will be advised on all aspects of campus life, ranging from the mundane (duplicating tests, reimbursing professional expenses, locating buildings), to the academic (publishing benchmarks, collaborating on research, assessing student outcomes), to the social (making friends, developing networks, living in the university and local communities).

The actions prescribed in the above steps convey a powerful message about the university's concern for new members of the community. In addition, they serve to clarify the tenure process and to enhance acculturation into university life. By respecting the professional, scholarly, and day-to-day concerns of new hires, RM prepares them for the discussion of mission, culture, and heritage. New hires will be more willing to focus on the latter issues if the former ones are clearly addressed first.

To reiterate an essential point: To be effective, RM presumes the enthusiastic support of the administration and senior faculty. They must see the value of assisting new hires in order for the latter to experience a successful and fulfilling introduction to university life, even if several hires are already experienced faculty members. In this way, the program encourages retention and should lead current faculty, administrators, and staff to reaffirm their own commitment to the mission and values of the university by serving as guides, mentors, or program leaders.

Practical Concerns

Budget

Financial support is fundamental. Some expected costs are related to the release time necessary for a program director of senior enough status to be taken seriously, and the retention of sufficient support staff. The MG needs to develop a budget and to be conscious of the university's budget-process timeline. The payoff for this investment can be enormous: namely, a faculty committed to the mission and vision of the university and interested in becoming the university's future leaders.

Establishing good relations and effective communication with the grants office will be an important factor in securing help in seeking and writing grant proposals. The communications campaign itself will attract interest in raising funds through proposals to outside sources. Of course, the office for advancement must be kept in the loop in all efforts at external funding.

Format

As noted, the Revisioning Mission program consists of an orientation program before the start of the academic year, followed by six sessions during the course of the year. The six sessions are evenly divided between fall and spring semesters, with three meetings each term of two hours' duration, each followed by a reception. Care must also be given to the amount of reading suggested for each session and to using the readings for discussion. The success of the program depends on new hires having time to reflect on all aspects of their appointment. An orientation for a weekend each semester or for a single week prior to the beginning of the school year does not provide adequate time for faculty to reflect on the impact of day-to-day life in the classroom, on campus, and in personal life. Time, reflection, and discussion over the course of the year are essential if the university is to fulfill its moral obligation to new faculty. If a Catholic institution or any faith-based university claims a "value-added" quality, what would be more fitting in its culture than Revisioning Mission, a program of hospitality toward those who may spend the rest of their academic lives in this one university?

Revisioning Mission accommodates a variety of academic schedules. A monthly two-hour themed meeting can be woven into the fabric of each semester and organized around participant schedules. The chairs may assist in scheduling their teaching sections such that the new hires are all free from 4:00 p.m. through the early evening on one day of the week. Participants will also be asked to read assigned texts, and to keep a journal based on their classroom and campus experiences as well as on readings and discussions. In addition to the regular monthly meeting, new hires will receive individual assistance as needed during their first year.

At the conclusion of the sixth session, participants will have the opportunity to enter the Mission Community. The Mission Community is composed of those who have committed themselves to preserve and enhance the Catholic culture of the university and the religious heritage of the founding congregation. Presumably, there will be individuals from the several divisions of the university who have already formed or joined a Mission Community prior to the entrance of the first group of new hires.

Schedule

At the beginning of each meeting month, send the RM group the readings for the gathering. Attach a reading guide that provides background and an explanation of unfamiliar terminology, and emphasize the importance of the discussion questions that will facilitate a well-organized program. The RM team should note that John Ford's *Glossary of Theological Terms* is a handy reference book that each participant will appreciate receiving during the orientation (see "Recommended Readings for All Participants" at the end of Part One).

Invite participants to speak with the director if there are problems with the readings or if they need additional clarification. This may be the case with religious literature in general, with which new hires from lay backgrounds may not be familiar.

At the meeting itself, discussion is best guided by a facilitator who utilizes discussion questions located throughout each essay[7] and encourages participation by all. The director and the committee should strategize on how best to engage the group, but enlisting faculty with expertise in group discussion is helpful and invites their buy-in to the RM initiative.

Logistics

Years of experience in organizing meetings suggest that Thursday afternoon gatherings held in September, October, November, February, March, and April are the ideal time to schedule RM sessions. Choose a room with adequate space, comfortable chairs, and a table that comfortably seats all the members of the group. Once you find a meeting space that works well, reserve it for all your meetings during the year. Schedule two hours for the actual meeting, and if possible, follow that with a brief reception. Provide refreshments during the meeting but not a meal. A meal prolongs the meeting, a concern of many new faculty who wish to be home for dinner, to spend time with spouses and children, or to work on course preparation. Of course, a celebratory meal after the final session will usually be appropriate, but the group should be surveyed on this point.

Beginning and ending the meeting and reception on time is important. People have busy lives, and keeping to schedules will help participants know what their expected commitment will be throughout the year. From time to time, senior administrators and deans should be invited to join the group for the reception, but the RM team and the FLC need to judge when these invitations are timely.

As you plan your first-year program, also consider how you want to bring it to an end. Manhattan College concludes its program with a year-end retreat held at a conveniently located hotel or conference center. The retreat begins at noon and ends at noon the next day. The dates are usually the same each year: the Tuesday and Wednesday after graduation. The new faculty report that their twenty-four-hour, end-of-the-year retreat was of great value. Participants are quite appreciative that the university provides this opportunity to review the year, develop a group SWOC analysis, and convey their assessment to the provost and academic deans.

The university president should be encouraged to join the group for dinner or part of the morning session. While not always possible, having the president present conveys to these new faculty members their value to the university. Get the event on the president's calendar as soon as possible. You may even want to schedule the event around the president's calendar.

Whatever is decided, make sure that the RM group has the dates for all commitments at the beginning of the academic year so they can reserve the time accordingly. Make sure that the RM schedule is also shared with all chairs and deans so as to avoid as many conflicting meetings or events as possible.

Meals, retreats, and meeting rooms all cost money. If an off-campus retreat is not feasible, don't let that deter you; a well-planned on-campus retreat with ample time for personal reflection and sharing can serve the same ends.

Cohort Size and Effectiveness

According to two experts in group work, Irvin Yalom and Molyn Leszcz (2005), a target cohort of seven to eight persons is optimal, with acceptable outside limits of five to ten (pp. 292-294). If there are only a few new faculty hires in a given year, a small class of two or three could be a negative factor in the program. One solution would be to invite recent faculty hires to participate with the new ones in order to have a reasonably sized group. Alternatively, a separate program may be developed, perhaps more tailored to the needs of both new and more experienced personnel from other divisions.

Whatever it takes to develop a sense of community through shared learning, networking, and collegial support is the standard against which this program should be measured. RM thus brings to life the spirituality of care that is fundamental to the mission of the founding religious communities. For instance, Saint John Baptist de La Salle, the founder of the Brothers of the Christian Schools and a pedagogical pragmatist, frequently worked in collaboration with the first brothers—fledgling teachers all—to determine what worked and did not work in the classroom. These conversations eventually led to his writing *The Conduct of the Christian Schools* (1720, 1996). De La Salle knew about the "wisdom of crowds," even if he did not use that expression.

RM is therefore much more than a cluster of monthly sessions. It creates a collaborative culture in which new hires work together for mutual benefit, but ultimately and most importantly, for the students. This strategy is straightforward, yet it requires imagination and time on the part of the program director and the team or steering committee. For instance, during the spring term of

RM, concerns about research, scholarship, or course development should be discussed in the context of university practice in these areas. Faculty mentors play an important role in these discussions.

Mentors

Recruiting faculty mentors is a challenging task, and one that is closely connected to obtaining buy-in from the university community. Ideally, there should be a one-on-one mentoring protocol, with the tally of senior faculty needed dependent on the size of each group of new hires. Personal meetings allow for more freedom in discussion and a closer bond between both parties. Practically speaking, having one mentor per hire will make scheduling of meetings easier than if the mentor meets with a group. Mentoring should continue beyond the program for some time, but as the new hires become acculturated to the university, the role of the mentor will diminish to some extent.

Mentoring presupposes a commitment to RM by tenured-track faculty. It also presupposes obtaining support from the academic deans and department chairs, as mentioned in Phase One (Crucial First Steps) above. Discussing RM at departmental meetings is time-consuming, but it is essential if buy-in is to be achieved. These meetings provide an opportunity to accurately describe the program. Developing a commitment to RM and openness to mentoring by tenured faculty will take a great deal of time—perhaps a year, if not longer.

Philosophical Concerns

Hospitality

Academics on the RM team will remember what it was like to sign that first contract. There was surely a sigh of relief after months and even years of searching for a position. That sigh was quickly supplanted, however, by the gasp of uncertainty about the place of employment where you would spend a good deal of the coming year and, hopefully, beyond the spring semester. Concerns about relocation, housing, family expectations, moving, leave-taking from colleagues and friends, teaching new courses, keeping the ever-pressing research agenda intact, meeting the department chair and new colleagues, and so many more challenges had to be dealt with, down to the level of locating one's office. Even if the new hire is an experienced faculty member from another institution, he or she brings a similar list, and will feel the anxiety and distraction shared by all newcomers.

What, then, is hospitality to these new hires? This virtue has ancient spiritual roots in Western civilization, playing an important role in monastery life. In monasticism, hospitality has perdured as a distinguishing characteristic of all monasteries, which were the only "inns" in medieval Europe and remain recognized throughout the world to this day as places of warmth, rest, and prayer. Benedict (2004) wrote in his Rule that "any guest who happens to arrive at the monastery should be received just as we would receive Christ himself" (p. 123). Benedict sought respect and deference in the monks' treatment of travelers. The superior should wash the feet of the visitors, with the community participating in this ritual (53.4). "The greatest care should be taken to give a warm reception to the poor and to pilgrims, because it is in them above all others that Christ is welcomed" (p. 123).

These directives are the benchmark for understanding hospitality in a Catholic university. It is a quality that reaches beyond Benedict's guest. Regardless of status or rank, every member of the university community, whether a senior professor or a brand-new assistant, professor is to be treated as if he or she were Christ. Such hospitality should be a feature of a Catholic institution. Although foot washing is not necessary today, special attention to the newcomer is the equal of the monastic attitude toward the newly arrived guest. Likewise, those in the university—the administrators, faculty, staff, and especially the students who might be most vulnerable economically, intellectually, or socially—should receive the warm reception that monks are to offer to the poor and pilgrims.

Practically speaking, hospitality should be embodied in the preparatory work of the RM team. The first gathering should be well thought out and have a solid agenda of consequential topics that is worked through with a certain rigor; it should be of great consequence. You want these new faculty members to be part of RM at the conclusion of the year, and you have to demonstrate the program's importance, beginning with the first meeting, in order to attain that goal. Your enthusiasm for their new role in this university community will be a good down payment toward the success of the program. The RM director and team are going to play a significant role in the faculty's lives over the coming years, helping them settle in and get comfortable with their new "home." As familiar faces, committee members will become regular contacts during other campus events and meetings.

Hospitality sets the tone of each RM meeting. While an "ice breaker" may not always be appropriate, warmth and attentiveness and a full response to all the questions and concerns are essential elements of hospitality. Questions that cannot be immediately answered can be written down and responded to at a later date.

Presume that the new hires do not know each other or members of the RM Team. Provide name tags for everyone (both to wear and to be placed on the table for ready reference) and focus the first part of the opening session around introductions. Besides helping people to put names and history to faces, this activity also helps to establish a feeling of comfort and ease among the group. Sharing personal stories will do this better than reciting academic achievements and research awards—although that is an important part of the conversation as well. Take the new hires' accomplishments seriously, congratulate them on their successes, and ask friendly questions to encourage in-depth conversations. Such gentle RM team leadership will establish a sense of welcome, let people know that what they have to say is valued, and set the tone for all future sessions.

Don't try to be overly familiar or overly serious. Too much humor or any irony or sarcasm can create dissonance and puzzlement, especially if these new faculty are from diverse locations nationally and internationally. Help those individuals who may need assistance with English as a second language. If there are new faculty whose English may be weak, invite a more experienced person from on or off campus who is sufficiently fluent in both the native language and English to accompany him or her, at least to the first meeting.

The most important role of the discussion leader is that of active listener, who maintains eye contact, encourages questions, and exudes ready acceptance. While getting through the agenda is important, how the leader does this is very important as well. The new hires need to feel comfortable in this group; they need to know that they are being understood and that they are not being judged or evaluated. Put them at ease by conveying complete acceptance of them as they are and helping them to see that everything will work out in time.

Another way to show hospitality is to provide an explanation of the nature and purpose of Revisioning Mission. Explain why it was created and made mandatory in the first year. Explain that the meetings will provide them with a knowledge base about Catholic universities in general and this one in particular. Clarifying the program's purpose will answer any questions or misconceptions they may have. Be positive in the presentation about this initiative to bring the Catholic university into and through the twenty-first century as a vibrant, powerful, and distinctive educational experience for the students and the faculty.

Make sure that the new hires understand that even though the RM program is mandatory, you hope that their experience will lead them to continue in other, similar programs and that, as a result of what they have come to know and feel about the university, their students, and their colleagues, they will be inclined to assume responsibility for the future of Catholic higher education.

Inclusiveness

Religion, spirituality, and worldview are topics that must be approached with sensitivity. The program director might consider having a conversation with each participant, prior to the first group meeting in the fall, about his or her religion or belief system. This will provide the RM team with valuable information about the diverse perspectives of the new hires. The program director and team can then determine a suitable way for respecting these beliefs and values.

One of the first times the subject of beliefs may arise is at the blessing before a meal or a meeting. If you choose to offer such blessings (follow whatever is standard practice at the university), consider asking various participants to share a blessing from their own traditions or humanist perspectives. If you do decide to offer prayers and blessings in this way, let the new hires know that this practice is standard at the university and that they are not expected to participate if they do not wish to. The challenge is to balance the traditional Catholic practices of the university with the faith and beliefs of faculty who are not Catholic. In this little practice you make clear the value of RM, help the new hires gain a taste of what being on the faculty of a Catholic university entails, and also show respect for the dignity and beliefs of the new hires.

Secular humanists (a more positive term than "atheists"), Buddhists, Hindus, Muslims, Jews, and persons of other religious persuasions on a Catholic campus will experience numerous situations where prayers are said, and they will welcome a conversation about such rituals and what is expected of them. The conversation itself may be more important than whether the prayer is actually said. People will generally be open to blessings, and not perceive them as insults or obstacles to participating in a meal, if the topic is treated with sensitivity and respectful listening.

The construction and use of a blessing requires attention, especially with participants from diverse traditions. Prayers offered by participants, except on particular occasions, should not be "vanilla," that is, so bland as to have little meaning for anyone. The prayer leader for a mealtime blessing or for a prayer before an RM session should draw on the riches of his or her tradition. As well as offering a short period of prayerfulness and reflection, the ritual gives the participants an insight into the religious or spiritual treasures that the individual holds sacred. The sharing promotes respect and friendship because something at the core of one's self, something deeply personal, has been offered to the group.

There are two reasons for seeking the assistance of the campus ministry team early in planning RM. First, the ministry team will often be familiar with constructing prayers or services respectful of other traditions. Make sure that the new hires are invited to help construct these services and to lead them. Second, securing the help of the campus ministry will also familiarize the ministry team with the program and make them more aware of the new hires and their needs. Having new hires involved in the process and as prayer leaders will increase their identification with RM.

In fact, the invitation to pray should become a "teachable moment," a discussion among all participants about public and personal prayer. Each of us, in his or her own way, pursues a spiritual path, as elucidated in the "Spiritual Journey" essay in Part Two of this book. Reading the essay provides a suitable setting for a broad discussion on prayer. Finally, remember to assess the prayer issue through individual feedback or a survey instrument.

Scholarship of Application

Participation in this program, here theory and practice interact, is a distinctive type of service, more comprehensive than a typical committee membership. In fact, given the nature of the participation, it is "scholarship of application" and should be evaluated as such by the promotion committee. Ernest Boyer's (1990) analysis of the several types of scholarship (discovery, integration, application, and teaching) provides a relevant reference in judging application or service as a type of scholarship.

Senior faculty and administrators who participate should also be acknowledged and rewarded for service to the university. Publicly recognizing participation as service demonstrates the importance of the program, and noting their work through a public presentation of plaques or other tokens of appreciation would remind the university community of the program's importance.

Recognition and encouragement of new hires as they progress during the year is important, but it is essential that participation not be perceived as a quid pro quo for tenure or promotion.

Conclusion

Practically speaking, as RM evolves over the years, the leadership team should enlist internal or external FLC experts to bring the experience to a high level of excellence. At the same time, RM should engage academic leaders in the FLC experience with the goal of spreading the initiative beyond the new hires program. Enlisting the support of learning centers on campus will also be an important strategy for activating FLCs in a number of projects throughout the university. Meeting with the principal investigators on research projects and presenting the FLC as an important methodology that enhances collaboration will also move the concept into an important area of the university.

Finally, what at first seemed to be an instrumental activity—the FLC—has evolved in this program into an integral part of the Mission Community, and then into an icon signifying fundamental characteristics of a Catholic educational endeavor: communities of learners transformed into responsible citizens committed to the common good.

While the program is intended primarily for new hires, a variation of RM can be used with any group on campus, because each person plays a role in shaping the educational and moral life of the student body and is therefore a candidate for RM. Think of the value added by coaches and cafeteria workers who know the students by name. Could the university succeed without effective residence-life and career-center personnel and counselors who are dedicated to the university, its mission, and its students? All sectors—administration, support staff, faculty—are essential to sustaining and enhancing the university's Catholic culture and religious heritage.

Faculty members, of course, play the key role in any university. By means of their interaction with the students, professors have a significant impact on their evolving worldview, values, and critical reasoning skills, as well as on their moral, psychological, and spiritual development. The essay on faculty learning communities will present a detailed picture of the FLC. As we shall see, a faculty learning community presents a secular template or framework for engaging new faculty. The FLC model will be the framework for each of the RM sessions.

Universities are about learning, the common good, civic responsibility, autonomy, and research. These attributes apply to all institutions of higher education, but I believe they are important ingredients for strengthening the culture of Catholic universities by enriching the concept of mutuality, subsidiarity, and social solidarity. In American society, where the individual and personal rights trump community, the FLC becomes a countercultural campus model for civic responsibility on the part of all university constituents. While the rational organization and the affective community are in tension in the university as a whole, it is possible to reduce the tension *within* the university. This reduction has always taken place where shared values and personal relations bring faculty together for problem solving, pedagogical and curriculum development, or classroom discussion. Students do the same in study groups or lab work. Community is not an alien concept, but one that needs to be seen in an intentional and transformative way. Let it become the "coin of the realm" in the Catholic university and it will propel these institutions through the twenty-first century.

References

Alexander, W., Astin, H. S., & Lindholm, J. A. (2010). *Cultivating the spirit: How college can enhance students' inner lives.* San Francisco: Jossey-Bass.

American Association of University Professors. (2006). *1940 statement of principles on academic freedom and tenure: With 1970 interpretive comments.* (Policy documents & reports.) Washington, DC: American Association of University Professors.

Benedict, Saint. (2004). The reception of guests. In P. Barry (Trans.), *Saint Benedict's rule* (pp. 123–125). Mahwah, NJ: Hidden Spring.

Boyer, E. L. (1990). *Scholarship reconsidered: Priorities of the professoriate.* New York: Wiley.

Clifford, A. M. (2008). Identity and vision at Catholic colleges and universities. *Horizons: The Journal of the College Theology Society, 35,* 355–370.

Cox, M. D. (2008). *Faculty learning communities: Recommendations for initiating and implementing an FLC at your campus.* Retrieved from Miami University of Ohio, Center for the Enhancement of Learning, Teaching and University Assessment Web site: http://www.units.muohio.edu/flc/recommendations.php.

Cox, M. D. (2009). *FLC Program director's and facilitator's handbook* (6th ed.). Oxford, OH: Miami University of Ohio.

Cox, M. D., Richlin, L., & Shulman, G. M. (2004). Institutional considerations in developing a faculty learning community program. In *Building faculty learning communities.* San Francisco: Jossey-Bass.

Ford, J. T. (2006). *Saint Mary's Press glossary of theological terms.* Winona, MN: Saint Mary's Press.

Gladwell, M. (2000). The law of the few: Connectors, mavens, and salesmen. In *The tipping point: How little things can make a big difference* (pp. 30–88). Boston: Little, Brown.

Higher Education Research Institute. (2003). *The spiritual life of college students: A national study of college students' search for meaning and purpose.* Retrieved from University of California, Los Angeles, Graduate School of Education & Information Studies Web site: http://spirituality.ucla.edu/docs/reports/spiritual_life_College_Students_Full_Report.pdf.

LaSalle, S. J. B., & Mann, W. (1720, 1996). *The conduct of the Christian schools.* Landover, MD: Lasallian Publications.

Massa, M. S. (2008). Myth buster. *Commonweal, 135*(14), 25–26.

Surowiecki, J. (2005). *The wisdom of crowds.* New York: Anchor Books.

Yolam, I., & Leszcz, M. (2005). *The theory and practice of group psychotherapy.* New York: Basic Books.

Recommended Reading for All Participants

Ford, J. T. (2006). *Saint Mary's Press glossary of theological terms.* Winona, MN: Saint Mary's Press.

Palmer, P. J., Zajonc, A., & Scribner, M. (2010). *The heart of higher education: A call to renewal.* San Francisco, CA: Jossey-Bass.

Recommended Reading for the RM Team

Cox, M. D. (2009). What is a faculty and professional learning community? Retrieved from Miami University of Ohio, Center for the Enhancement of Learning, Teaching and University Assessment Web site: http://www.units.muohio.edu/flc/whatis.php.

Cox, M. D., & Richlin, L. (2004). *Building faculty learning communities.* San Francisco, CA: Jossey-Bass.

Cox, M. D. (2009). *FLC program director's and facilitator's handbook* (6th ed.). Oxford, OH: Miami University of Ohio.

Notes

[1] On "Flatter Organizational Structures," see Simmering, M. (2012). Management levels. In *Encyclopedia of Business* (2nd ed.). Retrieved from http://www.referenceforbusiness.com/management/Log-Mar/Management-Levels.html; see also deliberative democracy: http://www.deliberative-democracy.net/.

[2] The term itself is derived from the Latin *limen*, meaning "threshold."

[3] For more information on the College Student Beliefs and Values Surveys in 2004 and 2007, see http://spirituality.ucla.edu/background/methodology/longitudinal-study.php#2007.

[4] Available at http://spirituality.ucla.edu/docs/results/faculty/spirit_professoriate.pdf.

[5] On the content and methodology of the Catholic Intellectual Tradition, see Hellwig, M. K. (2000). "The Catholic intellectual tradition in the Catholic university." In A. J. Cernera & O. J. Morgan (Eds.), *Examining the Catholic intellectual tradition* (pp. 1–18). Fairfield, CT: Sacred Heart University Press.

[6] Assessment queries look for answers such as: This is who we are, what we say we do, and here is the evidence of our success or lack of success.

[7] At the author's request, all questions for discussion are presented at the end of Essay Three, "The Spiritual Journey."

PART TWO

CORE THEMES FOR THE SESSIONS

INTRODUCTORY ESSAY
THE FACULTY LEARNING COMMUNITY:
NEW HIRES AND BEYOND

> Gen X faculty lack a sense of community,
> and are struggling to find it.
>
> —Robin Matross Helms

Faculty learning communities (FLCs) form the basis of the Revisioning Mission process. This essay addresses the importance of these learning groups while providing guidance for FLC formation and application during subsequent sessions of the program.

Soon you will teach your first class and attend your first department meeting. By now, however, you have already had to address practical questions related to office space and supplies, course outlines, and office hours, and probably stumbled onto a number of unanticipated work issues. Add these to the personal issues you've already dealt with, from getting settled in a new home to getting children enrolled in new schools, and it wouldn't be surprising if you were a bit overwhelmed by it all. While this program, Revisioning Mission, will not address any of these challenges as topics in themselves, it is designed to help you become more comfortable in your new position and provide you with an opportunity to become more knowledgeable about the university that you've now joined. There is a presumption, moreover, that you will have received the help you need to manage the challenges described above. I am confident in making this presumption because of the university's respect and concern for all members of the campus community, especially first-year students and newly hired faculty. However, if there is still some unfinished practical business that you or the group wishes to bring up, please do so.

In this essay we will discuss the great potential the FLC offers in overcoming faculty alienation, loneliness, stress, and anxiety, especially in the first few years of employment. Communities of all kinds are at the heart of the matter in education on all levels, especially in the university. As you are reading this essay prior to the orientation meeting, take some time to reflect on challenges that you wish to discuss at that meeting. Of course, if there are issues that you would like to address privately, please raise them with a Revisioning Mission team member outside the FLC. Also, if you have questions related to the university, its history, philosophy, charism, tradition, or standard practices, feel free to bring them to future sessions as you become more comfortable with and informed about the institution. Again, don't hesitate to raise any of your questions privately at any time with members of the Revisioning Mission team.

Questions for discussion follow many of the sections in this essay. They are intended to begin, not to limit, the conversation. Feel free to use the ones that most interest you or the group or to suggest others that may arise within the dynamics of the group meeting.

Community: The Heart of the Matter for New Faculty

Universities annually engage in a process that is both bureaucratic and academic: hiring new faculty to replace those retiring and leaving. These new hires often have many concerns and questions. Researchers Eugene Rice, Mary Sorcinelli, and Ann Austin (2000) report that prospective and new-hire "[i]nterviewees told us they want to pursue their work in communities where collaboration is respected and encouraged, where friendships develop between colleagues within and across departments" (p. 13). They put a high value on having "time and opportunity for interaction and talk about ideas, one's work, and the institution" (p. 13). Integration of academic and personal lives is also a core concern.

Most academics, whether newly minted or experienced, share the desire to master pedagogy, conduct meaningful research, and write for publication in one's field or in collaboration with faculty from other disciplines. Faculty learning communities promote these aspirations. These gatherings facilitate the development of a common body of knowledge along with a personal sharing of insights, values, convictions, and professional aspirations.

In her recent study for the Collaborative on Academic Careers in Higher Education (COACHE), Robin Helms (2010) notes, "Gen X faculty [born between 1964 and 1980] lack a sense of community, and are struggling to find it" (p. 18). She realized how critical community is, almost by happenstance, when she asked one of her interviewees, "Is there anything else you would like to tell me?" The answer was the beginning of a cascade of concerns raised by the new faculty in this study. She concluded, "Community—the lack of it and the quest to find it—provides a compelling storyline for Generation X. It is a unifying theme in their experiences, and may well hold the key to truly understanding X'ers. . . . In short, community, more than any stereotype or characterization, may well be the essence of X" (p. 20). Helms's (2010) recommendation: "To address the community issue, create as many opportunities for interaction among faculty members as possible" (p. 21). Moreover, her study, as a whole, is germane to all aspects of the FLC and should be a resource for all RM programs.

Concern for the acculturation of faculty is not a recent phenomenon. Paul Baker (Cox, M.D., 2004) voiced a sympathetic concern: "The heart of the crisis in American education is the lonely work of teachers who often feel disconnected from administration, colleagues, and many of their students" (p. 6). While Baker applies his concern to all faculty, there is little doubt that new hires require attention from the inception of employment, otherwise they may readily fall under the shadow of the "disconnect" that Baker notes. Cox (2004) responds with a significant remedy for this isolation: "Cohort-based Faculty Learning Communities address the teaching, learning, and developmental needs of an important group of faculty or staff that has been particularly affected by the isolation, fragmentation, stress, neglect, or chilly climate in the academy" (p. 8).

Learning communities have traditionally been associated with undergraduate students and find early expression in the writings of two influential educators, Alexander Meiklejohn and John Dewey. Cox (2009) defines the term in relation to other sectors of higher education: "A Faculty Learning Community is a group of trans-disciplinary faculty, graduate students and professional staff . . . engaging in an active, collaborative, year-long program with a curriculum about enhancing teaching and learning and with frequent seminars and activities that provide learning, development, transdisciplinarity, the scholarship of teaching and learning, and community building" (para. 2).

Questions for Discussion

- What types of community did you experience in graduate school or at other universities where you previously worked?
- What has been your experience of community at this university so far?
- What challenges and opportunities have you experienced so far in your teaching, department gatherings, conversations, and on campus more generally?

Faculty Learning Communities: Revisiting the Foundation of Catholic Higher Education

While faculty learning communities provide the framework for the Revisioning Mission program, the concept (used by thirty-eight universities in the United States and one in Scotland) has, in itself, no religious overtones. FLCs "develop empathy among members; operate by consensus, not majority; develop their own culture, openness, and trust; engage complex problems; energize and empower participants; have the potential of transforming institutions into learning organizations; and are holistic in approach" (Cox, 2009, para. 7). This is an important consideration, because many in academe react negatively to religious approaches. However, the FLC does provide a valuable but neutral space for a gradual unfolding of the concepts of mission, Catholic culture, religious heritage, spirituality, intellectual life, and the value-added dimension of Catholic universities.

These learning communities also place Catholic education in the larger context of higher learning in America, providing leadership opportunities among its secular public and private counterparts and among other Christian universities. While learning communities offer benefits for new faculty members, they also offer the added benefit of reenergizing the entire professoriate, and they can help to reinvigorate relationships with university administrators and staff. For instance, many professors and administrators share an interest in interdisciplinary research and publication, curriculum revision, and an institution-wide common body of readings and related discussions. Learning communities offer them an opportunity to exchange ideas, test theories, and engage in spirited debate with like-minded colleagues. It is a process that will also make the six essays that form the curriculum of the six sessions during the academic year both appealing and accessible as common reading. My hope is that the last essay and session, on the Mission Community, will lead new hires to choose to become part of that group.

Since the ultimate aim of the Revisioning Mission program is to establish the Mission Community, a working definition is in order: A Mission Community is a group of lay faculty and congregational members, as well as administrators and staff, who are committed to creating a new living endowment. Using the FLC model, the Mission Community is an intentional, transparent, religiously pluralistic group, open to all university employees, inviting all who are drawn to Catholic education to join a community committed to a robust future that is faithful to the mission of their university. This new living endowment or Mission Community will take a vibrant Catholic educational system into the future.

Questions for Discussion

- What experiences have you had with a faculty learning community? What were the format and goals? What opportunities and challenges did the FLC present? How did the format work? How were the goals achieved?
- How might a faculty learning community benefit the university with its great diversity and many divisions, such as academics, student life, or athletics?
- What thoughts or questions do you have about the concept of a Mission Community and its value for Catholic higher education?
- What are the challenges and opportunities of an FLC? What do you see as its strengths and weaknesses?
- How does the idea of an FLC compare to your own expectations of teaching in a Catholic university environment? What concerns does this strategy raise for you?

The Common Good and the Qualities of an FLC

Community is an important aspect of Catholic higher education, flowing as it does from Catholic social teaching, with its emphasis on the common good and on the community as the womb in which the individual is nurtured and becomes a person. The importance of community resonates with the concerns expressed by the Carnegie Foundation for the Advancement of Teaching and its president, Ernest L. Boyer, in the seminal report *Campus Life: In Search of Community*. As Boyer (1990) notes elsewhere, for professors "to be fully effective, [they] cannot work continuously in isolation. It is toward a *shared* vision of intellectual and social possibilities—a community of scholars—that the four dimensions of academic endeavor [the scholarship of discovery, integration, application, and teaching] should lead. In the end, scholarship at its best should bring faculty together" (p. 80).

A close, nurturing community plays an important role in recruiting and retaining new faculty. Research shows that "many early-career faculty and graduate students who aspire to join the faculty hold dear a vision of a 'culture of collegiality' in which they wish to work" (Rice et al., 2000, p. 13). As Rice and his colleagues indicate, "evidence supporting this is consistent across studies" (p. 13). Once again, a broad approach will eventually include all faculty as well as other staff, not only the newly hired.

Cox's (2008) description of the qualities necessary for building community in an FLC are very much in line with the goals of RM in a Catholic university (p. 103). Highlighting five of these qualities reinforces characteristics sought in Catholic academic culture: trust, openness, respect, hospitality, and responsiveness. Because the characteristics are so deeply human, they are also by their very nature inclusively "catholic," or universal. In themselves, therefore, these characteristics are not necessarily Catholic or even religious. Taken together in the context of a university's Catholic culture and congregational heritage, they are powerful reminders of the virtues that give vitality to the mission.

Cox underlines the importance of *trust* in creating a group in which individuals reveal weaknesses in teaching or in any aspect of faculty and administrative life that demonstrates personal vulnerability. *Openness* allows for sharing thoughts, impressions, or ideas that might normally be kept under wraps. *Respect* provides an even deeper foundation for the qualities already discussed and reinforces a central characteristic of the Catholic university in that "members need to feel as though they are valued and respected as contributors and as people" (Cox, 2008, p.103). An even more welcoming expression, characteristic of Benedictine spirituality and education, would be *hospitality*. Closely allied with respect is the imperative of *responsiveness* to one another by the members of the FLC along with a commitment to collaboration, as opposed to an individualistic or competitive approach to university learning and career development.

Empowerment flows from the above characteristics and is one of the most important goals of an FLC. "In the construction of a transformative learning environment, the participants gain a new view of themselves and a new sense of confidence in their abilities" (Cox, 2008, p. 103). Empowerment fosters the principle of subsidiarity, which is highlighted in Catholic social teaching. The principle "favors decision making and responsible social action at the lowest feasible level" (Ford, 2006, p. 179).

Questions for Discussion

- What do you know about Catholic social teaching and its emphasis on the common good?
- Cox presents five characteristics of FLCs that find a home in Catholic higher education. These characteristics are also "virtues" in Catholic social thought. What do you think are the values that give rise to these characteristics or virtues in a Catholic university?

The Potential of a Faculty Learning Community: Palmer, Senge, and Zajonc

A point made earlier, that "FLCs can profoundly affect campus culture and may represent a major institutional change," requires further elaboration. Three educational researchers, Peter Senge, Parker Palmer, and Arthur Zajonc, make important contributions to the study of learning communities, adding a great deal to our understanding of the FLC. Senge challenges an instrumental view of work with an understanding of the intrinsic benefits of work, while Palmer and Zajonc present the epistemological foundation of work as a communal activity.

The FLC bears a relationship to the "learning organization" model, a dynamic institutional change agent discussed by Senge in *The Fifth Discipline.* "Senge describes the learning organization as one that connects its members closely to the mission, goals, and challenges of the organization. These close connections are necessary for the organization to meet the demands of rapid change"

(Shulman, 2004, p. 45). While Senge is referring to organizations in general, for our purposes it is the university itself, as the learning organization that is of concern. However, it is a challenge to view the university as a gestalt. Faculty members tend to view their work through the lens of their particular department or academic guild of the discipline, resulting in what is often referred to as a "silo mentality." The department or discipline offers what are frequently the most important rewards that faculty value: recognition, promotion, acclaim from the disciplinary guild, and publication in premier journals. These accolades can be critical to the identity and self-image of the faculty member. With regard to learning communities, the challenge is to help senior faculty see the larger university picture, with the goal of understanding the FLC and its potential impact on the entire culture of the institution. Hopefully, they will value the aspirations of a learning community and will be more likely to speak up and defend its creation. There should be little doubt that winning wide support for a holistic view of the university is a formidable task.

In *The Fifth Discipline*, Senge (1990) offers a way of thinking that adds enrichment to developing FLCs. His thinking is based on reframing the notion of work from an industrialized "instrumental" view (work seen as a means to an end) to a more "sacred" view that emphasizes the intrinsic benefits of work as a practice, thereby drawing the practitioner into a "relationship" (pp. 4–5). A sacred (but not necessarily religious) view of work is commensurate with an understanding of the educator as one who embraces the intrinsic benefits of work—benefits that go beyond satisfaction of the basic needs for food, clothing, and shelter. He or she is a *professor*, one who professes to educate for the good of society, meaning those transcendent goals and higher aspirations that include personal satisfaction but move beyond that to the common good of human flourishing. In other words, the "workplace," or, in this case, the university, is not only a private good, but also a public good.

In *The Heart of Higher Education*, Palmer, Zajonc, and Scribner (2010) present an epistemology that reinforces Senge's perspective by providing the philosophical underpinnings of faculty learning communities and a practice that will animate them: collegial conversations. Education transforms students if it is integrative: "A truly integrative education engages students in the systematic exploration of the relationship between their studies of the 'objective' world and the purpose, meaning, limits, and aspirations of their lives" (p. 10). Knower and known become one. "Students," in its usage here, casts a large net to include the entire university community, but most importantly the faculty, and in this case, the faculty learning community.

Interestingly, Palmer and Zajonc take their cue from what they call the "new sciences" as opposed to the "old sciences" of Newton and Descartes. The authors look to "Einstein and Bohr, whose science is not of matter and mechanism but of relationships and dynamic processes" (p. 10). Professor and student are "participating observers," not "detached analysts." These authors present a striking alternative to the Cartesian paradigm by using terms such as "experiences, relationships, and the spectrum of human feelings," all of which challenge us to embrace a paradigm shift that focuses on the "heart" of higher education.

The capacity to be a participating observer is powered by what Martin Buber (1970) called the "I-Thou" relationship, whether it be with other persons or with the subject matter of a course. "We have all had the experience of a conversation shifting and becoming a deep, free exchange of thoughts and feelings that seems to reach into and beyond the individual participants. Something new emerges, a transcendent communal whole that is greater than the sum of its parts" (Palmer et al., 2010, p. 12). The intensity of the conversation raises the speakers to a level of "presence" that is rarely achieved between two people, let alone in the classroom. Yet presence is not limited to human discourse. "[T]here are parallel moments in the arts, as when a painting becomes so alive for us that an I-Thou relation is established with it: in that moment we behold the painting in ways that set the experience apart from a more objective or analytic study" (Palmer et al., 2010, p. 12).

The knower and the known enter into each other in a mysterious way: each is separate but they are one. For such "presence" to become the fundamental pedagogy of education requires a reconsideration of objectivism and detachment, without destroying these essential dimensions of research and teaching. They must partner with, or, better still, embrace a side of life that has been stifled and declared taboo in the university: relational knowing of the subject matter, the students, and one's colleagues, all of which belong to a learning community engaged in open-ended collegial conversations. The latter "allow us to explore shared concerns selflessly and achieve unexpected insights as our desire to 'win' as individuals yields to the desire that the full resources of the community be tapped for the common good" (Palmer et al., 2010, p. 12).

What gives this pedagogical paradigm its greatest power is the fact that it cannot be mandated by accrediting agencies, boards of trustees, administrators, or faculty committees. It is a paradigm shift nurtured into life by "caring and thoughtful human beings" who are genuinely interested in the *other*—whether persons or subject matter. It is a life-giving paradigm that engenders "soul" in education: "a quality of mutual attentiveness" without fear of the unexpected, the other, or creativity. To be "present" excludes fear, because presence begins with the serenity of self-love generating openness, attentiveness, and transparency in the embrace of the other.

Presence is a "social capacity" empowering "focused and disciplined conversation." The latter constitutes "bottom-up" social capital of the type Robert Putnam values in his writings (Putnam, 2000; Putnam, Feldstein, & Cohen, 2003). Palmer, Zajonc, and Scribner (2010) conclude: "[F]undamental change in institutions has always come from planting small communities of vision and practice within those settings; those communities can grow from good conversation; and those conversations can be started by individuals, whether or not they hold positional power" (p. 14). Such is the opportunity offered by FLCs.

Senge (1990) echoes Palmer's communal epistemology. The former offers five vital dimensions in building learning organizations and realizing their highest aspirations:

1. **Systems Thinking** is the first of the disciplines, but, as we shall see, it is the integrating or master discipline. Holistic thinking of this type calls us to see all the parts of a scenario if we are going to understand the scenario itself.

2. **Personal Mastery** mirrors the artist's embrace of his or her creation whereby the artist, the creative process, and the work of art are united as one. For the educator, it is a commitment to personal, lifelong learning; or, as Palmer would put it, the knower and the known become one. "Personal mastery is the discipline of continually clarifying and deepening our personal vision of focusing our energies, of developing patience, and of seeing reality objectively" (p. 7). This mastery is at one and the same time the individual's and the organization's spiritual foundation, a discipline found deep within Eastern and Western spirituality as well as in secular traditions. The challenge to personal mastery comes from deep within contemporary culture. The superficiality, materialism, instant gratification, and constant hum of media background noise are the fundamentals of a cultural system that block out reflection on our personal journey through life and our deepest aspirations. While personal mastery is more about the individual, lifelong organizational learning and individual learning or mastery must proceed in tandem for any group of persons who seek growth in the enterprise.

3. **Mental Models** are none other than the numerous applications of our epistemology, the taken-for-granted view of the world discussed by Palmer. It truly takes the "discipline of personal mastery" to recognize these assumptions and deeply ingrained beliefs within us, since so much is at stake in models that have guided us and provided a seemingly secure philosophy of life. Equally important, "it also includes the ability to carry on 'learningful' conversations that balance inquiry and advocacy, where people expose their own thinking effectively and make that thinking open to the influence of others" (p. 9). I do not believe these conversations can take place without the community of relatedness Palmer describes above.

4. **Building Shared Vision** in the university depends on a commitment to systems thinking, a striving for personal mastery, and the sharing of mental models. These disciplines make sense only in the community of relatedness built on trust and the communal epistemology, both of which transform the role of the individual and his or her place in the educational community. Proverbs 29:18 declares that "without a vision the people perish." Likewise, institutional or organizational vitality depend on what Senge calls "a common identity and sense of destiny." Vision that is shared is vision that is built from the bottom up. It is not solely a function of charismatic leadership. It is internally embraced and results in a shared sense of the future that engenders commitment, without which an institution muddles through, atrophies, or dies. Genuine vision is not the same as a "vision statement." Rather, it is a discipline freely embraced, evoking internal commitment because authentic vision wells up from the sharing, the consensus, and the assent of the community. It cannot be imposed from an external source.

5. **Team Learning** builds on Senge's previously described disciplines and Palmer's community of relatedness. The suspension of assumptions, attentive listening, and the yet-to-be-defined deliberative democracy also characterize team learning or thinking together. Team learning means the learning outcome is greater than the sum of its parts. To put it another way: The intelligence of the group is greater than the average IQ of the team itself. In other words, team learning goes hand in hand with systems thinking. The definition of the Greek word *dialogos* reinforces this line of thinking: "a free flowing of meaning through a group, allowing the group to discover insights not attainable individually" (p. 10). A common practice in "primitive" societies, it is largely unknown in our culture. It is not a heaving back and forth of ideas, as in a discussion. Dialogue is the art or discipline that animates team learning. Senge views the latter as the "fundamental learning unit in the modern organization."

While Senge sees the five disciplines as a unit, he considers systems thinking the "fifth" (that is, in his construct, the first, or key) discipline precisely because it fuses the others into a coherent whole. Furthermore, and most importantly, systems thinking reinforces the epistemological insight of Palmer: that in reality there are different, often conflicting worldviews, such as the objectivist or the relational. In other words, reality is not a given; it is constructed. Once we understand that the world as we perceive it is a construct of society, not of the individual alone, we are unshackled from that social construct, viewing it dispassionately from a distance (Kuhn, 1962).

Senge speaks of the disciplines as an "ensemble of five component technologies." "Discipline" may seem to be an unusual word to apply to each dimension of the ensemble; however, it derives from the Latin *disciplina*, meaning "instructions for a disciple" (Ford, 2006, p. 62). That original meaning applies to Senge's "ensemble" of disciplines: they are a set of instructions or beliefs for a disciple of systems thinking. An individual becomes a disciple of the latter only through what anthropologists might call "a rite of passage." In agreement with Palmer, Senge calls it "a shift of mind," but he equates the shift with the Greek word *metanoia*. Making that equation means it is not simply changing one's mind, as in deciding not to go to a ballgame. Metanoia is a fundamental shift, or, better still, transcendence. "To grasp the meaning of 'metanoia' is to grasp the deeper meaning of 'learning,' for learning also involves a fundamental shift or movement of the mind" (Senge, 1990, pp. 4–5).

Learning does not usually have that connotation today. Senge views "real learning" as getting "to the heart of what it means to be human." It has what John Haughey calls a "catholicity," or search for completeness. We have the potential of re-creation through learning. "Through learning we reperceive the world and our relationship to it." This is the essence of the learning organization and its ensemble of disciplines. "Discipline" can also mean "teachings" or "rules pertaining to a practice," such as Zen meditation. It can also mean the training itself. The point is that discipline and practice go together (Ford, 2006, p. 62). The five disciplines are a practice, and they require repetitive use in order to be mastered.

Thus, "discipline" itself has these two meanings that mutually reinforce each other. We cannot learn or (better still) practice the five disciplines without the sweat and tears of hard work in the cognitive and affective domains. Under the rubric of *The Fifth Discipline's* systems thinking approach, interpreting the world becomes more complex, for the globe's problems admit of no easy solutions. Personal mastery, likewise, does not come easily to any of us because it means profound reflection on the adequacy or inadequacy of our prevailing mental models. Questioning becomes the background music of our consciousness, requiring much discipline to allow it to continue. Finally, working with others or team learning to build a shared vision challenges a dominant dimension of the culture that is part and parcel of who we are: the individualism of the Lone Ranger, also epitomized by Frank Sinatra's "I Did It My Way."

Questions for Discussion

- Senge describes an instrumental view of work. What do you see as the "intrinsic benefits" of work? What is your view of your work? How do you envision it in terms of goals?
- Do you view work as a private good and a public good, or both? Why or why not? What tensions exist between these two goods? What is the hierarchy of values in the way you view your work?
- Ask senior colleagues about the existence of a "silo mentality" at this university. How do they assess this image? Do they see this as the most productive model for a university? What is their model?
- How is the epistemology that Palmer and Zajonc describe both valid and viable in university education? Or is it invalid and not viable?
- What conversations have you had that are of the type Buber describes?

- If relational knowledge is truly a paradigm shift, what challenges and opportunities do you see for the future of pedagogy in higher education?
- How do Senge's learning organization and the five perspectives that give it life "fit" in relation to your own view of learning?
- What are your "mental models" of the purpose, pedagogy, and student culture of higher education?
- What are the opportunities and challenges that result from a social-construction view of reality?
- In the section on "building a shared vision," Senge says that institutional vitality depends on "a common identity and a sense of destiny." In your time at this university, what examples have you seen of a "common identity and sense of destiny"?

Motivation: A Distinctive Characteristic of the Catholic University

For Catholic universities, the embrace of Palmer and Senge's thinking is not sufficient in itself. Motivation for so doing is critical to Catholic distinctiveness, and in this case the source of motivation for identifying with their ideas is deeply religious and finds its wellspring in the fundamental beliefs that all creation reflects the glory of God and that each person is made in the image and likeness of the Creator. Furthermore, the horizon, endpoint, or vision of Catholic theology is the coming of the Kingdom of God. This is the "good news" of the Gospel that gives direction and purpose to all Catholic thought.

Metanoia also plays a central role in Catholic spirituality, thereby adding another dimension of distinctiveness to Catholic higher education. Metanoia is the liminal moment—the crossing of a threshold (Latin, *limen*)—that is at once a conversion and the engine for the development of a deeply spiritual life. The concept of metanoia helps us better understand the culture of higher education. Spohn (2005) notes that "[t]o a degree not matched in contemporary spirituality, traditional writers appreciated the depth of resistance to radical transformation and the human capacity for self-deception that

66

are rooted in the abiding influence of sin" (p. 281). Although he is writing about Christian spirituality per se, I believe his cautionary advice applies to the type of resistance to radical transformation that one not infrequently finds in higher education.

Catholicism, through its members and institutional life (imperfect as both are), aspires to prepare for the coming of the kingdom by seeing the face of Christ in each person and treating each as he or she would treat Christ himself. From this theological worldview flow the moral imperatives of Catholic social teaching: community as the womb and home of the individual, respect for the dignity of each person as an end in himself or herself, care for others or the common good (especially, but not exclusively, the most economically vulnerable), as well as trust, hospitality, subsidiarity, and empowerment among several others. In a word, motivation is the critical factor in Catholic culture.[1] Remember, however, that there is no requirement that every member of the campus community share the motivation that arises from the Catholic faith and its embodiment in Catholic social teaching. Fortunately, a plurality of views converge at Catholic universities, in the sense that Catholic social teaching casts a wide net, appealing to administrators, faculty, staff, and students across the religious spectrum as well as the spectrum running from secular humanism through agnosticism and atheism.

Questions for Discussion

- In the previous section, Senge uses a classic religious term, "metanoia," to describe the fundamental shift or deeper meaning in understanding "learning." Palmer would say that in lifelong learning the knower and the known become one. The topic arises again in this section. Metanoia involves a fundamental reorientation of one's way of thinking and acting. In what ways is this feasible? What would the motive have to be for doing so? How can the knower and the known become one? How do these views impact learning in higher education?

- A Catholic epistemology or motivation appears to be the value-added or distinctive characteristic of the Catholic

university, setting it apart from secular institutions. Why is this, or is this not, a valid conclusion for your university?
- If you are not Catholic—if you are from another religious tradition or of a secular humanist persuasion—how do you align your values with the Catholic worldview? Does the concept of "metanoia" make sense to you?

Characteristics of a Faculty Learning Community

An FLC provides the framework for developing an environment of peer support, mutual understanding, and collaborative learning in a university setting. Based on my own experience as a graduate student writing a dissertation, I empathize with the recent PhD graduate who has spent many lonely days and nights on a writing project in which very few colleagues or even friends are interested. This phenomenon is not peculiar to the "ABD" (all but dissertation) graduate student; take note of how few people will ask a colleague engaged in any writing project what the topic is or how it is going. The proposed FLC will be an opportunity to transform the loneliness and isolation of writing into a celebration of achievement, insight, and creativity within a culture of academic hospitality, attentive listening, appreciative support, and dignified deliberative democracy.

The latter term, "deliberative democracy," calls for clarification in relation to an FLC. Deliberative democracy is often identified with a political methodology, but it has a variety of applications. The Web site for the Deliberative Democracy (DD) Project at the University of Oregon notes:

> Deliberative Democracy is founded on our belief that citizens care enough and are smart enough to participate meaningfully in the deliberative process of making public policy. We also believe that as citizens choose policy options they're willing to accept, they develop the political will to make needed changes. (Weeks, 1996)

These characteristics present a discussion method for the Faculty Learning Community (Weeks, 1996):

1. "DD involves the whole community in the decision-making process." While an FLC does not involve the entire university community, it is a whole unto itself. DD should characterize all FLC discussions.

2. In DD, as in the FLC, "an informed, stable consensus [is] reached through thoughtful deliberation." Both offer "substantial and relevant information," and while DD "tells policy makers what trade-offs citizens are willing to support," an FLC provides accurate information about challenges new faculty face and the solutions they offer to these challenges.

3. DD "gives citizens a realistic policy problem to work on, challenging them to make choices that reach past compromise to shared solutions." An FLC addresses real issues as well: pedagogy, curriculum, departmental collegiality, mentoring, research and publication, committee work, and personal issues such as spirituality, housing, spousal employment, and schooling and daycare for children. The hoped-for outcome is shared solutions, not compromise as a "forced option."

4. DD "allows governments to invest the time and money required for quality policy research. Only then will the results be accepted as credible and worthy of implementation; only then will policy makers be empowered to take strong, decisive action." The goal of an FLC is likewise to offer quality consensus and credible policies that will lead to administrative action that addresses the needs of new faculty.

In many ways, the FLC reinforces Palmer and Zajonc's epistemological grounding of the individual in community. Learning communities also highlight a foundational tenet of Catholic social teaching noted earlier: We are all created by God within the bosom of a community, the members of which have individual God-given rights but also God-given responsibilities toward one another. This principle stands in opposition to the worldview of the free-standing individual who, out of rational self-interest, enters into a social contract. The latter protects the person but does not organically or intrinsically connect one individual to the other because the social contract itself is a function of preexisting, individual inalienable rights and self-interest. Emphasis is on a negative understanding of rights, such as minimal government, rather than a positive understanding of rights, such as healthcare. This worldview of individualism is taken for granted by many persons in American society.[2]

Catholic higher education denies this "individual-trumps-all" worldview. While Catholic social teaching affirms the principle of human rights, it always assesses them in relation to the common good of the community. Thus, at its deepest level, the distinctiveness of the Catholic university lies in its countercultural stance vis-à-vis American individualism and offers the last century of social teaching by the Catholic Church in support of a communal worldview.

Such is the nature of a community as opposed to the distance, rationality, and impersonalism associated with the individualist, contractual understanding of the educator's role in higher education. Ideally, an FLC in a Catholic university embraces the common good of the students, faculty, administration, and staff. As a fundamental principle of Catholic social teaching, the common good places a premium on care for the most vulnerable members of the community, including those in an academic community. Within the FLC the members will come to know and appreciate one another as colleagues across schools and disciplines; and Palmer's notion of "relatedness" and care for one another will go far to assuage faculty alienation or loneliness. In focusing on the new faculty, the administration, other faculty, and staff may suffer similar alienation or loneliness.

Although this book does not focus on the student directly, I would be remiss not to attach the greatest importance to care for students. They are the reason for the Catholic university's existence. If Catholic social teaching does not motivate respect and love for the students, especially the most vulnerable, it is not a Catholic institution. This is a distinctively Catholic interpretation of an FLC and provides an instructive lesson in understanding and living in a Catholic university culture. The interpretation challenges the default mode in American higher education mentioned above: the contractual relationship among the individual professors with the university within an objectivist epistemology.

The FLC social model proposed here is an intentional community that finds its basis in Catholic culture and in most other, if not all, religions. In other words, it is Catholic and catholic (universal). The Catholic worldview gives rise to an intentional community of care, hospitality, and an unconditional respect for each person's dignity and intrinsic worth. However, one cannot reiterate sufficiently that there is no implicit agenda of religious proselytizing, a view that is incongruous with the contemporary Catholic culture of a university. The proposed FLC provides an environment for personal, social, and professional growth or flourishing. In a Catholic culture it aspires to be truly "catholic" in the sense of "universal." The community is intentional but not homogeneous. It seeks heterogeneity of persons and a pluralism of worldviews.

A first principle of Catholic theology is that God's creation is good and therefore all that is created, especially the human person, is good. If this were not the case, there would be no grounds for a doctrine of the Incarnation. This foundational understanding interprets creation as a manifestation of God—an insight into and a wellspring for understanding the unknowable, who transcends all creation and all humanity. This vision of an "other-regarding" community finds its Jewish counterpart in Buber's aforesaid understanding of the "I-Thou" relationship with God and with one another. An "I-Thou" relationship moves far beyond the legal guarantee of toleration to a heartfelt embrace of the other.

In sum, cohort-based communities are important in RM for the following reasons:

- The Catholic intellectual tradition, particularly in the area of social justice, stresses the communal nature of human beings. The starting point of human development is the community, in contrast to the Enlightenment view that the individual person is the beginning point and that the social contract creates society.

- New faculty constitute an important cohort that requires an active embrace by the university if isolation, fragmentation, and other challenges are to be overcome. Respect for human dignity and the needs of the individual are deeply embedded in the culture of the Catholic university.

- "Making a positive impact on the culture of the community" is an essential outcome of this mission program. By the beginning of the last session, the tenured class in the cohort will realize that the Catholic culture and the religious heritage of the founding congregation will be largely in their hands, in partnership with the founding group.

Question for Discussion

In your mind, what questions present themselves concerning faculty learning communities and their relationship with Catholic social teaching?

Conclusion

The Revisioning Mission process is based on structuring a faculty learning community during the initial meeting for new hires before the fall term begins. The FLC will be the format for the six sessions during the school year and will provide a structure that orients the participants to the Catholic university. There will also be a focus on the needs of an incoming faculty member during the entire year. In a sense, the medium of community conveys a message about these institutions, in that a culture of community and caring is a distinctive characteristic of Catholic education.

In the first session of the academic year, the FLC will discuss Catholic culture as the context for understanding the Catholic dimension of the university. In the second session, the meeting will focus on the Catholic university students and their search for meaning and purpose in higher education. The third session will address the nature of the adult spiritual journey. The FLC framework will likewise be in place for the fourth, fifth, and sixth sessions, the topics of which are the Catholic intellectual life, the university's founding congregation, and the Mission Community, respectively. As a whole, the program will serve as a rich introduction to Catholic education, and as an invitation to join the Mission Community and become a member of the new living endowment.

References

Boyer, E. L. (1990). *Scholarship reconsidered: Priorities of the professoriate.* Princeton, NJ: Carnegie Foundation for the Advancement of Teaching.

Buber, M., & Kaufmann, W. A., trans. (1970). *I and thou.* New York, NY: Scribner.

Carnegie Foundation for the Advancement of Teaching. (1990). *Campus life: In search of community; with a foreword by Ernest L. Boyer.* Lawrenceville, NJ: Princeton University Press.

Cox, M. D. (2004). Introduction to faculty learning communities. M. D. Cox & L. Richlin (Eds.), *Building faculty learning communities.* San Francisco, CA: Jossey-Bass.

Cox, M. D. (2009). What is a faculty and professional learning community? Retrieved from Miami University of Ohio, Center for the Enhancement of Learning, Teaching and University Assessment Web site: http://www.units.muohio.edu/flc/whatis.php.

Cox, M. D., Miami University, & United States. (2008). *Faculty learning community program director's handbook and facilitator's handbook.* Oxford, OH: Miami University.

Ford, J. T. (2006). *Saint Mary's Press glossary of theological terms.* Winona, MN: Saint Mary's Press.

Helms, R. M. (2010). *New challenges, new priorities: The experience of Generation X faculty.* Retrieved from Harvard University, Cambridge, Mass., The Collaborative on Academic Careers in Higher Education: http://isites.harvard.edu/

fs/docs/icb.topic436591.files/COACHE_Study_NewChallengesNewPriorities_20100304.pdf

Kuhn, T. S. (1962). *The structure of scientific revolutions.* Chicago, IL: University of Chicago Press.

Massa, M. S. (2003). *Anti-Catholicism in America: The last acceptable prejudice.* New York, NY: Crossroad Pub.

Palmer, P. J., Zajonc, A., & Scribner, M. (2010). *The heart of higher education: A call to renewal.* San Francisco, CA: Jossey-Bass.

Putnam, R. D. (2000). *Bowling alone: The collapse and revival of American community.* New York, NY: Simon & Schuster.

Putnam, R. D., Feldstein, L. M., & Cohen, D. (2003). *Better together: Restoring the American community.* New York, NY: Simon & Schuster.

Rice, R. E., Sorcinelli, M. D., & Austin, A. E. (2000). *Heeding new voices: Academic careers for a new generation.* Washington, DC: American Association for Higher Education.

Senge, P. M. (1990). *The fifth discipline: The art and practice of the learning organization.* New York, NY: Doubleday/Currency.

Shulman, G. M. (2004). Institutional consideration in developing a faculty learning community program. In M. D. Cox & L. Richlin (Eds.), *Building faculty learning communities* (pp. 5–25). San Francisco, CA: Jossey-Bass.

Spohn, W. C. (2005). Christian spirituality and theological ethics. In A. G. Holder (Ed.), *The Blackwell companion to Christian spirituality* (pp. 269–285). Malden, MA: Blackwell Publishing.

Volf, M. (2009). God, justice, and love: The grounds for human flourishing. *Books and Culture, 15*(1), 26–28.

Weeks, E. (1996). *Deliberative democracy.* Retrieved from University of Oregon, Eugene, Dept. of Planning, Public Policy & Management, Deliberative Democracy Project Web site: http://pages.uoregon.edu/ddp/

Recommended Reading

American Association of University Professors (AAUP). (2001). *1940 statement of principles on academic freedom and tenure: With 1970 interpretive comments.* (Policy documents & reports.)

Washington, DC: American Association of University Professors.

American Association of University Professors (AAUP). (2006). *1940 statement of principles on academic freedom and tenure: With 1970 interpretive comments.* (Policy documents & reports.) Washington, DC: American Association of University Professors.

American Association of University Professors (AAUP). (2006). *Statement on professional ethics.* (Policy documents & reports.) Baltimore, MD: Johns Hopkins University.

American Council on Education. (2003). *Statement on academic rights and responsibilities.* Retrieved from http://www.acenet. edu/AM/Template.cfm?Section=HENA&template=/CM/ ContentDisplay.cfm&ContentID=10672.

Boyer, E. L. (1990). *Scholarship reconsidered: Priorities of the professoriate.* Princeton, NJ: Carnegie Foundation for the Advancement of Teaching.

Bryant, A. N. (2009). College experiences and spiritual outcomes: An interview with UCLA Spirituality in Higher Education Project Director Jennifer Lindholm. *Journal of College and Character, X* (3), 1–6.

Carnegie Foundation for the Advancement of Teaching. (1990). *Campus life: In search of community.* Princeton, NJ: The Foundation.

Helms, R. M. (2010). New challenges, new priorities: The experience of Generation X faculty. *The Collaborative on Academic Careers in Higher Education.* Retrieved from http://isites.harvard.edu/fs/docs/icb.topic432240.files/COACHE_Tenured-and-TenureTrack_2011.pdf.

Nelson, C. (2010). Defining academic freedom. *Inside Higher Education.* Retrieved from http://www.insidehighered.com/ views/2010/12/21/nelson_on_academic_freedom.

Palmer, P. J. (1987). Community, conflict, and ways of knowing: Ways to deepen our educational agenda. *Change, 19* (5). Retrieved from http://www.couragerenewal.org/images/ stories/pdfs/rr_community.pdf.

Palmer, P. J., Zajonc, A., & Scribner, M. (2010). *The heart of higher education: A call to renewal.* San Francisco, CA: Jossey-Bass.

Notes

[1] In a recent review essay, Miroslav Volf (2009) grounds human rights theistically: "It is God's generative delight in and care for creatures that can themselves give and receive love that ultimately bestows worth on human beings" (p. 28).

2 On this point, see the classic works of Bellah, R. N., Madsen, R., Sullivan, W. M., Swidler, A. Tipton, S. M. (1985). *Habits of the heart: Individualism and commitment in American life.* Berkeley, CA: University of California Press; and (1991) *The good society.* New York, NY: Knopf. See also Putnam, R. D. (2000). *Bowling alone: The collapse and revival of American community.* New York, NY: Simon & Schuster; and Putnam, R. D., Feldstein, L. M., & Cohen, D. (2003). *Better together: Restoring the American community.* New York, NY: Simon & Schuster.

Essay One

The Catholic Culture of the University: A Work in Progress

The introductory essay was devoted to the practical details of creating a faculty learning community (FLC). As with every group, the FLC exists within a larger context—the university itself. While the learning community will develop its own culture, a discussion of the university's Catholic culture will provide an important insight into Catholic education. Examining the "Catholic" dimension of the culture will go a long way toward developing an understanding of Catholicism as more complex than merely an ecclesiastical structure. Embodied in a culture, the university ultimately speaks to the depths of the human search for meaning, which is the keystone of every society. An analysis of Catholic university culture will provide important insights into how the university functions and its potential in forwarding the mission of Catholic higher education. In this discussion, I take seriously the insight of the Second Vatican Council's (1996) Pastoral Constitution on the Church in the Modern World (Gaudium et Spes): "Man [sic] comes to a true and full humanity only through culture" (para. 53).

Cultural analysis as a phenomenological tool attempts to present an accurate picture of the university as it is. While this is an important first step, a cautionary note is necessary. This analysis is itself a creature of its own culture, and each analysis will have its own interpretation. It is never a neutral or totally distanced perspective, although this is an aspiration that should guide research. At the same time, Catholic higher education brings distinctive characteristics to cultural evaluation.

An analysis of the culture of the Catholic university is also a valuable means for understanding Catholicism as a church. Catholic culture is the lived experience on campus and, therefore, a palpable presence in which new faculty are immersed, but which often perplexes them. Further, this essay on Catholic culture and the university will analyze the relationship between the two entities and the impact of current trends in the Church on higher education. Such a discussion presents the strengths and weaknesses, as well as the opportunities and challenges, inherent in any university, while bringing to light the presence of cultural contradictions in an institution. Finally, an examination of an "ideal type" of the Catholic university, as described in Ex corde Ecclesiae, will round out the essay.

It is my hope that as a result of understanding Catholic culture and the Catholic Church, new faculty will join other colleagues and members of the larger university population as cultural citizens and cultural catalysts, committed to an inheritable, distinguishable, and distinctive Catholic culture and congregational heritage.

Understanding Catholic Culture

"Immersion" may best describe the new hire's experience of his or her new place of work. It is immersion into the Catholic culture of the university, a culture quite different from that of its secular counterpart. Entrée into this educational world has a liminal quality about it, a sense of crossing a threshold into a new space. Most importantly, this culture presents the opportunity for a new self-understanding as an academic.

Maureen O'Connell (2008), in a counterintuitive insight based on Charles Taylor's writings, would call this liminal opportunity an experience of "fullness": "To experience 'fullness' is not to be affirmed, or actualized, or integrated but rather to be interrupted, disrupted, or unsettled. A desire for fullness is a desire to break through the way things are, to move beyond the familiar and the ordinary, to be affected by alternatives to the mundane" (p. 337). This challenge to the accepted social construction of higher education, however, creates, as O'Connell (2008) notes, "the possibility for common ground, whether through the acknowledgement that all persons are looking for more, or through a shared critical examination of less authentic promises of fullness" (p. 337). Where better for the new hire to find a rich "common ground" than in the Catholic culture of the university itself?

The liminal experience is abetted by the stories (if not sagas) of institutional and congregational beginnings. These are compelling introductions to the Catholic culture and religious congregational heritage of the university. Culture and heritage in this case cannot be bifurcated. One does not exist without the other: a Dominican, Jesuit, Lasallian, or Mercy university cannot exist with integrity except within the context of the Roman Catholicism that shaped their founders and disciples.

In view of culture's huge significance, there is great relevance in a discussion of "thickness" in Catholic university culture. Clifford Geertz (1973), following Max Weber, perceives the individual to be "suspended in webs of significance that he himself has spun" (p. 5), cultural webs in need of interpretation in pursuit of meaning. Geertz goes on to say that "culture is not a power, something to which social events, behaviors, institutions, or processes can be causally attributed; it is a context, something within which they can be intelligibly—that is, thickly, described" (p. 5). Description is "inscription," and explanation is "diagnosis"; that is the difference "between setting down the meaning particular social actions have for the actors whose actions they are [inscription], and stating, as explicitly as we can manage, what the knowledge thus attained demonstrates about the society in which it is found and, beyond that about social life as such [diagnosis]" (p. 27).

While "Catholic culture" is a comprehensive term, "Catholic identity" is more frequently used in the literature on Catholic universities. However, as Melanie Morey and John Piderit (2006) note, "identity" does not lend itself to precision or analysis, whereas "'culture' has a variety of dimensions that can be explored concretely" (p. 8). "Culture" is also a useful term because these universities are located in the larger context of American Catholic and secular culture, the understanding of which facilitates insight into the Catholic university. "There is an osmotic cultural exchange between and among all these cultures that impacts and influences how Catholic colleges and universities understand themselves, adjust to the times, and shape their futures" (p. 10).

Morey and Piderit (2006) discuss culture in terms of actions and inheritance: "*Actions* are the present choices people within a culture make about activities—what to do and how to behave. *Inheritance* is the operative context for actions that resulted from previous choices made" (p. 21). New faculty arrive at a university that is, ipso facto, a culture—a cherished past, a reality in the present, and a future that is evolving. The evolution takes place slowly because culture does not change quickly—it is "thick," in a descriptive sense. The Catholic university lends itself to thick description because it is close to a thousand years old and intimately connected to the Roman Catholic Church, the oldest continuing institution in Western society. However, Catholic higher education also carries many of the values and aspirations of the wider American and global university cultures.

For instance, the heritage of the founding congregation is part of the inheritance Morey and Piderit identify. The heritage, however, is a key factor in a meaning system, a living reality that has evolved from the days of a sainted founder into an organization that the founder would be hard put to recognize but that, as a result of the Second Vatican Council, may actually be closer in spirit to the original vision or meaning. In fact, this book is a direct result of many congregations' reading of the "signs of the times," leading the members and their leadership to forge closer relations with lay people in university work.

According to Morey and Piderit, a culture will endure if two fundamental characteristics are present. First, it must be worth continuing—distinguishable from the culture of other universities. An observer can distinguish one Catholic university from another and from secular universities, but what is the "value-added" dimension that will lead the student to this or that Catholic university? In other words, while a Catholic university is distinguishable, what makes it distinctive among Catholic universities? Second, Morey and Piderit (2006) also inquire about the "inheritability" of the inheritance itself: "the ways of acting in a specific culture that assure authentic cultural assimilation by new groups that enter the culture" (p. 31).

Without action, inheritance will atrophy. For the inheritance to continue, a cadre of "cultural citizens" is necessary. They are "principled and high-minded actors, motivated and inspired by the beliefs, norms, stories, and rituals. These actors make almost daily decisions to do things in ways that reinforce the existing culture" (Morey & Piderit, 2006, p. 23). However, citizens do need leaders, those who not only "reinforce the existing culture" but who are proactive in integrating the inheritance into the culture as it continues to develop and evolve within the larger context of the local, national, and global environments, and the context of Catholicism, other Catholic universities, and American and global higher education. As the torch is passed to lay persons working in association with congregational leaders, "cultural catalysts" will need to take on a greater role because of the continuing increase in religiously pluralistic and heterogeneous lay faculty and the ongoing diminishment of the homogeneous congregational members. "Role models, knowledge experts, and heroic leaders are the *cultural catalysts* essential to any organization hoping to sustain, enhance, and transmit a vibrant culture. Without them, an organization's culture will surely dissipate and drift" (Morey & Piderit, 2006, p. 29).

"Citizens and catalysts" among the faculty who prize the university culture place great value on the inheritance. They embrace it and live it because it is a value—not simply an idea, but a belief leading to action. In the view of William R. Rogers (1989), more important than explicit articulation, values "function implicitly as operating principles and often need to be identified even in one's self by attempts to understand what gives unity or coherence to a pattern of action" (p. 5). He concludes that implicit values tell us where real values lie, much more so than spoken statements (p. 5). In other words, values are central to self-understanding or personal identity and erupt—or body forth, as it were—into action. As Richard Morrill (1980) puts it, "When persons take upon themselves and into their own identities the values of a community, they have *become* those values" (p. 117).

Questions for Discussion

Note: A number of questions for discussion in this essay may presume more experience than you have. These types of questions provide grist for future discussions and alert you to aspects of the culture that you might not normally consider. Some areas may lend themselves to separate presentations by experts and discussions on topics that cannot be adequately addressed in this session.

- How aware were you of the culture of your graduate program? How would you describe it?
- Would you characterize your work experience to date as liminal, or as an experience of "fullness," as Maureen O'Connell uses this term?
- Morey and Piderit conclude that cultural citizens and catalysts are necessary to bring the inheritance into the future. Whom would you name as such a citizen or catalyst in your previous or present university work? Why so?
- What does it mean to say that a person "embodies" the values of the university? How would you describe such a person? Have you met any such person or people?

Catholic Culture: Historical Background and Contrast with the Present

In the 1960s, the overwhelming presence in Catholic universities of the founding religious congregation and of the near one hundred percent Catholic student body—both nurtured in a highly central-ized, dogmatic "ghetto church"—virtually ensured homogeneity. A profound and unsettling religious and cultural shift began in the late 1960s with the diminution of the founding congregation. The shift was exacerbated by the growing religious and ethnic diversity of the student body, faculty, and administration. Even more importantly, con-tention over what it means to be Catholic characterizes the present-day Catholic university. Not only is the heterogeneity a result of cultural transformations and immigration within the context of the American Catholic community at large, it is also the result of rapid cultural shifts in the broader American and global culture. These multiple contexts easily blend into the university's culture and become part of the form-ative role in the students' education, although aspects of the formative role are at times hidden or unintended (such as aspirations to eco-nomic wealth and individualistic academic competitiveness).

It is not surprising, then, that many universities intentionally seek a core group of Catholics and other administrators and faculty who, while not necessarily Catholic, are committed to the Catholic culture, the Catholic intellectual life, a personal spirituality, and the religious heritage of the founding congregation. Recruiting a core group is a daunting task, one reason being the lack of una-nimity about how to measure an individual's Catholicity.

Questions for Discussion

- What are the explicit and hidden student formative responsibilities that the university articulates or demonstrates?
- If a colleague says he or she is a Catholic, what would that say to you? What "Catholic" characteristics would you expect that person to exhibit or embody?

What Is a Catholic?

The question "What does it really mean to be a Catholic?" is an important one to raise here. Catholicism has a strong institutional dimension, rituals, sacraments, and voluntary groups, but at the heart of the matter, Catholicism is about interiority and a spiritual life that is not necessarily correlated to all of the practices mentioned above. (This is, of course, true for other religions as well.) Individuals may be profoundly Catholic and yet be at odds with the Church over issues of polity, feminism, divorce, birth control, or its role in the public square. Should religiously committed gay, lesbian, bisexual, or transgender Catholics and other colleagues be automatically considered unacceptable as members of a core group? Might the university have a way of developing what it considers a core group of Catholics that is at odds with the evaluative method of the local bishop? All these questions bear consideration and are worth discussing.

Obviously, homogeneous Catholicism in the church or the university, the "center" as it were, is not holding as it did in the past. As a result, the Catholic culture and the religious heritage of the university receive great attention and scrutiny as the institution itself struggles to develop a clear articulation of the vision and mission that draw the institution into the future. If one takes seriously Philip Gleason's interpretation of how Catholic higher education has "contended with modernity," clarity of vision and mission require a distinctive context or culture to achieve vitality and dynamism. In 1995, he sought an overarching framework common to all universities, one that would serve as the catalyst for a robust Catholic university culture:

> The task facing Catholic academics today is to forge from the philosophical and theological resources uncovered in the past half-century a vision that will provide what Neoscholasticism did for so many years—a theoretical rationale for the existence of Catholic colleges and universities as a distinctive element in American higher education.
> (Gleason, 1995, p. 322).

Gleason's challenge to the Catholic academic community has still not been fully acknowledged or taken up, for many of the reasons discussed above. A brief description of Neoscholasticism brings home the challenge of developing a robust Catholic culture in the university today. Neoscholasticism promoted a philosophy of life and a Catholic worldview much at odds with elements of American culture during the interwar years of the 1920s and 1930s, as well as present-day American culture.

Philip Gleason offers several characteristics of Neoscholasticism, and they provide a framework for understanding a Catholic worldview, especially its clarity and solidity during a time of great cultural disillusionment. That worldview also provided the overarching philosophical and theological structure enlivening Catholic higher education for a good part of the twentieth century. Thus, Neoscholasticism offers a cultural case study, an opportunity to understand and learn from this philosophy and worldview as Catholic culture is evolving today in Church, university, and in society. Among the characteristics of that culture are the following:

1. Through the integration of faith and reason, the latter provides rational preambles to the supernatural gift of faith. Among the "preambles of faith" based on natural reason is the ability to establish the existence of God.

2. The mind has the capacity "to arrive at objective truth through the direct intuitions of the intellect and the exercise of discursive reason" (Gleason, 1995, p. 118). Modernism, subjectivism, pragmatism, and relativism stand in sharp contrast to the belief in the power of reason.

3. Neoscholasticism is not only a way of thinking, it is a worldview. It is a philosophy of life, since the way one thinks becomes the way one acts and lives. "A major Jesuit self-study [in 1932] admonished professors to 'bring out clearly how Scholastic Philosophy is a stable, universal, and certain system of thought, a real philosophy of life, something to which they [students] can anchor all their views and thoughts and knowledge'" (Gleason, 1995, p. 119).

4. Moreover, while appealing to the individual, Neoscholasticism, in the eyes of its supporters, "constituted the most appropriate cognitive foundation for the culture of a whole society with the natural law playing an especially important role in the culture-shaping process" (Gleason, 1995, pp. 119–120).

5. Neoscholasticism's power to mold culture goes hand in hand with its ability to create a sense of order in all things. Disorder, incoherence, and fragmentation are the salient characteristics of modernity that are challenged by the philosophical system of Catholicism. "By synthesizing natural truth and supernatural revelation, Neoscholasticism furnished the intellectual armature around which the unified fabric of an integrally Christian and therefore truly humane culture could be fashioned" (Gleason, 1995, p. 120).

6. At the heart of Neoscholasticism is a God-centeredness that moves beyond the parameters of a purely philosophical system. "For God's *being* did more than illuminate the human intellect. Once understood, the divine plan for humankind required action, a commitment to its fulfillment on the part of every believer . . . God's infinite perfection simultaneously awakened spiritual longings that could be satisfied only by personal union with God" (Gleason, 1995, pp. 121–122). Not a dry philosophy, Neoscholasticism "nourished, and was in turn nourished by, the literary, aesthetic, and even mystical dimensions of the [Catholic] revival (Gleason, 1995, p. 122).

It was during the interwar period that the Catholic revival or renaissance came into its own. With this renaissance came an emphasis on Catholicism as a culture, "the way of life of a people" (Gleason, 1995, p. 148). According to George Bull, SJ, a Fordham University philosopher, "the distinctive feature of Catholicism-as-culture was its totality of vision, the way it ordered all knowledge and values into a comprehensive organic unity" (p. 149). This Catholic moment, however, was not confined to higher education, although this period witnessed the founding of a number of academic and professional societies as further expressions of a flourishing Catholic cultural movement.

Gleason (1995) notes that an emphasis on Catholic culture reflected "a broader movement in American intellectual life . . . designating the way of life of a people" (p. 322). He further observes that the liturgical movement, under the leadership of Virgil Michel, OSB, and the theology of the Mystical Body of Christ reinforced the growing sense of Catholicism as a culture, a way of life that could redeem the rapidly secularizing Western civilization. Moreover, Catholic Action, epitomized by the rapid growth of the Sodality of the Blessed Virgin, was also instrumental in what Gleason calls "the campaign to create a Catholic culture."

Neoscholasticism made an important contribution to the development of a rich Catholic culture on university campuses. Thomist theology and, especially, philosophy, were keystones of the undergraduate curriculum. However, one must remember that the universities existed in multiple contexts, among which were the culture of the founding religious congregations, American Catholicism, and the broader context of American culture itself. Although the corresponding secular contexts of local civic and national life cannot be dismissed, Catholicism in its many forms was still foreign to American society, as demonstrated in the 1928 presidential election, in which the Democratic candidate, Al Smith, the first Catholic nominated for that office, was defeated largely because of his Catholicism. National parishes, the parochial primary and secondary school system, the emphasis on attending a Catholic university, and the local parish as the religious and social anchor for the laity—all of these factors directly or indirectly facilitated a Catholic campus culture.

To some extent, the evolving Catholic culture from the 1920s to the 1960s was an attempt to reduce what John Haughey calls the tension between "Catholicism and catholicity." The latter is the drive that seeks to make "wholes," to connect the dots between one's calling in life and one's interiority as a religious or spiritual person. Catholicism "is the faith that seeks to tell and celebrate a continually updated story about the relation between God and human beings" (Haughey, 2009, p. 78). In those forty years, Catholicism and catholicity were brought closer together within Catholic culture.

Within a short period of time, however, the apparent solidity of a homogeneous Catholic culture on the university campus and within the multiple contexts already described began to weaken. The rise of what Gleason (1995) calls Catholic liberalism in the 1940s and 1950s was a counterpoint to ecclesiastically driven Catholicism. "Staunchly orthodox and loyal to the church, mid-century Catholic liberals concentrated not on doctrinal questions, but on social, political, and cultural issues" (p. 285). They were "Americanizers" who challenged the ghetto and siege mentality then present in the Church. The turn to dialogue with, as well as acceptance and critique of, American society and also the Church itself characterized the preconciliar liberals—those proposing change in the Church prior to the Second Vatican Council (1963–65). Among this group are four whose profiles characterize this important movement: the clerics John Courtney Murray, SJ,[1] and John Tracy Ellis[2] and lay persons Daniel Callahan[3] and Rosemary Radford Ruether,[4] all of whom, with the exception of Murray (d. 1967), continued their work in the postconciliar period. Seen in hindsight through the lenses of Vatican II and the swift movement of Catholics into all categories of American life, especially the election of President John Fitzgerald Kennedy, the early 1960s signified that the American Catholic moment had arrived.

However, the American Catholic moment was short-lived, as was that of Catholicism's all-encompassing culture. This was so, Gleason (1979) observes, because

> Catholics who had absorbed the
> mentality dominant in the generation
> before the Council had about the worst
> possible preparation for the sixties
> because the main thrust in those years
> [before the sixties] was toward an
> organically unified Catholic culture in

> which religious faith constituted the
> integrating principle that brought all
> the dimensions of life and thought
> together in comprehensive and tightly
> articulated synthesis.
> (p. 189)

He concludes "that the stress on unity and integral Catholicism from the 1920s through the 1950s heightened the disintegrative impact of changes in the postconciliar years and made those changes particularly unsettling to the faith of persons whose religious character had been formed during the earlier period" (p. 189).

American society underwent profound changes in the 1960s (e.g. the Vietnam War, feminism, and campus ferment), and the Catholic Church and Catholic higher education were equally affected. Within Catholicism, the renewal that resulted from the Second Vatican Council was followed by significant dissent from papal teaching on birth control beginning in 1968, and by the exodus of clergy and religious from dioceses and congregations, also beginning in the late 1960s; all became part of the unsettled American landscape.[5] Writing about the effects of these upheavals on Catholic higher education, Philip Gleason (1995) noted, "it was clear from an early date [in the 1960s] that the old ideological structure of Catholic higher education, which was already under severe strain, had been swept away almost entirely" (p. 285).

As a result, the overarching Neoscholastic synthesis that provided the unifying, transcendent framework of the Catholic university fragmented. Survival without its deeply rooted meaning system profoundly affected Catholic identity and, as Gleason notes, that was still the case as recently as 1995. As we shall see, the publication of *Ex corde Ecclesiae* in 1990 attempted to construct an overarching meaning system, but "identity" or "Catholic culture" remains a central issue to this day.

As such, Gleason's Neoscholastic framework is relevant to Catholic culture and intellectual life in the twenty-first century. Catholicism still maintains an overarching meaning system, one reflective of Haughey's view that "Catholicism and catholic were brought closer together." Nevertheless, the Catholic meaning system today lacks the strong cultural support of a homogeneous Catholic community kept intact by the pressures of Protestant American society. The Catholics have saturated the larger culture and have been absorbed by it. Ironically, the larger American and Western culture itself has unraveled over the last forty to fifty years. The Church, in this same period, has been strongly ecumenical and interreligious in its outreach to the global community and more knowledgeable about and open to the worldview of other societies and civilizations. The collapse of the Enlightenment project and the rise of postmodernism have eroded the possibility of an overarching philosophical or theological worldview or culture that is meaningful to contemporary society. As a result, "a totality of vision, and of ordering all knowledge and values into a comprehensive organic unity," as George Bull notes above, could be seen as more of an ideal type than an achievable reality. However, openness to the other and attentive listening through interreligious dialogue, coupled with humility in the face of other religions and their many adherents, may lead to the realization of a "common ground" between the Catholic worldview and that of other believers.

Questions for Discussion

- What would be a viable present-day vision for the existence of Catholic higher education?
- What are the contributions Neoscholasticism can make to a viable vision for the existence of Catholic education?
- What meaning would such a vision have among a religiously pluralistic and ethnically diverse faculty, administration, staff, and student body?
- How would ecumenical or interreligious groups contribute to this vision?
- As an academic new to Catholic education, what mental models or unexamined beliefs do you have about Catholicism and the Catholic Church?

The Catholic Church and Catholic Culture

In discussions of Catholic higher education, an equation is often made between the Catholic Church and the Catholic university. Understanding Catholicism is an important part of the new professors' introduction to Catholic education, and they have much to gain from a deeper understanding of the Catholic Church as such. A heterogeneous faculty will experience Catholicism primarily by immersion in campus culture; this underlies the importance of culture as an analytic tool. The study of, critical distance from, and continual nurture of Catholic culture are essential for new hires. New faculty and students in the classroom and across the campus relate to one another within the received culture of the Catholic university. They are shaped by and shape that culture and one another, ensuring continuity and newness over time.

William P. Leahy (2008), SJ, the president of Boston College, defined culture thus: "Culture is like a fine mist. If you stand in it long enough, you will be soaked." A Catholic university culture provides a dynamic context in which faculty learning communities, the Catholic intellectual life, and student development will thrive. The particularity of each university's religious congregational heritage is also a significant part of the culture and catches the imagination by the "story" that heritage tells.

Church Trends and the Catholic University

Understanding the contemporary Catholic Church and the direction it is taking is akin to looking into a "cloudy crystal ball" (p. 36), to quote Patrick Jordan (2009) in his review of John Allen's *The Future Church*. There are trends, to be sure: Allen notes ten that he claims are "revolutionizing the Catholic Church." As trends, they call for serious consideration. Whether they are in fact revolutionizing the Church will only be answered over time. For our purposes, *The Future Church* does present new faculty with a contemporary snapshot of Roman Catholicism as a culture that is both local and global, an important consideration in itself for understanding Catholic higher education.

Allen (2009) states that "the issues, party lines, and ways of doing business that have dominated Catholicism in the forty-plus years since the close of the Second Vatican Council in 1965 . . . are being turned on their head by a series of new forces reshaping the global church" (p. 17). For Allen, trends are currents, not headlines. They are present in the contemporary Church and, as with a river current, they change surface contours as well as submerged landscapes. While not often noticed, the effects of trends may be far-ranging if there are no countervailing forces. Scanning present trends and projecting possible future scenarios is at the heart of his book. For our purposes, two of Allen's trends are discussed below. I have chosen them because of their relevance to understanding Catholic culture.

"A World Church"

The first trend Allen (2009) discusses is the most obviously empirical fact of contemporary Church life: the global reach of Catholicism. Although Catholicism has always been missionary as a religious movement, the worldwide network of parishes, dioceses, seminaries, dispensaries, hospitals, universities, schools, orphanages, and other social service agencies astounds any observer of things Catholic. At the same time, Catholicism is a church populated by the "world at large," no longer a Caucasian, European/North American entity. "Projecting forward to the year 2025, only one Catholic in five in the world will be a non-Hispanic Caucasian. This is the most rapid, and most sweeping, demographic transformation of Roman Catholicism in its two-thousand-year history" (p. 17).

For new faculty, understanding the global nature of Catholicism presents an institution—the Church—with which the university is a partner. In fact, many of the universities have founding congregations that have affiliated universities throughout the world, presenting a global context in which faculty at American institutions teach. This realization complements the global perspective so many disciplines now bring to their teaching and research. Many faculty are actually working at one campus of a complex international group of universities founded in turn by a subset of Catholics—the religious congregation—bound together by a common set of characteristics, values, and mission. This fact challenges their self-understanding as individual teacher/researchers within a discipline or subspecialty. Hopefully, it will shift their perspective in curriculum development and interdisciplinary teaching and research. Finally, the international scope of Catholic higher education will broaden faculty fields of research and writing through the many collaborative possibilities with colleagues in African, Asian, and Latin American universities.

As a result of this deeper understanding of the global reach of the Church and Catholic education, I now describe myself, first and foremost, as a member of the international Catholic education community. In particular, I am a member of the Lasallian Education Movement, composed of the De La Salle Christian Brothers and lay partners, commissioned by the Catholic Church and committed to the education of young people, especially the poor.

Questions for Discussion

- How does the above description of the global Catholic Church compare to your previous understanding?
- What are some of the opportunities that could accrue from your university's being a part of a global group of higher education institutions?
- How does this presentation contribute to your understanding of your role as an academic in a worldwide educational movement?
- What significant research opportunities could result from this information?

"Evangelical Catholicism"

The second trend is what Allen calls evangelical Catholicism. The tension between secularization and Catholicism is one aspect of the evangelical trend within the Church. For most new faculty, the secular is the dominant paradigm of graduate education and will be welcomed into the Catholic university by many colleagues who share a belief in secular dominance within their disciplines. Allen offers a description of secularization that is helpful in understanding this significant aspect of university life that Catholic institutions share with other universities. "[Secularization is] more like a transition from a socially dominant religious system to a bewildering variety of impulses, movements, and currents, often pulling in different directions, and with little apparent regard for internal coherence" (Allen, 2009, p. 61). New hires will also find much in their Catholic place of work that they can identify as secular. Though not necessarily expressed as such, the secular paradigm dismisses or sidesteps the perspectives of religion or theology in the sense that they could be conversation partners on an equal footing with other disciplines.

The secularity of academic disciplines has, in many instances, been hard-won, and this is not the place to discuss a revisionist view of religion in academic life. What is of note in the Church and among some students is the rise of evangelical Catholicism among the university population. Understanding this cohort of students is of importance, especially to new faculty, and Allen offers three characteristics of this group: (1) They will *stand out* in their willingness to assert Catholic identity; (2) they will *distinguish themselves* by their "clear embrace of traditional Catholic thought, speech, and practice" (Allen, 2009, p. 56); and (3) they are different from most Catholic students in the sense that they are *intentional about their faith.* They do not see themselves as cultural Catholics. In the vast majority of cases, they are not the dominant group of Catholic students on a campus, but they offer an insight into an important segment of Catholicism.

Discussing evangelicalism will help new faculty listen attentively to and have a sympathetic understanding of vocal evangelicals who may challenge their classroom content or perspective. Appreciating the religious commitment of these students will facilitate understanding evangelical Catholics when they join with "traditional" Catholic students and alums in objecting to invited academic speakers, degree honorees, certain political candidates, film series, or policies related to gay, lesbian, bisexual, or transgender students. Bringing critical distance to this segment of Catholic, as well as evangelical Protestant, students will lead to a deeper understanding of why this embrace of religion is so vital to them: "[F]rom a sociological point of view, the evangelical Catholic movement is one way of coping with the losses imposed by secularization" (Allen, 2009, p. 76). In a world of relativism, evangelical Catholicism offers a robust sense of personal identity.

Questions for Discussion

- What are some examples of secularity at the university? What challenges and opportunities might they present?
- To what extent has your university moved from a "religious" model to a "professional" (secular) model? How well has it blended the two? *(Note: you may need help from senior faculty or administrators to gather the information you need to discuss this topic.)*
- What place does religion have in a predominantly secular curriculum?
- At a Catholic university, what are the proper roles of religious studies and theology as academic disciplines with equal standing among all departments?
- What would be the benefits, challenges, opportunities, and risks of teaching evangelical Catholics?

Cultural Analysis: Opportunities and Challenges

Achieving even a modicum of critical distance from one's own culture can be either, or simultaneously, liberating or threatening to the individual's sense of self and of her or his place in the culture. The point of view assumed by the cultural critique itself must also be accounted for in evaluating the analysis. Individual self-understanding is shaped by nature but also strongly influenced by nurture—that is, by culture. The cultural critique should appeal to new faculty since each of them is a cultural actor in higher education. They will find the differentiation and distinctiveness of Catholic education in relation to American higher learning to be of great help in adjusting to and embracing their new position.

In the case of Catholic higher education, as with other institutions, distancing oneself culturally can never be fully and finally achieved. However, cultural critique is valuable and has at least two possible but divergent outcomes. It may result in freedom to accept, question, or reshape the culture, thereby giving rise to new understanding and direction; it may also result in anxiety, rigidity, or a search for employment in an institution characterized by a more suitable culture. As a result, the RM team should be sensitive to the impact and unintended consequences cultural analysis may have on new faculty or other members of the university community. Some new faculty, for instance, may become quite confused or upset by a discussion of Catholic culture.

The description of culture goes far in providing a heuristic for understanding the challenges and opportunities Catholic universities are facing today. Aspiration to a robust, dynamic Catholic culture is the premise of the Revisioning Mission program. A thorough grasp of the inheritance is essential, but without action in support of making the inheritance a vibrant reality, the drift toward secularity is unavoidable. Thus, a well-conceived retention program in an "inheritable" and "actionable" culture has a threefold cumulative effect: New faculty commit themselves to taking a leadership role by *treasuring* the university inheritance, *working* to make it the animating feature of the institution's culture in the present, and *transmitting* it to future generations by retaining a new generation of faculty. (See Morey & Piderit, 2006, p. 37)

When inheritance and action are in synchronicity, culture lends itself to thick description. Harmony between inheritance and action results in continuity and enhances culture. Dissonance between the two develops conflict and weakens both. In any case, even a revolution does not sweep away a culture. The latter evolves, but the change may hardly be noticed in any given time period. It is almost as if social groupings have a genetic resistance to rapid cultural change even though culture is nurture, not nature.[6]

Thus, rapidity of change, "things falling apart," is a great challenge, given the need for a workable level of stability and continuity in the critical areas of social life in a community: physical survival, nourishment, childbearing, personal identity, trust, and economic exchange, among the many other interactions of a social group. In the case of the university, regular contact between students and faculty, predetermined semesters or quarters, regular examinations, general education, major fields of study, an end point or graduation, administrative leadership and service, and work contracts are among many areas of stability and continuity that are foundational to education.

A university president described the Catholic university as life-giving:

The heart and soul of [Catholic] institutions are transformational in nature, not just transactional. They are not just credit bearing, but life giving. These institutions teach people not only how to earn a living but how to live a life in a moral sense, an ethical sense, in a value sense. They give a moral compass that enables students to get through life's crisis situations. (Morey & Piderit, 2006, p. 11)

This statement reflects the summative goals of Catholic education. These goals are achieved through faculty relationships, curriculum development, and classroom learning, along with the informal learning that occurs across the campus: in the dining hall and the dormitory, among other places. In other words, whether the university articulates it or not, the campus culture in which the entire community is immersed is the locus for achieving these goals, and worthy of examination.

The Peer Group and Catholic Culture

Nevertheless, among all elements in campus culture, it is the peer group that is most influential in university life and, therefore, essential in this discussion of Catholic culture. Alexander Astin (1993) concludes that "the student's peer group is the single most potent source of influence on growth and development during the undergraduate years" (p. 398). The peer group, then, is more powerful than faculty, curriculum, or institutional type. In terms of affective development, Astin concludes, "students' values, beliefs, and aspirations tend to change in the direction of the dominant values, beliefs, and aspirations of the peer group" (p. 398). Astin's conclusion about peer influence is backed by the respect given his research. Yet he also believes that faculty influence is powerful in the development of the students: "Next to the peer group, the faculty represents the most significant aspect of the student's undergraduate development" (p. 398). For instance, service learning is a highly regarded tool for student development in higher education. The quality of the learning in this pedagogy is determined by two factors that cannot be separated: the experiential and the reflective. "To serve is to learn" is accurate only when faculty and other adults in service learning centers and campus ministry accompany and guide the students in a service or immersion experience. Reflection needs guidance through the use of relevant questions and respectful dialogue among all participants. As mentors, faculty and staff are catalysts for the innumerable life-changing student service learning experiences.

I posit that peers do have an enormous influence on one another, but the towering role that faculty and staff can play in student development cannot be discounted and deserves more study. After all, faculty and staff bring a wealth of personal development, education, and life experience to their calling, all resulting in hard-earned beliefs, values, and commitments. Their lives speak to the students in unfathomable ways. It is said that Francis of Assisi told his followers, "Preach the Gospel. Use words if necessary." That maxim applies equally well to faculty and student-life staff in their work with students.

New faculty should have some insight into the highly nuanced culture of campus life, especially peer-group impact. Attention to peer groups in terms of identifying, understanding, communicating with, educating, and influencing them is of significant importance to the future of all universities. This would seem more the case in a Catholic university, where attention to culture plays a critical role in achieving a distinctive mission. As already indicated, on average, the majority of students at Catholic universities are indeed Catholic (65 percent), but their Catholicity runs the gamut, with many students religiously illiterate, unchurched, disaffected, or rejecting of all religion and accepting of a broader, if somewhat "therapeutic," spirituality.

How does this fact impact university culture, and, reciprocally, how does the culture impact these students, and especially peer groups? These are important questions, and ones that remain to be addressed. I see the Catholic university as the last, best *institutional* opportunity to bring students to a fuller awareness of Catholicism, the Church, and their relationship to it. You will note my emphasis on "*institutional* opportunity." This is so because the Catholic Church traditionally has not invested itself in ministry to young Catholics after confirmation or in early adulthood.[7] This contention about the role of the university in bringing some religious stability to the lives of Catholics and other religiously affiliated students is supported to some extent by Astin's research on faculty. However, he does caution "that most effects of institutional type are indirect, that they are mediated by faculty, peer group, and involvement variables" (Astin, 1993, p. 413).

Astin (1993) concludes "that institutional *structure*, as such, is not the key ingredient; rather, it is the kinds of peer groups and faculty environments that tend to emerge under these different structures" (p. 413) (i.e. small, private, residential colleges, large public or private colleges and universities, or major research universities). As noted by Astin, the faculty exert great influence on their young adult students, second only to the influence of peers. While this is portrayed somewhat globally, faculty influence on students in terms of relationships with institutional religion must be intentional. Hopefully, the presence or emergence of a Mission Community will enhance this influence. With the growing prevalence of the residential campus, the professionally trained student-life staff also brings increasing influence to bear on twenty-four-hour student life and is becoming an important counterweight to peer influence.

The complex problem of young adult Catholics falling away from active involvement in the Church has arisen from many other sources, among which are:

- Distrust of institutional religion and voluntary associations more generally, yet correlated with an attraction to therapeutic, emotive religiosity associated with evangelicalism and Pentecostalism.

- Knowledge of diverse religious and spiritual traditions, learned in comparative religion courses, on Web sites, and from peers, leads students to conclude that religions are relative as a result of their "social construction." Thus, young adults choose or combine, without much institutional baggage, religions and free-floating spiritualities, leading to characterizations such as Jewish Buddhism.

- Along with the overwhelming influence of a secular, consumerist, sexually promiscuous, and technology-encrusted culture, bound up with a confident, optimistic individualism, many young adults do not have a sense of direction or understanding of commitment. As a result, adult maturation has been pushed into the third decade of their lives.

These characteristics should not be taken as blanket generalities about all young adults between the ages of eighteen and thirty-five, as we shall see in the next essay, "Students at Catholic Universities." But they do shape the profile of the many whose deep unease with the direction of their lives is not easily healed because they lack the time and solitude to address their deepest needs. There are significant numbers of young adults, however, whom one seldom hears of because their lives and commitments are invisible in a gaudy, spotlight-obsessed society. These are university graduates who continue the service learning experience through full-time work in nonprofit organizations, part-time work with Catholic Charities, Catholic Big Brothers and Sisters, or longer-term commitments to the ministries of Catholic Relief Services and to the founding religious congregations.

Questions for Discussion

- How do you react to this statement: "While a cultural critique of the university may be appealing, it may not be well received by senior faculty, staff, or administration, who may consider it an attack on the 'way the university operates.'"

- How are the university's vision and mission in line with its policies and their implementation? What gaps have you experienced so far? What examples can you offer to show agreement between vision and policy?

- Give some examples of the impact of peer influence on university life. What parallel examples of faculty impact can you offer?

- What opportunities might offer you a better understanding of student culture?

- What impact do the words and actions of faculty have on students? Give some examples from your own experience.

- How might you have a spiritual impact on your students? What would be your response to this query?

- What reasons exist for the religious disconnect of students?

Cultural Strains on Catholic Higher Education

Cultural analysis of Catholic higher education reveals the challenges these universities face. *One of the cultural strains* on the Catholic university today is the embrace of diversity among faculty, administrators, staff, and students as an intrinsic good, at a time when the institution is working to preserve and clarify its distinctive Catholic culture and the heritage of the founding religious congregation. The university is caught in the bind of hospitality to a heterogeneous population, over and against what many new and long-standing faculty, staff, and administrators mistakenly see as a return to homogeneity due to emphasis on the Catholic culture and the heritage of the founding congregation. They do not understand the profound shift to ecumenism and interreligious cooperation brought about by the Second Vatican Council, and so misinterpret the support for a Catholic culture as a return to the years before the Council, thus contradicting a turn to diversity. Other members of the university community may see the apparent contradiction as forging a new frontier in institutional self-understanding and, as a result, are energized and participative in the process.

A second cultural strain is the emphasis placed on the mission to the poor in the context of such challenges as costly competition for brighter students and upgraded campus facilities. Catholic universities have had a historical mission to the underserved and first-generation undergraduate students. This mission has been reinforced by Church social teaching, especially its declaration of a "fundamental option for the poor." While Catholic institutions with significant endowments can address this mission with considerable resources, this is not the case for many less-well-off universities. All Catholic universities are subject to the pressures of enhancing reputation, SAT scores, enrollment, endowment, facilities, and the recruiting of star faculty. The annual ranking by national publications casts a shadow over the efforts of Catholic institutions to give priority of place to the religious heritage and Catholic culture over and against these pressures and the resulting impact they have on parents, high school students, guidance counselors, Catholic undergraduate admissions offices, and the orientation and rigor of the curriculum.

A third cultural strain is the religious makeup of the student population in relation to the professed Catholicism of the university. Although, as previously noted, Catholics still represent a majority of the student population, their profile is quite different from that of previous generations, thereby presenting another cultural contradiction: Catholic students are valued, but in what sense are they Catholics? Will they need religious remediation? Two to three generations ago the vast majority of Catholic university students were Catholics, came through the Catholic school system, and matured within its culture; this isn't the case today. There are significantly fewer elementary and secondary Catholic "feeder" schools, and they are mostly staffed by a heterogeneous lay faculty whose commitment to teaching is not at issue, but who do not have the Catholic cultural experience and the religious heritage of the homogeneous congregation that founded and conducted the elementary and secondary schools, some for a century or more.

A fourth strain is that Catholic graduates of these high schools, with few exceptions, lack a nuanced understanding of Catholicism. In fact, some observers of Catholic university life go so far as to say that the incoming classes are religiously illiterate. Even more significant is the fact that many of the incoming first-year students, whether Catholic or Christian, are also unchurched. It does not help the students that Catholicism itself is not easily understood and does not appeal to their "spiritual" sensitivities. Preconciliar solidity in Catholic culture no longer exists. More importantly, the Church itself would appear to be crumbling: "three Catholics leave the church for each one who enters" (Steinfels, 2010, p.19).

Question for Discussion

What experiences have you had so far of the four strains described above? What do you think has caused these strains?

Cultures on a Collision Course

The fact that the vast majority of students opt to live on campus means they have more time to be influenced by one another about religion and spirituality or politics and sex, among many other areas of life. Academic learning is the reason the students are on campus, but their growth as persons is influenced by the many dimensions of university life, especially peer culture. If the Catholic culture is a "fine mist," a majority residential population could actually assist in fulfillment of the university's mission, but at the same time, these students are not cultural blanks. To a greater or lesser extent, as with the rest of the American university population, they embody the culture of the society and its value system, especially the emphasis on human rights, individualism, material-ism, consumerist capitalism, and the personal good, in contrast to the public good of society.

The Catholic university itself is immersed in American culture for good and for ill. The valued-added dimension that makes it distinctive, however, is the countercultural, prophetic dimen-sion of Catholicism exemplified in Catholic social teaching and the heritage of the founding congregation. A culturally reflective institution will be aware that the tension between these two value systems will never disappear and needs constant attention. Cam-pus ministry, social justice initiatives, and curriculum offerings are most often the sources of prophetic voices and cultural reflection.

These same tensions will assert themselves among the trust-ees, in most instances alums who are financially successful and lead major corporations. They will consciously and unconsciously bring to bear on the university's short- and long-term planning the values of the market system and their political convictions. Their values are at times on a collision course with the mission of the university, the heritage of the congregation, and Catholic social teaching. At the same time, these individuals possess, or have wealthy contacts that possess, the financial resources to increase the endowment-fund scholarships for the needy and to contribute to capital campaigns or building projects.

Highlighting the cultural tensions, contradictions, nuances, and unintended consequences of university life presents an edu-cational opportunity to discuss with new faculty the evolution of Catholicism over the last several decades. Catholicism is too fre-quently misunderstood within American graduate education, either viewed as alien territory or interpreted as a threat to per-sonal and academic freedom. These interpretations occur because Catholic culture is all too often equated with the media's emphasis on controversy related to the Church hierarchy as well as its politi-cal positions and teachings, both of which are perceived as author-itarian and inhospitable to the core value of academic freedom. Because of high-profile issues such as clerical child abuse, the con-sequent cover-up by the hierarchy, and episcopal pronouncements in the political arena, the Church has indeed lost both social capital and moral suasion among many Catholics. (Universities would do well to offer programs addressing the state of the contemporary Catholic Church as well as evaluating the positive role Catholic higher education can assume in restoring the Church's credibility, and not only for new faculty.)

In sum, the heterogeneity of the Catholic university, its aspirations to a competitive niche in American higher education, its fidelity to a mission to serve first-generation students, the absence of an informed Catholic majority in the university community, the cultural power of residence life among the majority of students, and memberships on the board of trustees, are all salient characteristics of these institutions. As a result, there are disputed questions, flash points concerning decisions and actions based on values and principles that are part and parcel of each person's cultural stance in the university, much of which they bring with them when they enter the university community. The taken-for-granted certitude that pervaded the Catholic university has given way to a marketplace of ideas, values, and lifestyles, in part because the university population is no longer the homogeneous enclave it was fifty or sixty years ago, and neither is American society or the global community.

In retrospect, the discussion of Catholic culture in this essay is a result of the upheaval in the 1960s and the Neoscholastic collapse previously described. There is also a direct line between the "Land o' Lakes" Statement on the future of Catholic higher education (1967) and the Apostolic Constitution, *Ex corde Ecclesiae*, promulgated by Pope John Paul II on August 15, 1990. The latter was the product of almost two decades of protracted discussion among (and multiple drafts composed by) university administrators, faculty, and church leaders in Rome and globally. The document presents the vision and mission of Catholic education that virtually all Catholic college administrators (and many faculty) support. That is not necessarily the case with the final section on implementation of Part II, "General Norms," especially the request that each Catholic theologian seek a personal mandate (*mandatum*) by which he or she pledges to explain accurately the teachings of the Catholic Church. Needless to say, both the theologians' call for privacy and hierarchical requests for head counting lent fuel to the fire of what counts as a truly Catholic university. This contention is a sidebar to the larger context of a Catholic Church in turmoil.

Question for Discussion

In what ways do you experience the Catholic university as counter-cultural? As a part of its surrounding culture? As above the reach of culture? As influencing and challenging culture?

Ex Corde Ecclesiae (From the Heart of the Church)

While giving Allen his due as a journalist and trend spotter, a discussion of the papal document *Ex corde Ecclesiae* (ECE)[8] offers a vision or ideal type of what the Catholic university aspires to be. It is an important document that paints a nuanced picture of Catholic university culture.

In reviewing ECE, my intention is to highlight several important points that relate to the Catholic culture of the university and the Catholic intellectual life. The document itself, of course, should be required reading for the Revisioning Mission cohort. We will address one issue at length in the essay on Catholic intellectual life: "the conflict between the search for truth and the certainty of already knowing the fount of truth" (John Paul II, 1990, para. 1).

The Culture of the Catholic University in Ex Corde Ecclesiae

In analyzing the identity of the Catholic university, ECE begins by stating that each one is an academic community and that its first obligation is to assist "in the protection and advancement of human dignity" (John Paul II, 1990, para. 12). Community and human dignity are starting points of Catholic social teaching and are foundational to higher education. The university also protects and advances "a cultural heritage through research, teaching, and various services offered to the local, national, and international communities" (para. 12). In higher education, the Catholic university is a "Christian presence," possessing the following characteristics, all of which speak to the culture of the institution:

The first characteristic is a "Christian inspiration," on the part of individuals and the community. The inspiration is not only the founding worldview but the present-day self-understanding of the university: recognizing itself as an institution built on Catholic culture and intellectual life as well as on the heritage of the founding congregation, resulting in a vision or ideal to which it is drawn. The task of elucidating "Christian inspiration" is an ongoing one that should involve new faculty and their senior colleagues.

Morey and Piderit (2006) contribute to a fuller understanding of "Christian inspiration" by way of their definition of Catholic culture as "groups of practices and behaviors, beliefs, and understandings" (p. 33) that play a central role in the lives of Catholics. Experiencing the culture offers a Catholic environment in which those who are Christian or of other belief systems pursue their work. A robust Catholic culture has indirect consequences: It is a way of living Catholicism, or, as has already been discussed, living espoused values. From a Catholic perspective it is a profound form of "preaching the Gospel" without using words. In other words, culture has "content." "If cultural content is clear and present in the forefront of the organization and in the minds of those who work there, the culture will be vibrant and affect the life, behavior, and tone of the organization" (Morey & Piderit, 2006, p. 25). Of course, the university must always critically search for signs of a "shadow" culture that might have devastating consequences on the credibility of the culture to which the university commits itself. As Morey and Piderit also note, a rich Catholic culture is also laden with symbols (the crucifix and statuary) and rituals (liturgies and commencements). Creators of a vibrant Catholic culture, or any culture for that matter, include icons such as role models, knowledge experts, and heroes. Likewise, "stories are the connective tissue of culture, giving it its depth, breadth, and texture" (Morey & Piderit, 2006, p. 26-27). (Although not intended as a book on culture,

Malcolm Gladwell's [2000] *The Tipping Point* offers important insights into the indicia of cultural richness.)

The beliefs and assumptions are not necessarily articulated and not necessarily shared by all members of the community. They are most often taken for granted—like wallpaper—creating an environment but unseen to the eye, as it were. A prime example would be: "How does this decision affect the students?"

A second characteristic is that the Catholic university reflects on "the growing treasury of human knowledge, to which it seeks to contribute by its own research" (John Paul II, 1990, para. 13). The reflection is distinctive in the sense that it is carried on "in the light of Catholic faith" (para. 13), a distinction that will be discussed in the essay on the Catholic intellectual life, epistemology, and the transcendental horizon of the university.

The third characteristic is that of "fidelity to the Christian message as it comes to us through the Church" (John Paul II, 1990, para. 13). If the "university is where the Church does its thinking" (Hesburgh, n.d.), then this characteristic suggests that higher education is a partner in crafting the message for the present generation in continuity with Christian tradition and teaching. Joseph A. Komonchak, a leading authority on the Second Vatican Council, offers a qualification on Hesburgh's apothegm above. While he agrees that it is one of many places, he points out that "the Church does her thinking also in the pews, in convents, monasteries and seminaries, in retreat centers, on the Bowery, in hospitals and prisons, in homes and workplaces, etc." (Komonchak, 2006).

Komonchak's observation is well taken, but doing such work inevitably leads both to creativity and to conflict in the university and elsewhere, as illustrated by the history of religious and theological thought since the early Church. Wherever there is an academic community struggling with meaning—which certainly includes the theological and philosophical disciplines—there is bound to be conflict, out of which new insight or understanding develops. If each academic pursues research freely, there is no guarantee that all will come to conclusions welcomed by the teaching authority (the magisterium) of the Catholic Church. As a result, these disciplines constitute the lightning rod of academic freedom in the Catholic university.

Clearly, a professor has no right to present his or her own perspective on Catholic doctrine as authentic teaching. However, as a critique of a Catholic position presented in comparison to Church teaching in a lecture or in the classroom, the professor's perspectives are protected by academic freedom. There is little doubt that this characteristic of the Catholic university will lead to interesting conversations among faculty.

The fourth characteristic presents the university as having "an institutional commitment to the service of the people of God and of the human family in their pilgrimage to the transcendent goal which gives meaning to life" (John Paul II, 1990, para. 13). Giving meaning to life is a fundamental quest for all humanity, a quest that is addressed by the Catholic university and that goes to the core of its distinctiveness. However, the university views the quest as the human pilgrimage to "the transcendent goal" that alone gives meaning to life. The core distinction, then, is the transcendent horizon, a horizon common to all religious traditions but understood within Catholicism as the kingdom of God. Respecting and embracing the pilgrimage of the human family, the Catholic university is institutionally committed to the service of the human race, without restriction. It is a commitment founded on Catholic social teaching; one that is, as we have seen, welcoming and welcomed by the spectrum of faculty and other members of the university community. The religious heritage of the founding congregation is likewise committed to Catholic social teaching, thereby enriching this fourth characteristic of the university.

The Pope synthesizes these characteristics in a description of university culture: "Catholic ideals, attitudes, and principles penetrate and inform university activities" (John Paul II, 1990, para. 14). The university is at once a "community of scholars . . . and an academic institution in which Catholicism is vitally present and operative" (para. 14). It is a place of research, which, along with knowledge, has an "intrinsic value," but a distinctive element is that "the various disciplines are brought into dialogue for their mutual enhancement" (para. 15).

Reinforcing the four essential characteristics of the Catholic university are four dimensions of research. These perspectives give further insight into the at times elusive understanding of Catholic culture. They present a contrast to the Enlightenment-driven scientific methodology in a secular environment precisely because they are dismissed by many, but not all, scientists as irrelevant and even hostile to research in itself. "In a Catholic university, research necessarily includes (a) the search for an integration of knowledge, (b) a dialogue between faith and reason, (c) an ethical concern, and (d) a theological perspective" (John Paul II, 1990, para. 15).

Note, however, that these perspectives are brought to bear on the research project but do not constitute the research work. "Integration of knowledge" is characteristic of the Catholic intellectual life because all that is—creation—ultimately originates in one source, God, with a transcendent horizon or teleology that is also God. The scientific method itself is not in dispute. This search complements the scientific model of objectivism and the challenges of disciplinary specialization because it seeks context and meaning beyond the particularity of empirical evidence and a specialized subdiscipline. There is the presumption of "social embeddedness" (Palmer, Zajonc, & Scribner, 2010) in the Catholic academic culture, a "community of knowledge" in research, just as there is the presumption of a "community of persons" in social teaching. Theology plays a role in research because it seeks a "synthesis of knowledge" as well. "It serves all other disciplines in their search for meaning, not only by helping them to investigate how their discoveries will affect individuals and society, but also by bringing a perspective and an orientation not contained within their own methodology" (p. 59).

Ex Corde also addresses the characteristics of the university community, the Catholic university in the Church, service to Church and society, pastoral ministry, cultural dialogue, and evangelization. These areas present important resources for discussion by the Mission Community on campus.

Remember that Parker Palmer and Arthur Zajonc also address another, perhaps more fundamental perspective on the integration of knowledge. From the scientific side, Zajonc, the physicist, discusses the integration of knowledge in a more personal sense by seeking to overcome the "divided self." He speaks not so much about the integration of content as about the "division and reification of fact and value." Writing more positively, he notes: "Our colleges and universities need to encourage, foster, and assist our students, faculty, and administrators in finding their own authentic way to an undivided life where meaning and purpose are tightly interwoven with intellect and action" (Palmer et al., 2010, p. 56).

Likewise, establishing "a dialogue between faith and reason" is considered irrelevant by many in the scientific community because two diametrically opposite perspectives on empirical evidence are involved. Following the thread of thought established by Zajonc, we find the "new sciences" taking the lead in laying the foundations for spirituality/reason and faith/reason dialogues. According to Zajonc, the outmoded scientific paradigm is characterized by manipulation of evidence, deduction and induction, models of reality, and distrust of direct experiential knowledge. Truth is equated with reductionism. He challenges this methodology: "I argue that the new physics opposes this misguided view, and I show how modern science asserts the primacy of experience and relations that are not reducible to entities and mechanisms" (Palmer et al., 2010, p. 56). Environmental catastrophe and global warming impel us to view our delicate blue planet suspended in space from a much more holistic viewpoint, reinforcing the new science's relational paradigm, one that evokes compassion and "ethical concern," the latter a characteristic that should imbue science research in the Catholic university. The educational imperative is to value "the self-consciousness of the new science" and other disciplines "while also affirming the possibility of a way to truth, meaning, and purpose" (Palmer et al., 2010, pp. 63–64). Essential to this valuing is "participatory epistemology, an introspective methodology," or what Zajonc simply calls "attention," a concept that goes to the heart of spirituality and faith. "Inclusion of the contemplative training of attention has already begun to gain ground in higher education under the name of contemplative pedagogy" (Palmer et al., 2010, p. 74).

Questions for Discussion

- Among the characteristics of a Catholic university described in ECE, which ones do you find appealing? Which ones are challenging for you to embrace?
- What characteristics or topics raised by ECE do you not yet feel you understand?
- What is your understanding of a "synthesis of knowledge"? Of an "integrated education"? Practically speaking, how will they be achieved?
- What challenges and opportunities present themselves with regard to the relationship of faith to reason?

Conclusion

In this overview of Catholic university culture, there has been no focus on sociological and anthropological studies, nor has an ethnography of a specific Catholic university been provided. The purpose of this essay has been to raise awareness of the critical role that culture plays in higher education, and especially in the Catholic university. The charge to the RM leader and to the FLC is to become conscious of the uniqueness of the local culture and its impact on the workforce and student body of the institution. With the assistance of faculty in sociology and other behavioral sciences, the FLC will determine the most appropriate tools to obtain local knowledge of their university's Catholic culture.

References

Allen, J. L. (2009). *The future church: How ten trends are revolutionizing the Catholic Church.* New York, NY: Doubleday.

Astin, A. W. (1993). *What matters in college? Four critical years revisited.* San Francisco, CA: Jossey-Bass.

Geertz, C. (1973). *The interpretation of cultures: Selected essays.* New York, NY: Basic Books.

Gladwell, M. (2000). *The tipping point: How little things can make a big difference.* Boston, MA: Little, Brown.

Gleason, P. (1979). In search of unity: American Catholic thought 1920–1960. *The Catholic Historical Review, 65*(2), 185–205.

Gleason, P. (1995). *Contending with modernity: Catholic higher education in the twentieth century.* New York, NY: Oxford University Press.

Haughey, J. C. (2009). *Where is knowing going? The horizons of the knowing subject.* Washington, DC: Georgetown University Press.

Hesburgh, T. M. (n.d.). Mission statement. Retrieved from Notre Dame, Department of African Studies Web site: http://africana.nd.edu/our-graduates/

John Paul II (1990). Apostolic constitution of the supreme pontiff John Paul II on Catholic universities (commonly known as *Ex corde Ecclesiae* (ECE)). Retrieved from the Vatican Web site: http://www.vatican.va/holy_father/john_paul_ii/apost_constitutions/documents/hf_jp-ii_apc_15081990_ex-corde-ecclesiae_en.html.

Jordan, P. (2009). Cloudy crystal ball. *Commonweal, 136*(19), 36–38.

Kaveny, C. (2010). Long goodbye. *Commonweal, 137*(18), 8.

Komonchak, J. A. (2006). Where does the Church do her thinking? [Web log post] Retrieved from http://www.commonwealmagazine.org/blog/?p=157

Leahy, W., SJ. (2008). Address at annual meeting of the Association of Catholic Colleges and Universities.

Morey, M. M., & Piderit, J. J. (2006). *Catholic higher education: A culture in crisis.* New York, NY: Oxford University Press.

Morrill, R. L. (1980). *Teaching values in college.* San Francisco, CA: Jossey-Bass.

O'Connell, M. (2008). Theological roundtable: Rethinking the secular. *Horizons: The Journal of the College Theology Society, 35*(2), 334-343.

Palmer, P. J., Zajonc, A., & Scribner, M. (2010). *The heart of higher education: A call to renewal.* San Francisco, CA: Jossey-Bass.

Rogers, W. R. (1989). Values in higher education. In C. T. Mitchell (Ed.), *Values in teaching and professional ethics* (pp. 3–8). Macon, GA: Mercer University Press.

Steinfels, P. (2010). Further adrift. *Commonweal, 137*(18), 16–20.

Vatican Council. (1965). *Pastoral constitution on the church in the modern world (Gaudium et spes); Promulgated by His Holiness Pope Paul VI.* Retrieved from the Vatican Web site: http://www.vatican.va/archive/hist_councils/ii_vatican_council/documents/vat-ii_const_19651207_gaudium-et-spes_en.html

Recommended Reading

Abbott, W. M. (1966). *The documents of Vatican II.* Piscataway, NJ: America Press. See also www.vatican.va/archive/hist_councils/ii_vatican.../index.htm.

Allen, J. L. (2009). *The future church: How ten trends are revolutionizing the Catholic Church.* New York, NY: Doubleday.

Gleason, P. (1995). *Contending with modernity: Catholic higher education in the twentieth century.* New York, NY: Oxford University Press.

Vatican Council. (1965). *Pastoral constitution on the Church in the modern world (Gaudium et spes); Promulgated by His Holiness Pope Paul VI.* Retrieved from the Vatican website: http://www.vatican.va/archive/hist_councils/ii_vatican_council/documents/vat-ii_const_19651207_gaudium-et-spes_en.html

Notes

[1] John Courtney Murray (1904–1967) championed an understanding of religious liberty at the Second Vatican Council that was based on American religious freedom and separation of church and state. His was the greatest influence on the *Declaration on Religious Freedom* (*Dignitatis Humanae*) at the Council. In print in Abbott, W. M. (1966). *The documents of Vatican II.* Piscataway, NJ: America Press. Or online at http://www.vatican.va/archive/hist_councils/ii_vatican_council/documents/vat-ii_decl_19651207_dignitatis-humanae_en.html

[2] John Tracy Ellis was the dean of Catholic historians (1905–1992). He wrote a groundbreaking essay, "American Catholics and the Intellectual Life," that has influenced Catholic universities from its first appearance in *Thought*, 30(3), pp. 351–388, available at http://alumni.online.bc.edu/content/dam/files/offices/mission/pdf1/cu25.pdf

[3] Daniel Callahan (b. 1930), co-founder of the Hasting Center with a focus on bioethics and public interest (1969), editor (1961–1968) of *Commonweal, A Review of Religion, Politics & Culture* (a lay-edited Catholic weekly) and author of 30 books and 250 articles, many of which address policy and ethical issues in the health sciences.

[4] Rosemary Radford Ruether (b. 1936) is a theologian, scholar, teacher, and Roman Catholic activist who has written groundbreaking books on feminist and liberation theology. Dr. Ruether taught at Garrett Evangelical Seminary, the Pacific School of Religion, and the Graduate Theological Union (Berkeley). An eminently readable Catholic theologian, she has written more than 30 books and approximately 500 articles.

[5] On the history of American Catholicism in the twentieth century, see Morris, C. R. (1997). *American Catholic: The saints and sinners who built America's most powerful church.* New York, NY: Times Books.

[6] Those sociologists or political scientists who contest the value or authenticity of thick cultural descriptions opt for a "thin" description of culture.

[7] The challenges facing the Catholic Church in the area of young adult ministry are discussed in Steinfels, P. (2010). Further adrift: The American church's crisis of attrition. *Commonweal*, 137(18), 16–20. See also Smith, C., & Denton, M. L. (2009). *Soul searching: The religious and spiritual lives of American teenagers.* Oxford: Oxford University Press. See also Smith, C., & Snell, P. (2009). *Souls in*

transition: The religious and spiritual lives of emerging adults. Oxford: Oxford University Press.

[8] The document is divided into numbered paragraphs. All references are in parentheses following the quote and are cited by paragraph number. The reference for the text itself is: John Paul II (1990). Apostolic constitution of the supreme pontiff John Paul II on Catholic universities (commonly known as *Ex corde Ecclesiae* [ECE]). Retrieved from the Vatican website: http://www.vatican. va/holy_father/john_paul_ii/apost_constitutions/documents/ hf_jp-ii_apc_15081990_ex-corde-ecclesiae_en.html

[9] More information is available on the website for the Association for Contemplative Mind in Higher Education at http://www. acmhe.org. See also Zajonc, A. (2009). *Meditation as contemplative inquiry: When knowing becomes love.* Great Barrington, MA: Lindisfarne Books.

ESSAY TWO

STUDENTS AT CATHOLIC UNIVERSITIES: THEIR SPIRITUAL DEVELOPMENT

By Jennifer A. Lindholm

Introduction by John Wilcox

The discussion of Catholic culture as the context for faculty learning communities leads to a profile of the students who attend Catholic universities. You will be disappointed if you anticipate a significant number of characteristics that set these students far apart from the vast majority of university undergraduates. However, the first-year men and women who do enter Catholic universities have a clear expectation of a focus on spiritual growth by these faith-based institutions— as do many of those attending other, sectarian universities. This expectation is present among three-quarters of the students, as opposed to two-thirds among their peers at secular public and private universities. Virtually all of them come from homes, high schools, and communities that are part and parcel of the American demographic landscape.

At the same time, many readers may be surprised at the depth of the students' spiritual life. This chapter and its related reading will greatly assist faculty in gaining a better understanding of the inner life of these young people. The result should lead to great insight, respect, and compassion for them. Knowing more intimately the inner life of eighteen- to-twenty-two-

year-olds also has the potential for a significant pedagogical payoff. Since research has demonstrated a similar spiritual journey by the faculty and others who study this chapter, greater personal reflection and self-understanding will hopefully result in powerful adult role modeling for students at the beginning of their own life journeys.

Background

Since the fall of 1966, data gathered annually through the Cooperative Institutional Research Program (CIRP), founded by Alexander Astin, have reflected the experiences, perspectives, expectations, and aspirations of the nation's entering college freshmen.[1] To date, more than 12 million students at public, private, religiously affiliated, and nonsectarian four-year institutions have completed the freshman survey. Each year, those data are statistically weighted to reflect all first-time, full-time, first-year students entering college that fall (currently, roughly 1.5 million). Staff from the Higher Education Research Institute (HERI), which is housed within UCLA's Graduate School of Education and Information Studies, prepares annual reports that highlight key survey findings.[2] Additional, periodic reports offer trends and perspectives. Taken together, these normative profiles are used broadly by a wide range of individuals who have vested interests in higher education, including policy analysts, campus administrators and faculty, and educational researchers, not to mention current and prospective college students and their families.

Since its inception, a fundamental purpose of the CIRP has been to conduct longitudinal research on undergraduate student development by following up on various entering classes. This essay focuses on one of those longitudinal research projects: a seven-year effort to explore students' spiritual inclinations, examine how spiritual qualities change during the undergraduate years, and consider what role the college experience plays in facilitating students' spiritual development. The chapter draws from material contained in *Cultivating the Spirit: How Colleges and Universities Can Enhance Students' Inner Lives* (2011), my recent book (coauthored with Alexander Astin and Helen Astin) based on our longitudinal

Spirituality in Higher Education study, and from an accompanying reference guide for practitioners entitled *A Guidebook of Promising Practices: Facilitating College Students' Spiritual Development* (Lindholm, Millora, Schwartz, & Spinosa, 2011). The essay provides perspective on the importance of understanding and attending to the spiritual dimension of college students' lives, highlights key findings from our recent longitudinal study, and offers insights for how faculty in particular may contribute to student learning and development within this realm.

Undergraduate Student Inclinations and Expectations

Today's traditional-age undergraduates enter college under the weight of tremendous social and economic pressures. For example, nearly two-thirds report that the current economic situation has "significantly" affected their college choice. Increasing numbers also have "major" concerns about financing their college education (Pryor, Hurtado, DeAngelo, Sharkness, Romero, & University of California, Los Angeles, Cooperative Institutional Research Program, Graduate School of Education & Information Studies, 2008). Perhaps at least in part reflective of their tenuous economic plight, fully three-quarters identify being very well off financially as a "very important" or "essential" goal (Pryor et al., 2008). In recent years, record (or near record) high self-ratings on drive to achieve and academic ability are also evident (Pryor et al., 2008). These findings are paralleled by an apparent decline in students' self-perceived emotional health, coupled with a rise in the proportion who report feeling frequently "overwhelmed" by all they have to do (Pryor et al., 2008). Rising expectations to seek personal counseling while in college are also evident (Pryor et al., 2008). Also noteworthy is that following a more than two-decades-long decline in the personal importance placed on "developing a meaningful philosophy of life," freshmen cohorts over the past several years have attributed resurging value to this pursuit (Pryor et al., 2008). Students attending Catholic universities tend to mirror their peers at other types of institutions with respect to personal, academic, and professional interests, concerns, and considerations.

Like the generations of students who preceded them, students today bring with them to college a range of talents, interests, anxieties, and aspirations. Increasingly, though, they come from diverse racial, ethnic, socioeconomic, and religious backgrounds, and they experience widely varying life circumstances and cultural traditions prior to their matriculation. And yet, amid all these differences and dimensions of potential division, they share many common hopes, concerns, passions, and responsibilities. They also ask the same existential questions: Who am I? What are my most deeply felt values? What do I want to do with my life? Why am I in college? What is the value of what I am learning both in and out of the classroom? How does this learning relate to what I will be doing in my work and life later on? What kind of person do I want to become? What sort of world will I help to create?

These are, at heart, spiritual questions. Their answers are rooted in a lifelong internal process of seeking personal authenticity; developing a greater sense of connectedness to self and others through relationship and community; deriving meaning, purpose, and direction in life; being open to exploring a relationship with a higher power that transcends human existence and knowing; and valuing the sacred. How students deal with these questions has important implications for the many very practical decisions they will have to make, including their choices of courses, majors, and careers, as well as whether they opt to stay in college or drop out, or whether they decide to pursue postgraduate study.

The process of seeking answers to these types of existential questions is also directly relevant to the development of personal qualities such as self-understanding, empathy, caring, and social responsibility. Over time, however, the relative amount of attention that universities devote to the "inner" and "outer" aspects of students' lives has become significantly imbalanced. The development of self-understanding, in particular, receives very little attention in many of our schools and colleges today, even though most of the great literary and philosophical traditions that constitute the core of a liberal education are grounded in the maxim "Know thyself." Self-understanding, of course, is a necessary prerequisite to our ability to understand others and resolve conflicts. It is difficult to imagine how most of our contemporary domestic and world problems can ever be resolved without a substantial increase in our individual and collective self-awareness. And yet, as a society, we nonetheless continue to heavily prioritize outcomes that are unrelated—even antithetical—to the enhancement of self-awareness and understanding (Astin, et al., 2011).

We know that for traditional-age college students, the undergraduate years are commonly characterized by an intensive period of cognitive, social, and affective development.[3] As they refine their identities, formulate adult life goals and career paths, test their emerging senses of self-authority, independence, and interdependence, and make decisions that will significantly impact their own and others' lives, young adults often grapple with issues of meaning, purpose, authenticity, and spirituality. Consequently, it is not surprising that while today's first-year students clearly expect their institutions to play an instrumental role in preparing them for employment (94%) and graduate or advanced education (81%), they also have high expectations that college will help them develop emotionally and spiritually. Looking at the institutional expectations of entering freshmen aggregated across different types of four-year institutions, we see that roughly two-thirds consider it "essential" or "very important" that their college enhance their self-understanding (69%), prepare them for responsible citizenship (67%), develop their personal values (67%), and provide for their emotional development (63%). Moreover, nearly half (48%) say that it is "essential" or "very important" that their campus encourage personal expression of spirituality (Astin et al., 2005).

As noted earlier, there are far more similarities than differences between students attending Catholic universities and their peers who attend other types of institutions. Relative to their peers at other institutions, however, students attending Catholic schools are even more inclined to expect the college experience to support their development within this realm. More than three-quarters, for example, indicate that it is "essential" or "very important" that their undergraduate experience develop their personal values (77%) and enhance their self-understanding (76%). Nearly three-quarters also place similar levels of importance on the role college should play both in providing for their emotional development and preparing them for responsible citizenship (73% for both measures). When asked specifically whether they expect the college or university they are attending to encourage their personal expression of spirituality, 61% concur that this expectation is either "essential" or "very important" (Astin et al., 2005). This finding is not necessarily surprising, given that students attending a Catholic institution are likely well aware of its faith-based tradition, and consequently are more inclined than they would be otherwise to "expect" a focus on spiritual growth. Indeed, relative to their peers at large, students attending other types of sectarian institutions also tend to show comparatively greater institutional expectations within this realm.

The *Spirituality in Higher Education* Study

Motivated by the existing climate within higher education, the myriad societal and global conditions that affect our lives today and that will inescapably shape the lives of future generations, and our shared belief that diversity can only be truly understood, appreciated, and embraced through acknowledging and celebrating our common humanity, Alexander Astin, Helen Astin, and I began work on the *Spirituality in Higher Education: A National Study of College Students' Search for Meaning and Purpose* Project in early 2002. Generously funded by the John Templeton Foundation, guided by technical panel and national advisory board members, and supported by a terrific cadre of graduate student and postdoctoral research analysts, we have collected survey information and conducted interviews with students and faculty across the country aimed at answering a number of questions concerning undergraduate students' spiritual life: How do students view their own spirituality? What priority does it have in their lives? How do students develop and change spiritually during college? How is their spiritual development affected by the kind of college they attend, their peer group, the different curricular and cocurricular programs to which they are exposed, and their relationships with faculty? What role do students feel their colleges *should* play in facilitating their spiritual development? How do they view the connection between spirituality and religion? How do the spiritual and religious aspects of students' lives relate to other aspects of their lives, including their politics, academic interests and performance, physical health, and psychological well-being?

The main portion of the longitudinal study detailed in depth within *Cultivating the Spirit* began in fall 2004 with a national survey of 112,000 first-year college students at 236 diverse institutions nationally. These students completed an extensive four-page CIRP Freshman Survey that included more than 200 questions about their backgrounds, high school experiences, expectations about college (including majors and careers), and attitudes about social issues. A special two-page addendum, entitled the College Students' Beliefs and Values (CSBV) Survey, contained 160 specially designed questions that pertained directly to students' perspectives and practices with respect to spirituality and religion.

In spring 2007, we surveyed a subsample of this same cohort again, specifically querying their college experiences. Repeated in that questionnaire were most of the questions related to spiritual and religious beliefs and practices that we originally asked in 2004, thus enabling us to develop measures of change in 15,000 students' spiritual and religious qualities during college. Respondents included sizable numbers of students from most religious denominations and racial/ethnic groups, and their colleges represent all types of public, nonsectarian, and religiously affiliated institutions (Roman Catholic, mainline Protestant, and evangelical). A complex weighting scheme allowed us to estimate how the entire population of students attending baccalaureate institutions would have responded to the survey (Astin et al., 2011). Our interpretation of survey data was informed further by student focus group discussions and individual interviews.

In an effort to understand the role that college faculty currently play in affecting students' spiritual development, as well as the potential role that they might play in the future, the study also examined how faculty view the intersection between spirituality and higher education and assessed how their beliefs and behaviors shape the spiritual lives of their students. Toward that end, during the 2004–2005 academic year we also collected extensive data from 8,000 faculty at many of the same institutions where we collected longitudinal student data. These data were collected as part of the 2004–2005 HERI Faculty Survey, a triennial national survey which, that year, generated responses from over 60,000 faculty employed at more than 500 diverse types of educational institutions nation-wide (Lindholm et al., 2005).

A fundamental reason for concerning ourselves with the spiritual dimension of educators' lives, their views on students' spiritual development, and associated behavioral implications is that the attitudes and behavior of faculty, staff, and administrators shape many of the structural and cultural characteristics of campus life. In return, the campus life they create shapes them and, by extension, impacts students' experiences and developmental trajectories. Among college and university personnel, student affairs educators have an especially rich legacy of concern for holistic education and personal development, and the significance of their contributions should not be underestimated or overlooked. To be sure, student affairs and religious life professionals have played key leadership roles in facilitating student development in this realm and should continue to do so. However, for spirituality to have a central place in campus life, the essential tenets of an institution's role in students' spiritual development should also be reflected in the core values, beliefs, and commitments of academic affairs educators, including faculty.

Questions for Discussion

- In your experience on this campus (and on others if applicable), how have students expressed their interest in the spiritual search?
- How have you experienced differences among students from a variety of religious backgrounds?

Defining Spirituality

Spirituality is a dynamic construct that involves the internal process of seeking personal authenticity, genuineness, and wholeness; transcending one's locus of centricity in order to develop a greater sense of connectedness to self and others through relationship and community; deriving meaning, purpose, and direction in life; being open to exploring a relationship with a higher power that transcends human existence and human knowing; and valuing the sacred.[4] Spirituality can also be thought of as an animating, creative, energizing, and meaning-making force—a "dynamic expression" of who we are (Chickering & Reisser, 1993). Some contend that although it may be manifest through highly variable personal mechanisms, spirituality is a biologically integral component of being human.[5] It is the impetus that compels us to ask why we do what we do, pushes us to seek fundamentally better ways of doing it, and propels us to make a difference in the world. Within the spiritual domain, human development can be characterized both by one's capacity to integrate the many other aspects of development (cognitive, social, emotional, moral), and by one's capacity for integrity, wholeness, openness, self-responsibility, and authentic self-transcendence (Fuller, 2001).

From the project's outset, our research team has conceptualized spirituality as pointing to our inner, subjective life, as contrasted to the objective domain of observable behavior and material objects. Spirituality involves our affective experiences at least as much as it does our reasoning and logic, and it is reflected in the values and ideals that we hold most dear: our sense of who we are and where we come from, our beliefs about why we are here—the meaning and purpose we see in our lives—and our connectedness to each other and to the world around us. Spirituality also captures those aspects of our experience that are not easy to define or talk about, such as intuition, inspiration, the mysterious, and the mystical.

We acknowledge that each individual will view his or her spirituality in a unique way. For some, traditional religious beliefs compose the core of their spirituality; for others, such beliefs or traditions may play little or no part. For those of us who conducted the *Spirituality in Higher Education* study, how students define their spirituality or what particular meaning they make of their lives was not a primary issue. The focal point of the research project was simply to identify the level and intensity of spiritual experience among college students and to understand how colleges can support students within this developmental realm.

Questions for Discussion

Spirituality is defined as a multifaceted concept, having to do with personally integrative capability, affective impact on the way we live our lives, and the realm of the mysterious.

- Which of these elements make the most sense to you, and why?
- Which of them have an impact on your discipline, and how do you draw on them in your teaching?

Examining the Intersections Between Spirituality and Higher Education

Within American society the spiritual dimension of our lives has traditionally been regarded as intensely personal, an innermost component of who we are that lies outside the realm of socially acceptable public discourse or concern. Consequently, it is not surprising that many colleagues and friends have asked us—in tones at some times genuinely inquisitive and at others unmistakably disapproving—whether spirituality has a rightful place within the modern academy. Our response is a resounding "yes," particularly in an era in which there seems to exist an inherent disconnect between the dominant values of contemporary American society and the perspectives and practices that will enable us to respond effectively not only to our individual needs, but also to local, national, international, and global challenges. The myriad ways in which our higher education institutions are evolving also compel us to reconsider long-standing expectations and deeply held assumptions about undergraduate education and our work as educators, as well as the associated effects that our beliefs and behaviors have on life, both within and ultimately beyond the academy.

In *Cultivating the Spirit* we argue that for too long, academic culture has encouraged students, faculty, and staff to lead fragmented and inauthentic lives in which people act either as if they are not spiritual beings or as if their spiritual side is irrelevant to their vocation or work (Astin et al., 2011). Moreover, we contend that while academics are understandably proud of their "outer" accomplishments in the fields of science, medicine, technology, and commerce, universities have, on the whole, increasingly come to neglect students' "inner" development—the sphere of values and beliefs, emotional maturity, spirituality, and self-understanding. Within such an environment, academic endeavors can become separated from students' most deeply felt values, and students may hesitate to discuss issues of meaning, purpose, authenticity, wholeness, and fragmentation with one another and especially with faculty (Astin et al., 2011). Those who study the history of higher education and its modern-day evolution have written extensively about the founding of American universities— their strong early ties to religious orders, their close connections with local communities, and their mission not only to enhance the breadth and depth of students' knowledge, but also to foster "a sense of purpose that included an awareness of the soul's relationship to God."[6] Whereas spiritual aspects of student development were cornerstones of early American college curricula, the Enlightenment ideals, positivistic modes of thinking, and scientific worldviews that began to exert powerful influence on American thought in the late nineteenth century have continued to dominate societal values and individual goal orientations. One manifestation of the resulting worldview is that rather than providing a developmental context characterized by self-reflection, open dialogue, and thoughtful analysis of alternative perspectives, many of today's college and university environments mirror instead the strong societal emphasis on individual achievement, competitiveness, materialism, and objective knowing. These orientations, coupled with the post–World War II emphasis on a more "business model" approach to education that emphasizes productivity and cost-effectiveness, have resulted in both a devaluing of the liberal arts and a shift away from holistic, integrative approaches to teaching and learning (Murphy, 2005).

Examining the evolution of higher education, one observes that the debate over the role of religion within higher education has been central to any discussion about curricular mission and purpose from the founding days of universities to the present. These questions persist: Can rational science coexist with one's religious faith? What about academic freedom and the need for the separation of church and state? How can we reconcile critical thinking and inquiry with religious faith and spiritual beliefs? For many years, our rote answers to these questions left little, if any, room for addressing issues of both the head and the heart in the standard modern-day undergraduate curriculum.

In the past few years, however, higher education has come under increasing criticism for what many see as its impersonal and fragmented approach to undergraduate education. Growing numbers of educators are calling for a more holistic education, speaking of the need to connect mind and spirit and of the need to return to the true values of liberal education—an education that examines learning and knowledge in relation to an exploration of self.[7] Such a reinvigorated liberal arts curriculum necessarily would pay much closer attention to the existential questions that we know are prominent in students' minds. At the same time, we have seen a movement gradually emerging in higher education in which many academics find themselves actively searching for meaning and trying to discover ways to make their lives and their institutions more whole. This movement likely reflects a growing concern with recovering a sense of meaning in American society more generally. The growing unease about our institutions and our society has led some of us to start talking much more openly about spirituality. The particular "spiritual" questions that give rise to these concerns encompass a broad set of issues:

- How do we achieve a greater sense of community and shared purpose in higher education?
- How can we provide greater opportunities for individual and institutional renewal?
- What are the causes of the division and fragmentation that so many academics experience in their institutional and personal lives?
- What does it mean to be authentic, both in the classroom and in our dealings with colleagues?
- What are some of the practices and traditions that make it difficult for us to be authentic in an academic setting?
- What are some of the disconnections that higher education is experiencing in relation to the larger society? How might we better serve the public good?
- How can we help our students achieve a greater sense of meaning and purpose in their academic and personal lives?

Questions for Discussion

- How might each of the above questions serve as a discussion question or research assignment for students?
- How might the answers to these questions affect your role on the faculty or in student life at this university?

Spirituality and Higher Education: Challenges and Opportunities

Our difficulties in achieving a greater sense of wholeness and spirituality in higher education have been exacerbated by many competing stresses: the need to secure adequate resources vs. the need to preserve institutional autonomy and academic freedom; the commitment to advance the frontiers of knowledge vs. the commitment to educate students well and to serve the community; the commitment to academic excellence vs. the commitment to educational opportunity and equity; and the quest for individual professional development and recognition vs. the desire to nurture and sustain an intellectual community. In recent years, these conflicts have been exacerbated by declining resources and public pressures for greater "accountability" and—at a more personal level—by the divisions and tensions that often emerge between family and work. These stresses and tensions have serious implications for the academic community—not only for those of us whose lives have become increasingly fragmented and disconnected, but also for our students (Astin et al., 2011).

On one hand, the prevailing orientations described briefly here and detailed in *Cultivating the Spirit* (Astin et al., 2011) paint a discouraging portrait of the higher education landscape and its corresponding capacity to facilitate students' holistic development. On the other hand, however, the broad formative roles that universities continue to play in our society position them well as a critical focal point for responding to the question of how we can balance the "exterior" and "interior" aspects of life more effectively; how we can support the development of students' inner qualities so as to better enable them to live meaningful lives and to cope with life's inherent uncertainties and discontinuities; and how we can more thoroughly and more intentionally prepare students to effectively serve their communities, our society, and the world at large.

Envisioning campus communities in which the life of the mind and the life of the spirit are mutually celebrated, supported, and sustained necessitates that our higher education community reconsider our traditional ways of being and doing. We must be open to broadening our existing frames of reference and willing to look closely not just at what we do (or do not do) on a daily basis, but *why* we do it, considering the motivations behind our thoughts, beliefs, and actions. Those both within and beyond the academy must also reflect on the origins of existing presumptions about the nature and purpose of higher education, as well as their own academic experiences and the resulting effects on their lives and others' lives.

Granted, the process of developing answers to these questions is not simple. The potential benefits of wrestling with such challenges, though, are well worth the effort, at both the individual and the institutional level. In fact, existing research indicates that developing people's abilities to access, nurture, and give expression to the spiritual dimension of their lives impacts how they engage with the world and fosters within them a heightened sense of connectedness that promotes empathy, ethical behavior, civic responsibility, passion, and action for social justice.[8] Healthy spiritual development has also been positively linked with physical, mental, social, and emotional well-being (Ellison & Levin, 1998).

Questions for Discussion

- How would you characterize the culture on your campus when it comes to recognizing and providing opportunities for spiritual development and nourishment?
- What are the opportunities on your campus for self-reflection, open dialogue, and thoughtful analysis of alternative perspectives?
- Are more opportunities for such reflection and discussion needed? How might they be provided or enhanced?

Spirituality Measures

One of our goals in conducting the *Spirituality in Higher Education* study was to develop measures that address various dimensions of spirituality and religiousness. Toward that end, our research team searched for clusters of survey questionnaire items that formed coherent patterns in terms of how students responded. Through this process we identified five spiritual measures: Spiritual Quest, Ecumenical Worldview, Ethic of Caring, Charitable Involvement, and Equanimity.

Spiritual Quest

Spiritual Quest is at the heart of students' spiritual development and captures the degree to which an individual is actively searching for meaning and purpose, desiring to find wisdom, and seeking answers to life's mysteries and "big questions." Each of the individual items that compose this heavily process-oriented measure includes words such as "finding," "attaining," "seeking," "developing," "searching," or "becoming."

Ecumenical Worldview

Ecumenical Worldview reflects a global worldview that transcends ethnocentrism and egocentrism. It indicates the extent to which the student is interested in different religious traditions, seeks to understand other countries and cultures, feels a strong connection to all humanity, believes in the goodness of all people, accepts others as they are, and believes that all life is interconnected and that love is at the root of all the great religions.

Ethic of Caring

Ethic of Caring reflects our sense of caring and concern about the welfare of others and the world around us. These feelings are expressed in wanting to help those who are troubled and to alleviate suffering. It includes a concern about social justice issues and an interest in the welfare of one's community and the environment, as well as a commitment to political activism.

Charitable Involvement

In contrast to Ethic of Caring, which emphasizes "caring about," Charitable Involvement emphasizes "caring for." This behavioral measure includes activities such as participating in community service, donating money to charity, and helping friends with personal problems.

Equanimity

Equanimity may well be the prototypic defining quality of a spiritual person. It measures the extent to which the student is able to find meaning and purpose in times of hardship, feels at peace or is centered, sees each day as a gift, and feels good about the direction of his or her life. Equanimity plays an important role in the quality of undergraduate students' lives because it helps shape how they respond to their experiences, particularly those that are potentially stressful.

Framed by five of the measures created through longitudinal research, we developed the following definition:

> *Spirituality is a multifaceted quality that involves an active quest for answers to life's "big questions" (**Spiritual Quest**), a global worldview that transcends ethnocentrism and egocentrism (**Ecumenical Worldview**), a sense of caring and compassion for others (**Ethic of Caring**) coupled with a lifestyle that includes service to others (**Charitable Involvement**), and a capacity to maintain one's sense of calm and centeredness, especially in times of stress (**Equanimity**).*

These five spiritual measures help to conceptualize various aspects of individuals' experiences that can also pertain to college-student development. By studying how these measures interface with students' college experience, our research team has been able to gain a deeper understanding of the impact that higher education has on students' spiritual development.

Insights into the Spiritual Lives of College Students

In *Cultivating the Spirit*, the Astins and I detail how students change during college on each of the five spiritual measures: Spiritual Quest, Ecumenical Worldview, Ethic of Caring, Charitable Involvement, and Equanimity. Changes over time on five religious measures—Religious Commitment, Religious Engagement, Religious/Social Conservatism, Religious Skepticism, and Religious Struggle—are also examined. Ultimately, we consider how student change on each measure affects traditional undergraduate education outcomes and how different college experiences tend to impact student development within this realm. Findings from the longitudinal study show that when they enter their first year of college:

- Students have very high levels of spiritual interest and involvement. Many are actively engaged in a spiritual quest and are exploring meaning and purpose in life. They also display high levels of religious commitment and involvement.
- Students also have high expectations for the role their institutions will play in their emotional and spiritual development. They place great value on their colleges' enhancing their self-understanding, helping them develop personal values, and encouraging their expression of spirituality.

Additionally, during college:

- Religious Engagement declines somewhat, yet students' spiritual qualities grow substantially.
- Students show the greatest degree of growth in the five spiritual qualities if they are actively engaged in "inner work" through self-reflection, contemplation, and/or meditation.
- Students also show substantial increases in Spiritual Quest when faculty members encourage them to explore questions of meaning and purpose or otherwise show support for their spiritual development.
- Growth in Ecumenical Worldview and Ethic of Caring enhances students' interest in postgraduate study, self-rated ability to get along with other races and cultures, and commitment to promoting racial understanding.
- Engaging in most forms of Charitable Involvement—community service work, helping friends with personal problems, donating money to charity—promotes the development of other spiritual qualities.
- Growth in Equanimity enhances students' grade point average, leadership skills, psychological well-being, self-

rated ability to get along with other races and cultures, and satisfaction with college.

- Educational experiences and practices that promote spiritual development—especially service learning, interdisciplinary courses, study abroad, self-reflection, and meditation—have uniformly positive effects on traditional college outcomes.

- Providing students with more opportunities to connect with their "inner selves" facilitates growth in their academic and leadership skills, contributes to their intellectual self-confidence and psychological well-being, and enhances their satisfaction with college.

These selected findings offer insights as to how specific experiences and involvement in college life can influence the spiritual growth and development of traditional-age students during the undergraduate years.

Supporting Students' Spiritual Development: Perspectives for Faculty Consideration

As elaborated in *Cultivating the Spirit*, findings from the *Spirituality in Higher Education* Project support the notion that many, if not most, students come to college today seeking spaces where their contributions and self-worth matter beyond how large their salary will be, what their GPA is, or the prestige of their future careers.[9] When they enter college, many first-year students also express high expectations for their own spiritual development. More than eight in ten, for example, report that "to find my purpose in life" is at least a "somewhat" important reason for attending college. Fully half say it is a "very important" reason. Two-thirds of first-year students also say that it is either "very important" or "essential" that college "helps you develop your personal values" and "enhances your self-understanding" (Astin et al., 2011).

The undergraduate experience offers students numerous potential opportunities to explore issues of meaning, purpose, and faith as they engage with peers, faculty, and staff that embody various backgrounds, beliefs, and practices. Exposure to new and diverse perspectives is valuable in challenging students to compare, examine, and clarify their own personal beliefs and values in a communal setting (Palmer, 1999). *Spirituality in Higher Education* Project findings support the notion that exposure to diverse people, cultures, and ideas through study abroad, interdisciplinary coursework, leadership education, service learning, and other forms of civic engagement helps students better understand, and value, multiple perspectives. These capacities are especially critical given the complex social, economic, and political challenges of our time.

As students encounter differences in college, they are challenged to grow and change. For many, college may be the first time they have questioned "truth" and "reality." Indeed, the college experience can be critical in helping students clarify their faith, beliefs, and values. Experiencing "disequilibrium," or spiritual struggle, provides students with opportunities to analyze their life circumstances and the deeper meaning and purpose that they are seeking as they strive to live more connected, integrated lives (Fowler, 1981).

Findings from our longitudinal study indicate that many students are eager to explore their own spiritual identities and come to a deeper understanding of meaning, purpose, and faith in their lives. These findings echo the call of other scholars who wish to amplify the importance of spiritual growth, authenticity, purpose, and meaning. This school of thought views spiritual issues and considerations as legitimate concerns within our campus communities—not only for students, but also for faculty, student affairs professionals, staff members, and administrators (Braskamp, Trautvetter, & Ward, 2006). The challenge for campus personnel, then, becomes how to effectively address issues related to the spiritual dimension of students' lives (Lindholm, et al., 2011).

As detailed in *Cultivating the Spirit*, findings from the *Spirituality in Higher Education* Project reveal multiple curricular and cocurricular experiences that support or hinder students' spiritual development. Importantly, we also find that faculty's own behavior and practices can also play a significant role in how students change and grow with respect to spiritual qualities. Growth in levels of Spiritual Quest, Ecumenical Worldview, Ethic of Caring, and Equanimity are all positively affected when faculty directly encourage students to explore questions of meaning and purpose. Similarly, if faculty encourage discussions of religious and spiritual matters, support students' expressions of spirituality, and act themselves as spiritual role models, students also show more positive growth in the same four spiritual qualities, as well as in Charitable Involvement (Astin et al., 2011).

Contrary to what many—including a majority of students who participated in our study—presume, findings from the 2004–2005 HERI Faculty Survey revealed that many faculty at both Catholic and secular institutions view the spiritual dimension of their own lives as important. For example, within today's professoriate, four out of five faculty describe themselves as "a spiritual person." Nearly half say they are spiritual "to a great extent." In addition, seven in ten faculty view "developing a meaningful philosophy of life" as an "essential" or "very important" goal. A similar proportion say they "seek opportunities to grow spirituality" to at least "some" extent and that they engage in self-reflection to a "great" extent. Moreover, for nearly half of today's faculty, "integrating spirituality in my life" is "essential" or "very important." Finally, although faculty are inclined to describe themselves as "spiritual" rather than "religious," more than three in five college professors say they consider themselves to be "a religious person," either "to some extent" (29%) or "to a great extent" (35%). Only about one-third of faculty (37%) say they are "not at all" religious.

However, while many faculty view the spiritual dimension of their lives as important, we nevertheless observe considerable ambivalence within faculty as to the place of spirituality in higher education and, more specifically, uncertainty as to how they individually might play a role in facilitating students' spiritual growth.

Indeed, across all different types of campuses, more than six in ten students report that their professors "never" encourage discussion of religious/spiritual matters, and only 20 percent report that their professors "frequently" encourage exploration of questions of meaning and purpose.

Certainly within each campus there are multiple ways for campus personnel to support students' spiritual development. Appreciating that many effective institutional practices are the products of collaborative efforts, below are a few suggestions extracted from *A Guidebook of Promising Practices* for how faculty can promote students' spiritual development by:

- Learning more about spiritual development and the role it plays in students' lives;
- Encouraging students to take time away from their busy lives to reflect on their experiences in light of their beliefs and values;
- Encouraging spiritually related discussions within the classroom (e.g. including course content about the "Big Questions" or spiritual practices);
- Exposing students to different values, belief systems, and different ways of living to build respect for differences within various academic environments;
- Sharing personal examples of spiritual struggles and questing for meaning, purpose, and truth with colleagues and students when appropriate;
- Providing emotional support for students in crisis and making appropriate referrals to student service professionals;
- Recognizing that students have lives beyond the walls of the classroom where these issues come into play, and exercising compassion; and
- Challenging students to search for ways to live with meaning and purpose within their field of study and beyond.

These ideas offer merely a snapshot of the many potential ways in which faculty can more intentionally support the spiritual dimension of students' lives. In these challenging times for higher education and society at large, questions of meaning, purpose, authenticity, and connection are especially critical. Through encouraging faculty and other campus personnel to reflect on their own spiritual perspectives and journeys and to engage in collective efforts to consider how their institution's mission and goals are manifested in their daily practice, universities can take important steps toward contributing more fully to the well-being of their institutions, their students, and the broader community.

Questions for Discussion

- Reflecting on the above suggestions from the *Guidebook of Promising Practices*, what are some examples from your work with students that have seemed particularly effective?
- What types of activities have seemed particularly ineffective?
- What support from the university or other faculty members would you welcome in this area?

Conclusion

Now that you have a clearer picture of student spirituality, a further challenge presents itself to the FLC in its third session. The faculty learning community exists in the context of Catholic culture, and the students who choose a Catholic university have high expectations that faculty and student-life personnel will assist them in their search for meaning and purpose. It is important, then, that those participating in a Revisioning Mission program or a Mission Community take seriously the challenge of examining their own spiritual lives, not just as individuals but in the FLC or an equivalent group. Given the American predisposition to regard religion as a private matter, this will not be an easy task.

References

Astin, A. W., Astin, H. S., & Lindholm, J. A. (2011). *Cultivating the spirit: How college can enhance students' inner lives.* San Francisco, CA: Jossey-Bass.

Astin, A. W., Astin, H. S., Lindholm, J. A, & Bryant, A. L. (2005). *Spirituality in Higher Education: A National Study of College Students' Beliefs and Values.* Retrieved from University of California, Los Angeles, Higher Education Research Institute, Graduate School of Education & Information Studies Web site: http://spirituality.ucla.edu/docs/reports/Spiritual_Life_College_Students_Full_Report.pdf.

Braskamp, L. A., Trautvetter, L. C., & Ward, K. (2006). *Putting students first: How colleges develop students purposefully.* Bolton, MA: Anker Pub.

Chickering, A. W., & Reisser, L. (1993). *Education and identity.* San Francisco, CA: Jossey-Bass.

Ellison, C. G., & Levin, J. S. (1998). The religion-health connection: Evidence, theory, and future directions. *Health Education and Behavior, 25,* 700–720.

Fowler, J. W. (1981). *Stages of faith: The psychology of human development and the quest for meaning.* San Francisco, CA: Harper.

Fuller, R. (2001). *Spiritual, but not religious: Understanding unchurched America.* New York, NY: Oxford University Press.

Lindholm, J. A. Millora, L., Schwartz, L.M., & Spinosa, H.S. (2011). *A guidebook of promising practices: Facilitating college students' spiritual development.* Los Angeles, CA: Regents of the University of California.

Lindholm, J. A., Szelenyi, K. Hurtado, S., & Korn, W. S. (2005). *The American college teacher: National norms for the 2004–2005 HERI faculty survey.* Los Angeles, CA: Higher Education Research Institute, University of California, Los Angeles.

Murphy, C. (2005). The academy, spirituality, and the search for truth. *New Directions for Teaching & Learning, 104,* 23–29.

Palmer, P. J. (1999). *The active life: A spirituality of work, creativity, and caring.* San Francisco, CA: Jossey-Bass.

Parks, S. D. (2000). *Big questions, worthy dreams: Mentoring young adults in their search for meaning, purpose, and faith.* San Francisco, CA: Jossey-Bass.

Pryor, J. H., Hurtado, S., Saenz, V. B., Santos, J. L., Korn, W. S., Higher Education Research Institute, & Cooperative Institutional Research Program. (2007). *The American freshman: Forty-year trends, 1966–2006.* Los Angeles, CA: Higher Education Research Institute, Graduate School of Education & Information Studies, University of California, Los Angeles.

Pryor, J. H., Hurtado, S., DeAngelo, L., Sharkness, J., Romero, L. C., University of California, Los Angeles, Cooperative Institutional Research Program, Graduate School of Education & Information Studies. (2008). *American freshman: National norms for fall 2008.* Los Angeles, CA: Higher Education Research Institute, University of California, Los Angeles.

Recommended Reading

Astin, A. W., Astin, S., & Lindholm, J. A. (2007). *Spirituality and the professoriate: A national study of faculty beliefs, attitudes, and behaviors.* Retrieved from University of California, Los Angeles, Higher Education Research Institute, Graduate School of Education & Information Studies Web site: http://spirituality.ucla.edu/docs/results/faculty/spirit_professoriate.pdf.

Notes

[1] For a complete history of the CIRP, see Astin, A. W. (2003). Studying How College Affects Students. *About Campus, 8*(3), 21–29.

[2] Pryor, J. H., Hurtado, S., DeAngelo, L., Blake, L. P., Tran, S., Cooperative Institutional Research Program, & Higher Education Research Institute. (2010). *The American freshman: National norms, fall 2010.* Los Angeles, CA: Higher Education Research Institute, University of California.

[3] Pascarella, E. T., & Terenzini, P. T. (2005). *How college affects students: Vol. 2.* San Francisco, CA: Jossey-Bass.

[4] Love, P., & Talbot, D. (1999). Defining spiritual development: A missing consideration for student affairs. *NASPA Journal, 37*(1), 361–361; Zinnbauer, B. J., Pargament, K. I., & Scott, A. B. (1999). The emerging meanings of religiousness and spirituality: Problems and prospects. *Journal of Personality, 67*(6), 889–919; Hill, P. C., Pargament, K. I., Hood, J. W., McCullough, M. E., Sawyers, J. P., Larson, D. B., & Zinnbauer, B. J. (2000). Conceptualizing religion and spirituality: Points of commonality, points of departure. *Journal for the Theory of Social Behavior, 30*(1), 51–77.

[5] Backer, D. C. (2003). Studies of the inner life: The impact of spirituality on quality of life. *Quality of Life Research, 12*(Suppl. 1), 51–57; Zohar, D., & Marshall, I. N. (2004). *Spiritual capital: Wealth we can live by.* San Francisco, CA: Berrett-Koehler.

[6] Cohen, A. M. (1998). *The shaping of American higher education: Emergence and growth of the contemporary system.* San Francisco, CA: Jossey-Bass; Marsden, G. M. (1994). *The soul of the American university: From Protestant establishment to established nonbelief.* New York, NY: Oxford University Press.

[7] Chickering, A. W., Dalton, J. C., & Auerbach, L. S. (2006). *Encouraging authenticity and spirituality in higher education.* San Francisco, CA: Jossey-Bass; Braskamp, L. A., Trautvetter, L. C., & Ward, K. (2006). *Putting students first: How colleges develop students purposefully.* Bolton, MA: Anker Pub; Trautvetter, L. C. (2007). Developing students' search for meaning and purpose. Kramer, G. L. (Ed.). *Fostering student success in the campus community* (pp. 236–261). San Francisco, CA: Jossey-Bass.

[8] De Souza, M. (2003). Contemporary influences on the spirituality of young people: Implications for education. *International Journal of Children's Spirituality, 8*(3), 269–279; Harris, M.,

& Moran, G. (1998). *Reshaping religious education: Conversations on contemporary practice.* Louisville, KY: Westminster John Knox Press; Astin, A. W., Astin, H. S., Lindholm, J. A., & Bryant, A. L. (2005). Spirituality in higher education: A national study of college students' beliefs and values. Retrieved from University of California, Los Angeles, Higher Education Research Institute, Graduate School of Education & Information Studies Web site:
http://spirituality.ucla.edu/docs/reports/Spiritual_Life_College_Students_Full_Report.pdf.

[9] Howe, N., & Strauss, W. (2007). *Millennials go to college: Strategies for a new generation on campus: Recruiting and admissions, campus life, and the classroom.* Great Falls, VA: LifeCourse Associates.

ESSAY THREE

THE SPIRITUAL JOURNEY: WAYFARING AT THE UNIVERSITY

By Suzanne Dale Wilcox

It seems to be common knowledge within higher education that "Know thyself" is a central guiding tenet of the intellectual life. And, upon reflection, we are aware that the dictum has deep implications for how and what we teach and for how we approach students. Inwardness is crucial to the success of our endeavors; this much we know. So, it's worth taking time to reflect on the spiritual in the context of Revisioning Mission. Weaving a seamless connection between one's inner and outer lives has the potential to further both institutional mission and personal growth, which are equally important as colleges move through the twenty-first century.

Overview

This essay addresses the spiritual journey by looking at recent research dealing with spirituality on campus, and then by sketching out some of the many stages of the spiritual path. An explicitly nondoctrinal approach has been taken, out of respect for the diversity on a typical campus. The great minds and respected thinkers in the philosophical and religious realms all seem to point to a common rootedness among religions and spiritual paths. Although the languages and rituals differ, the familiar themes of setting out, liminality, and return repeat themselves in the literature worldwide—and in the research on student spirituality today. Each tradition offers something unique and yet essentially similar. Is this really surprising? Aren't people of every race and time different and yet universally human? If common ground is to be found anywhere, it is in our spirituality, which takes us beyond the apparent separateness of things to a vision of oneness, lifting us beyond our personal differences to the unifying knowledge of God (Freke, 1998).

And yet, despite the underlying unity of religious and spiritual traditions, most of us have committed to a particular path based on life history, personal trajectory, and serious adult decisions not easy to undo or too valuable to deconstruct (Plaskow, 1990). This program is based on deep respect for each chosen path and intends to foster a community based on reverence for all. Such an approach has the potential of providing a unifying force on campus. Increasingly, as incoming students place significant emphasis on the interior dimensions of their lives (Lindholm, 2007), spirituality may have the additional benefit of offering a space where adults might come together on campus, regardless of their religious persuasion.

Overall, this essay is emphasizes the importance of spiritual practice among faculty and administrators as essential to the Revisioning Mission program. We offer a nudge toward campus planning in this direction, for the college campus environment offers many opportunities for spiritual growth, both inside and outside the classroom, and these opportunities can be maximized with intentional leadership and planning. Underlying all this are the questions: How do we create a personal and communal atmosphere friendly to the spiritual? What is the inherent value of fostering the spiritual? And how does all of this relate to the new cosmology and to our sense of connectedness with one another and with the natural world (Corcoran, 2010)?

As a partial answer to these questions, consider this case study from academia, a first-person account of a faculty member following a spiritual path. While she was a faculty member at Cal Poly–San Luis Obispo, Paula Huston (2010) became a Catholic and later

experienced a "third conversion," a call to a more totally committed spiritual life. She expresses the challenge of juxtaposing her
personal life and her life as a professor in the following words:

> Many obstacles held me back, some
> of them mundane. One was simple
> embarrassment: I was nervous about
> what others thought, especially my
> university colleagues. It was bad enough
> that I'd become a Catholic after years
> of loyalty to secular liberalism. Most
> of them had forgiven me; with much
> eye-rolling they had accepted my
> wacky, medieval-sounding Christian
> pilgrimage. But could they handle
> whatever was coming next? I myself
> couldn't imagine what this might be,
> only that it boded ill for my good name
> on campus.
> (Huston, 2010, p. 32)

Coming to terms with spirituality in a postmodern culture is
not an easy task for anyone, and it may be more difficult for academics, whatever their religious or spiritual persuasion. Paula's
new level of call to the spiritual life led her to become an oblate of
a religious congregation of monastics, the Camaldolese Benedictines. Her change of heart and ensuing involvement with a contemplative congregation has resulted in a very different way of life
for her. Immersed in academia, she nevertheless follows a daily
regimen of prayer practice followed by monks since the fourth
century. All of us in academia have real lessons to learn from her
attentiveness to the Spirit of God working in her life and from her
dedication to contemplation.

It is important, however, to insert some rather mundane real-
ism into this picture. There are challenges when it comes to
emphasizing the spiritual on a campus. Although students are

quite explicit in expressing their spiritual questions, many are as fearful as faculty about "going public" with their real questions about spiritual realities. But things may be changing. In a newly released book summarizing a decade of research on student spirituality, Alexander Astin, Helen Astin, and Jennifer Lindholm (2010) found that student religious engagement declines somewhat during college, but student interest in the spiritual tends to increase through the undergraduate years. How to address and foster student interest in spirituality remains a challenge for faculty and administrators, who may tend to see their spiritual lives as something private and personal. Even when a campus has the rich tradition bequeathed by a founding religious congregation, adults on campus may feel that addressing the spiritual is an intrusion into their hidden lives. Whether they are seekers or agnostics, similar dynamics come into play, despite the fact that their daily tasks are carried out in a carefully constructed, verbally laden "goldfish bowl." Not unlike professionals in other fields in some ways, their very work puts them on display. Personal values enter into classroom lectures and discussions; campus decisions are framed by ethical and value-laden principles. In other words, the spiritual life of faculty and administrators is visible because they work in a tightly knit community of scholars and have daily contact with students in a meaningful way.

Looking at issues of personal spirituality and at the related values of integrity and ethics from an institutional perspective, it is not difficult to see the challenges inherent in this area. To reiterate the essential question: To what extent ought the spiritual life of faculty, administrators, and staff be the concern of the college's professionals charged with carrying out the essential mission of the institution? How can the Revisioning Mission program have lasting effects without the personal commitment of individuals to a spiritual path? To what extent ought a concern with spirituality be fostered by specific offerings, perhaps by campus ministry? Or, to look at it another way, should adults on the campus remain outside the scope of the mission? And what difference would attention to the spiritual make, both to the individual and to the institution?

These questions are best answered by referring to the existing literature dealing with faculty spirituality.

The Literature on Faculty and Spirituality

With some intensity over the last ten years, researchers have been gathering data in the area of student and faculty spirituality. The primary emphasis had been the student, and then, because of the connection between student growth and classroom instruction as well as campus climate, a growing research agenda has been looking at adult spirituality. In reviewing the literature, I have gathered the findings into six thematic clusters, each highlighting an area of interest and research relevant to growing the emphasis on adult spiritual life and the college campus. The themes will be stated first, and then the research dealing with each is summarized. Following a treatment of the six themes found in research, I will address positive steps that have been taken, and that should still be taken, to bring about a more focused spirituality on campus.

1. There is a resurgence of interest in studying spirituality on the college campus—both the spirituality of students and that of the teaching faculty and administrators.
2. Students have high expectations regarding the university's role in their spiritual growth and development.
3. There are reasons why colleges are doing very little to foster the spiritual life of adults and students on campus.
4. Where spiritual interests have been encouraged, there is a spillover effect into teaching and mentoring behavior of adults.
5. Religion and spirituality are viewed as deeply and essentially different.
6. There is deep-seated resistance to the spiritual on the college campus.

1. There is a resurgence of interest in the spiritual on campus.

Research into what's happening in higher education, among both students and faculty, has been largely driven by studies by Alexander and Helen Astin and their associates at the University of California, Los Angeles. Over the past ten years, surveys have included questions for students dealing with values and spirituality. Faculty surveys have been added to the agenda in an effort to measure attitudes and practices related to the inner life of members of the academy. Much can be learned from this research. For certain, students give priority to things spiritual (Lindholm, 2007): they indicate that they are engaged in a spiritual quest, discuss matters of spirit with their friends (Chickering, Dalton, & Auerbach, 2006), and increasingly want colleges and universities to assist them in their search. Likewise, four in five faculty members describe themselves as "spiritual persons" (Astin, Astin, Lindholm, & Bryant, 2007). And faculty members report feeling a great divide between their work in the academy and their personal values (Astin, Astin, & Lindholm, 2011).[1] There seems to be a movement emerging in higher education to recognize the experience and needs of both students and faculty in this regard. Academics are actively searching for meaning and trying to discover ways to make their lives and their institutions more whole (Astin, 2004). Other research, somewhat less empirical, points to "the silence around the topic of spirituality in the academy" as being "increasingly drowned out by the emphatic chorus of those whose underlying versions of truth cry out: 'We are a spiritual people'" (Shahjahan, 2009). Conferences have multiplied, such as the one sponsored by the Johnson Foundation at Wingspread on "Religion and Public Life: Engaging Higher Education," at which professors have debated their role in helping students along the spiritual path (Rice, 2007).

2. Students have high expectations of the university's role in their spiritual growth.

Several recent studies conducted at New York University (Lee, Matzkin & Arthur, 2004) and at four diverse campuses around the country (Cherry, DeBorg, & Porterfield, 2001) have looked into the impact of college on students' attitudes and beliefs. Students report that they expect colleges and universities to play a role in their spiritual and emotional development. At the same time, only one-third of faculty members agree that they should be concerned with students' spiritual development. The data deal with faculty at institutions public and private, secular and religious, Catholic and other denominations and faiths. Overall, the number of faculty concerned with the spiritual development of students is greater in some fields (the humanities and the health sciences) than in others (the traditional sciences), and also higher among faculty on Catholic campuses and religious campuses (Astin et al., 2007). Scholars point to the deep rationality underlying higher education instruction, to the exclusion of the experiential and the spiritual (Chickering, Dalton, & Auerbach, 2006). This finding is all the more puzzling, Alexander Astin notes, because many of the core literary and philosophical traditions are grounded in the maxim "Know thyself." More than two-thirds of faculty members responding to the Higher Education Research Institute (HERI) survey seek opportunities to grow spiritually "to some extent" and engage in self-reflection "to a great extent." While HERI's student surveys reveal a shift in student value structures more focused on making money than on developing a meaningful personal philosophy of life, there is nonetheless a deep current of interest and concern with the personal spiritual quest.

3. There are reasons why colleges are doing very little to foster the spiritual life.

It is no surprise that the culture on campuses reflects that of society as a whole. Jennifer Lindholm points to the prevailing culture's emphasis on individualism and achievement, rather than self-knowledge and reflection, as having a serious impact on the emphasis given to learning on the campus. Her surveys reveal that faculty are open to conversations dealing with meaning and spirituality, but are held back by the demands of the professoriate, with its time constraints, research agenda, and publication schedule. Accrediting groups and scholars of higher education tend to think of faculty largely in terms of external matters, reports Astin (et al.,1999), such as scholarly activities, teaching techniques, and service to the institution and community. Elizabeth Dreyer and John Bennett (2004) refer to the "dog-eat-dog" world of the academy Bennett (2004) argues that the academy has elevated self-interested autonomy (what he calls "consistent individualism") to a level of competition that emphasizes self-promotion and self-protection In a series of case studies of faculty who are teaching in a transformative (more experiential, more rooted in the spiritual) mode, West Georgia State faculty member Tobin Hart faults cynicism, inertia, fear, scientism, and utilitarianism as constituting significant barriers to linking pedagogy with spirituality (Duerr, 2002). A body of qualitative research conducted among diverse faculty members at a Jesuit university (allegorically called Holy University for purposes of the study) spells out why faculty find it difficult to foster Ignatian spirituality. Participants cite multiple challenges: lack of faculty commitment, insufficient personal time for spiritual development, increased faculty and student secularization on campus, and the lack of a formal system to reward mission-related activities. In other words, while publications and university service are factors in the tenure process, commitment to Ignatian spirituality (perhaps because it is so difficult to measure) is not (Peck & Stick, 2008). And this may be true at colleges and universities founded by other religious communities as well.

4. Where spiritual interests have been encouraged, the teaching and mentoring behavior of adults is enhanced.

Where there is attention paid to the spiritual on campus, studies reveal interesting and diverse results. Among students who come to campus with a high level of spiritual interest, qualities such as compassionate self-concept, charitable involvement, and ecumenical worldview emerge in personal profiles. In addition, twice as many spiritually inclined undergraduates (as compared with those less spiritually inclined) disagree with the statement "You cannot bring about change in society" (Lindholm, 2007). Even more startling are the results as they apply to faculty. Four in five faculty members describe themselves as "a spiritual person." And on HERI surveys, faculty who report themselves as being deeply spiritual are high scorers on six desirable qualities:

- Focus on students' personal development;
- Civic-minded values;
- Diversity advocacy;
- Student-centered pedagogy;
- Civic-minded practice; and
- Positive outlook on work and life.

Significant in these findings are these facts: that those who are more spiritual are more likely to use "student-centered" pedagogy (Astin et al., 2007), mentor students in higher numbers, and interact with students in ways that foster identity awareness and moral development (Astin et al., 2007). Arthur Chickering points to current emphases on learning rather than on teaching as conducive to and flowing from a more spiritually oriented faculty. Reflection, meditation, and personal growth seem to be fostered by experiential learning—indeed, by all pedagogical practices—leading to what Parker Palmer calls

- The precious inwardness of the things of the world,
- Our sense of community with each other, and
- Humility that makes teaching and learning possible (Palmer, 2004).

John Haughey's (2009) recent publication *Where Is Knowing Going?* underscores the importance of this shift in modes of thinking, knowing, and learning.

5. Religion and spirituality are viewed as deeply and essentially different.

Here we rely on some of the distinctions made by Elizabeth Tisdell (2003) in thinking about the nature of spirituality in reference to education (pp. 48–50). Based on qualitative research (interviews with thirty-one adult educators), Tisdell notes that "spirituality and religion are not the same, but for many people they are interrelated." She notes that spirituality honors the wholeness and the interconnectedness of all things through the mystery of what many refer to as the Life-force, God, higher power, higher self, cosmic energy, Buddha nature, or Great Spirit. Spirituality is more personal, related to experience and meaning construction and communal experience of attention to the former. This notion of interconnectedness is further developed by Riyad Shahjahan (2009) as "a way of being in the world where one is connected to one's cultural knowledge and/or beings (e.g. one's community, transcendental beings, and other parts of creation) and allows one to move from inward to outward action" (p. 122). Religion, as noted by Lerner (2000), has to do with an organized community of faith that has written doctrine and codes of regulatory behavior. So, while religious experience and spiritual experience may intersect, they are not the same. According to Palmer (2007), spirituality is one way in which "the human soul yearns eternally for connection." (p. 59) Scholars, as well as people in the street, agree that the religious experience is highly complex and quite varied in interpretation. J. Milton Yinger, a socialist (1946) notes that "religion is defined as the totality of man's attempts 'to bring the relative, the temporary, the disappointing, the painful thinks in life into relation with what is conceived to be permanent, absolute, and cosmically optimistic." (p. vii) James Fowler (1996) looks at religion from a theological perspective. He talks about religion (cumulative tradition made up of beliefs and practices), belief (acceptance by individuals of the truth of the doctrines or ideological claims of a particular religious tradition or denomination), and faith (more personal and existential). In *The Illustrated Book of Sacred Scriptures*, Timothy Freke (1998) describes the concept of spirituality as being a complex phenomenon when explored through a perspective based on ancient scripture and wisdom. While there may be a tendency for religion, with its reliance on dogma and distinctive tradition, to separate people, there is as well the potential for spirituality to bring academics and others together around a common vision.

6. There is deep-seated resistance to the spiritual on the college campus.

Some of the reasons why there is resistance to the spiritual (and to the religious) among faculty on the campus have already been detailed. The rewards for faculty are elsewhere: publications, research, teaching expertise, and service have been integrated into the tenure process and are well respected and rewarded. Because it is viewed as soft and outside the respected disciplines, spirituality provokes a kind of fear within academics, a sense that they may be ridiculed. And yet, despite this, scholars have spoken out regarding the importance of their spirituality in maintaining a sense of purpose and emancipation (Dillard, Abdur-Rashid, & Tyson, 2000). In fact, the disconnect between the spiritual and the academic may well lead to the alienation of those scholars who speak out, both for themselves and for the students whom they view as being deprived of a truly unified education.

What Can Be Done—Spiritual Solutions for the Campus and Beyond

The Ox-Herding Story engages us in reviewing the "mysticism of life," the presence of the Holy One in our search for becoming our true selves. It is this metaphor, as encapsulated in the Ox-Herding Pictures, which will serve as a framework for discussing the spiritual journey with its seminal stages, "letting go, letting be, letting grow" (Dorff, 1988).

Looking at some religious traditions, Roman Catholicism in particular, the journey is clearly organized around a central figure and a clear path that is challenging to follow. In all Christian traditions, not just the Roman Catholic one, Jesus Christ is the figure who followed a humble path, spent a lifetime of teaching in word and deed, and died a salvific death at the hands of his enemies. In so doing he demonstrates the way to live: self-sacrifice, gradual self-understanding, and prayer (through connection with the Father). There are varied traditions across other faiths, and this variety of traditions will also be found among faculty and administration even on deeply Catholic campuses. For that reason, I have chosen a story to serve as backdrop for the spiritual search. The story is Buddhist but sufficiently archetypal and fresh to enliven the discussion among adults of many different faiths and belief systems.

The Spiritual Search and the Ten Ox-Herding Pictures

The Ox-Herding Story provides an imaginative framework for exploration into the challenge of encouraging reflection on college campuses. The songs and accompanying pictures detail ten phases in the process of enlightenment. The tale joins a host of myths and hero stories that spell out the archetypal journey of the seeker who starts out, becomes enmeshed in a liminal period of struggle, and ultimately returns with something of a new identity. Various religious traditions call this whole process by other names: the paschal mystery, Passover, pilgrimage, the hajj. In its ecumenical document, *Nostra Aetate*, the Roman Catholic Church points to the paschal mystery as the common event among faiths around the globe. We share the journey; let us set out.

Figure 1
Searching for the Ox

Alone in the wilderness, lost in the jungle,
The man is searching, searching,
The swelling waters, the faraway
mountains, and the unending path,
Exhausted and in despair, he knows not
where to go.

The ten Ox-Herding Pictures begin with a sense of the ordinary state of humanity. Prior to conscious searching, our spiritual search is couched in the ordinariness of daily life with its ups and downs and challenges. This seems true for all of us, from whatever faith tradition or religious persuasion we come. All of us, faculty and staff and students, are on a search, more or less conscious, whether we are Buddhist, Christian, Hindu, Jewish, Muslim, humanist, deist, or atheist. The object of our search is unknown, some say unknowable. Through the ages, mystics and holy ones have used metaphors and allegories to identify and name the Holy One, the Mystery. Augustine of Hippo said, "Our hearts are restless, O Lord, until they rest in thee." Francis Thompson in his poem "Hound of Heaven" tells us "he fled him down the nights and down the days." Ronald Rolheiser (1999) delineates spiritual desire in his book *The Holy Longing*.

We are all aware in our moments of greatest honesty that desire fuels much of our activity, and perhaps it is the mimetic desire spoken of by René Girard (2001). Aware or not, this desire at its deepest level seems blunted in this twenty-first century by the gradual process of secularization in our culture and in our society. Rolheiser summarizes this state of affairs in quoting Frederic Neitzsche: "God is dead, and we have killed him." We live, and perhaps academics even more so, in a culture that denies another dimension, that relies on scientific fact, that leans heavily on the relativistic truth of each discipline. But we are all nonetheless on a search. As Thomas Merton (1915–1968), a Cistercian monk of Gethsemani Abbey in Kentucky, commonly known as Trappist, writes in his "Untitled Poem,"

All theology is a kind of birthday
Each one who is born
Comes into the world as a question
For which old answers
Are not sufficient.

Deeply concerned about the loss of soul in the modern age, Merton became a monk in order to face his own soul, his deepest identity, his true self, and in so doing, to address the wrenching concerns of the day. He embarked on a journey much like that of the ox herder, probing his own (and thereby our) existential predicament in the world. Merton (1949) envisioned the entire spiritual life as progress away from a false self and toward the self God intended us to become:

> Every one of us is shadowed by an
> illusory person: a false self. This is the
> [person] I want myself to be but who
> cannot exist, because God does not
> know anything about him. And to be
> unknown to God is altogether too much
> privacy. My false and private self is the
> one who wants to exist outside the reach
> of God's will and God's love—outside
> of reality and outside of life. And such a
> self cannot help but be an illusion
> (p. 34).

What Merton calls "our life in God" is more than a state of affairs. It is a work in progress, born of the sweat and tears of human labor and human suffering. The true self is the whole self, emerging from the Adam of our false selves, rooted in sin and distance from God. Key to Merton's (2000) insight about the emergence (the first sighting) of the True Self is that the sighting is God's work, born of meditation, and "the secret of my identity is hidden in the love and mercy of God" (p.37).

Embarking on one's journey, beginning the process of going deeper, will not be an easy path, either for faculty or for administrators. Faculty in the Revisioning Mission program will undoubtedly experience the "silo" nature of academic life in their disconnectedness from other faculty in their own disciplines as well as from faculty across the campus. Reflection on the spiritual commonalities ought to bring RM folks a little closer together, sure in the realization that each is searching in his or her own way for the Ineffable, for the Deep Meaning of things.

With a comparative theological emphasis, Paul O. Ingram (1997), in his *Wrestling with the Ox*, likens the first of the Ox-Herding Pictures to postmodern religious pluralism, highlighting two models—the "theology-of-religions" model and the "primordial" model. In essence, Ingram's synthesis of the personal search for the Ultimate points to the unity of many approaches. The theology-of-religions model takes seriously an accurate description of the impact of religious experience on the social and individual lives of people. The emphasis here, as it is for Richard Rohr (2009) in his "Emerging Church" series on the Web (*National Catholic Reporter*, July 2009) is on experience and praxis rather than dogma. The primordial or perennial model, one spelled out by the theologians John Cobb, Huston Smith, and Stephen T. Katz, takes the position that there are certain universal truths common to all religions. Ingram reminds us that the usual goal of a "science of religion" or theology is "an accurate description of the effects of religious experience on the social and individual lives of human beings." He talks about Buddhists and Christians encountering religious persons whose faith and practice are other than their own. Because of the common truths (outlined below), people can make an intellectual assent to the deep truths of, say, Buddhism (for example, God as self-emptied-of-self) while remaining Christian. Raimundo Panikkar, quoted in his obituary in *The New York Times* on September 6, 2010, says of his journey, "I left Europe as a Christian [his mother was Roman Catholic], I discovered I was a Hindu [his father was Hindu and he studied Indian philosophy in Mysore] and returned as a Buddhist, without ever having ceased to be Christian." How is this possible? Those who favor the primordial model, which points to the unity of religions, list the following common beliefs·

- "God" or "Godhead" or "Absolute" or "Sacred";
- human beings possess the capacity to ascertain truth about this Sacred reality;
- the most important of these truths is the Sacred's ultimacy in comparison with the world's finitude;
- the Sacred, however named, is beyond all names and predicates;
- and the *neti-neti* (not this, not that) nature of the Sacred is the only point, where the primordial model sees the various religious ways of humanity converging indistinguishably.

In other words, whatever the religious persuasion of the believer, there is some universality to the search. The moment of being a formal spiritual seeker is the moment we have been discussing: Searching for the Ox. Now we will proceed with the ensuing pictures.

Figure 2
Seeing the Traces

By the stream and under the trees, scattered are the traces of the lost. The sweet-scented grasses are growing thick; did he find the way? However remote, over the hills and far away the beast may wander,

his nose reaches the heavens and none can conceal it. Seeing the traces of the truth of a religious Way's faith and practice.

Commentators note that coming to this point is a crucial step in the process of enlightenment; it seems to be preceded by the process of quieting and focusing the mind, finding the center of one's being, returning easily to the still point again and again. John Loori et al. (2002) reminds us that it can take many years to settle into knowledge of the true self, years of practice and meditation and awareness. We must remember that "the struggle is the path." (p. 19). Some commentaries identify the tracks as the wisdom teachings of various traditions that, while not being the True Self or Enlightenment, are testimonies to others' having been there, and are thus motivating factors for the seeker.

The second of the Ox-Herding Pictures points to the importance of "seeing," probably in the concept known in Hindu wisdom literature as *darshan,* or keeping our eyes open. And this picture also points to the importance of scripture, for "no scripture
tells the whole story; only traces of it . . . and scripture can help us
see other traces of the Sacred in other scriptures." (Ingram, 1997,
p. 48).

"Seeing the traces" of the ox—of the true self—is a task for
each person. Earlier seekers, giving evidence in scriptures and
personal tales, enlighten us in our search and give us hope. Plotkin's (2008) wilderness journeys take people along a circuitous
trail in imitation of the real-life search. He notes that each person must take the long and twisting path to their true center.
Descent into the deep soul world often begins with a personal
crisis of some sort: the death of a loved one, the destruction of
a home, loss of religious faith, or even suicidal depression. The
work of really seeing beneath surface realities involves paying
attention and slowing down. Many times it means surrender of
one's beliefs about how we are supposed to be and surrender to
the deepest and wildest passions. By giving up a grip on a former
identity and surrendering to some people, places, and roles, we
come to live in the present and can *really see* ourselves as well as
others more clearly.

What are the characteristics of this "seeing," presented in
the second ox-herding song and illustrated in the picture? Who
can come to our aid in delineating its characteristics? Some clarity about truly "seeing" can be found in the writing of Christian
monks and mystics and in the insights of the Sufis. This "seeing"
is a glimpse of the beyond in the ordinary, the daily work (Norris, 1998). It presents the "beyond" through the scriptures and
through literature (Casey, 1996). It shines through the natural
world. Thich Nhat Hanh (1991) calls this living with deep seeing,
a sort of mindfulness, a kind of paying attention. Merton gives us
an example when he writes:

O land alive with miracles!
O clad in streams,
Countering the silver summer's pleasant arrows
And beating them with the kind armor
Of your enkindled water-vesture.
O brilliant wood!
Yours is the voice of a new world;
And all the hills burn with such blinding art
That Christ and angels walk among us, everywhere.

Ingram (1997) recounts the illusive nature of the glimpse or trace given him by the *Bhagavad-Gita*, by the New Testament, and by the Buddhist Pure Land texts. *Lectio divina*, for centuries a practice among Christian monastics, leads the reader from careful reading of Scripture (or any text) through meditation to personal prayer and even to wordless contemplation of the truth revealed to the reader.[2]

Many faculty have found glimpses of the Transcendent within the riches of their chosen discipline, whether it be in the insights of its literature, the wonder of its scientific discoveries, or the marvel of creating structures to make travel smoother. Sharing of the connection between discipline and spirituality can surely benefit participants, if only to set them out in search of the contemplative dimension of their respective disciplines.

Figure 3
Seeing the Ox

On a yonder branch perches a nightingale cheerfully;
The sun is warm, and a soothing breeze blows,
on the back the willows are green;
The ox is there all by himself; nowhere is he to hide himself;
The splendid head decorated with staring horns—what
painter can produce him?

The third picture in our series pivots on getting the first glimpse of the ox, the True Self. We catch a glimpse, but we're not there yet, cautions Loori (2002), who likens the step to going out with a jar in April, capturing some air, and giving it a definitive name. It's an inebriating glimpse that we catch. We do not have the breeze, nor do we have the True Self. We have only caught a glimpse.

And what is this True Self of which the ox seems so powerful a symbol? Thinkers and spiritual gurus alike have plumbed the depths of this question and come up with answers that enrich and strengthen one another. Ken Wilber (2010), the contemporary philosopher of integrative thinking, in his vast work of meshing together all the systems of structures of philosophy and theology through the ages, talks about three different definitions of "self" that call out for clarification in the integration of Eastern and Western philosophy: the False Self (the broken or illusory self), the Actual Self (the authentic or healthily integrated self at any stage of development), and the Real Self (the timeless self beyond all manifestation.) Merton centers his thinking about finding the True Self on personal religious experience. Inspired by Merton's work, Palmer plumbs the deep self in his work *A Hidden Wholeness*, giving it what he considers an essential twist, an emphasis on community, specifically mentioning some Quaker practices such as Circles of Trust and Clearness Committees. In providing a framework for the individual, reflecting on life and vocation in a small group, people can gain new insights about where one is and what challenges require attention in the moment. Seeing the ox, for Palmer (2004), yields a requirement for community. It is a step on a journey "toward inner truth too taxing to be made solo; lacking support, the solitary traveler soon becomes weary or fearful and is likely to quit the road" (p. 26).

Figure 4
Catching the Ox

With the energy of his whole being,
the man has at last taken hold of the ox;
But how wild its will, how ungovernable its power;
At times it struts up a plateau,
When lo! it is lost again in a misty impenetrable mountain pass.

The boy catches the ox in order to transform it, and the end is in sight—of this round of the struggle, at least. If we think of the ox as standing for the True Self, the deep center of ourselves, this grasp is a crucial step in reigning in the divergent elements that cover and cloud and obfuscate it. This is a victory of sorts, the result of discipline and growing self-knowledge. And the rewards extend beyond the individual person. For "every time we get in touch with the truth source we carry within, there is net moral gain for all concerned," Palmer (2004) tells us in recalling searches undertaken by individuals in *A Hidden Wholeness*. But we are dealing with the wild strength of the ox, requiring the reining in with whip and rope of total compassion, perfect nonviolence, and unwavering truthfulness. And the resistance of the ox is clear, "for its wild nature refuses domestication." (Ingram, 1997, p.73) that have evolved over time are at last recognized, and the person is about to do something to overturn these. The moment of "catching the ox" is described poetically by Merton. After sixteen years of struggling to be the perfect monk, he decides at last to let the best (and worst) of who he is, in all its strength and weakness, emerge. Merton's poem "When in the Soul of the Serene Disciple" illustrates this:

> When in the soul of the serene disciple
> With no more Fathers to imitate
> Poverty is a success,
> It is a small thing to say the roof is gone;
> He has not even a house.
> Stars, as well as friends,
> Are angry with the noble ruin.
> Saints depart in several directions.
> Be still:
> There is no longer any need of comment.
> It was a lucky wind
> That blew away his halo with his cares,
> A lucky sea that drowned his reputation.

The bittersweet success of self-discovery in all its glory and unmasking emerges in Merton's poem. There is work to be done, but a new plateau has been reached. Participants may catch such glimpses in their own contemplative practice, or in the rigorous research of their own subject matter, or even in the faces of the students they teach. Wherever the revelation takes place, it is important that the program give people a chance to share their insights and their "Aha" moments, either in person or online.

Figure 5
Taming the Ox

The man must not separate himself from his whip and tether,
Lest the ox wander away into a world of defilements;
When the ox is properly tended, it will grow pure and docile;
Without a chain, nothing binding,
it will by its own free will follow the man.

The ox has been caught; now the novice must learn to tame him. Soul practice becomes essential here, helping the seeker to dissipate the illusory distinction between spiritual life and ordinary life, a distinction that is no longer useful. The point of the taming is to untether the ox, to release the primal awareness that we have focused as a particular body and mind. Lex Hixon (1995) helps us see that here is where the ox becomes a free companion, not a tool for plowing the field of Enlightenment.

Soul work helps (some would say is essential) in the process of taming. Bill Plotkin, in his insightful work on the journey into the soul, lays out several practices of use to those of us imbued with Western culture, separated from nature where ancient civilizations found "soul." Called as he is to be a Cocoon Weaver, a creator of "beautiful contexts for transformation," Plotkin reminds us that the movement toward soul is a journey of descent, or what Thomas Berry calls "inscendence," a journey that deepens. The shamanistic traditions of indigenous cultures and the twentieth-century depth psychologists like Jung, Hillman, Robert Johnson, and James Hollis emphasize the discovery of soul, while the world's major religions focus on the realization of union with spirit.

The work of reining in the ox may well be facilitated by practices referred to collectively by Plotkin as "soulcraft" (the work of evoking soul): dreamwork, deep imagery journals, self-designed ceremonies and traditional rituals, wandering in nature, and conversing with birds and trees, the wind, and the land itself. Perhaps a college might sponsor a retreat, designing ceremonies and practices that enable individuals to seek the deeper part of themselves. Seton Hall University, for example, sponsors a series of such faculty retreats throughout the academic year.

Helpful as well are spiritual practices embedded within the major religions, each tapping into the soul and enabling the seeker to integrate the wildness of soul into the personality. Some of these include Zazen meditation from the world of Buddhist practice, yoga with its accompanying asanas and world-embracing philosophies, *lectio divina* from the world of Western monasticism, and many practices drawn from religious congregations in the Roman Catholic tradition and in Protestant traditions. Modern meditation practices such as Centering Prayer and John Main's "Christian meditation" form useful soul-enriching practices.

There are two books (among many) from the Protestant traditions that describe practices designed to keep alive the life of the soul. Both *Practicing Our Faith*, edited by Dorothy C. Bass, and *An Altar in the World* by Barbara Brown Taylor are chock-full of ideas for daily practice. Bass, director of Valparaiso University's Project on the Education and Formation of People in Faith, has gathered articles from many experienced authors on practices such as honoring the body, household economics, keeping Sabbath, shaping communities, dying well, and singing our lives. Brown Taylor has a gift for weaving her personal experience into such practices as "Vision: The Practice of Waking Up to God" and "Wilderness: The Practice of Getting Lost."

Within the Roman Catholic tradition, there are many spiritual practices designed to keep people "soul-full" on a daily basis, many having their origins in religious congregations. These faith-filled communities, founded through the centuries by charismatic leaders with a spiritual emphasis, have found their way into colleges through the congregations that established such institutions of higher education. Some currently used practices:

- From the Dominicans we have inherited a commitment to the study of theology; Saint Thomas Aquinas wrote a systematic treatise on God and the things of God entitled *Summa Theologica*. Dominicans also passed on to us a deep devotion to Mary, the mother of Jesus, and the praying of the rosary, a set of prayer beads enabling the pray-er to meditate on mysteries of the life of Christ.

- From the Franciscans comes the deep-seated commitment to serving the poor, providing the root of our current emphasis on social justice.

- The oldest of the monastic congregations, the Benedictines, founded in 490, has bequeathed the call to hospitality and to the seven sacred pauses during the day to chant the Psalms—the Divine Office (Liturgy of the Hours)—as well as *lectio divina,* prayerful reading of Scripture that leads to contemplative practice. A variation on this practice is a currently popular method of meditation known as Centering Prayer.

- From the Jesuits, we learn about the Examen, a practice of reflecting on one's actions at the end of each day, and the Spiritual Exercises, written by their founder, Saint Ignatius of Loyola, best used over a thirty-day period of reflection, accompanied by a spiritual guide.

- The Brothers of the Christian Schools and Saint John Baptist de la Salle have built on these spiritual practices to develop a pedagogy relying on deep respect for each student.

- In all of these congregations, the need for a spiritual guide is emphasized, giving rise to having a spiritual companion or Spiritual Director. Revisioning Mission participants who are committed to spiritual growth will become gradually aware that practice is important, that once awareness of the "something more" is accomplished—in self, in work, in relationships—it must be nurtured. Practice is the key: a daily regimen of reflective prayerful time, a commitment to examining one's faults and efforts at growth, the recitation of the Psalms.

Figure 6
Riding the Ox Home

Riding on the ox, the man leisurely winds his way home;
Enveloped in the evening mist,
how tunefully the flute vanishes away!
Singing a tune, beating time,
his heart is filled with joy indescribable!
Because he is now one with those who know, need it be told.

The rancher rides the ox with leisure. This stage is the start of "walking the talk," living one's life immersed in another dimension. It is not enough to *start* spiritual practice; one must bring it home, incorporate it into living. There is effortlessness in this stage of the spiritual journey. An ancient commentary on this stage says, "The struggle is over. Gain and loss are assimilated. I sing the song of the village woodsman, and play the tunes of the children. Astride the ox, I observe the clouds above. Onward I go, no matter who may wish to call me back." The sage, having untethered his own being and the being of all phenomena, begins to blend with the ordinary flow of life. Loori et al. (2002) call our attention to the transformation that is beginning to show itself at this stage. The three poisons of greed, anger, and ignorance are beginning to morph into the virtues of compassion, wisdom, and enlightenment. It is possible to link the insights of this stage to the notion of *wu wei*, one of the most important Taoist concepts. People learn the ease and non-doing of the Tao—the creator and sustainer of everything in the Universe. Non-doing means the actionlessness of Heaven, illustrated in the following abstract from the *Tao Te Ching*: "Tao abides in non-action, yet nothing is left undone" (Lao-tzu, Feng, & English, 1997). Alan Watts refers to non-doing as "what we mean by going with the grain, rolling with the punch." He takes some trouble to point out the simple yet complicated experience of realizing that the immediate now, whatever its nature, is the goal and fulfillment of all living:

It is not that he loses his identity to the
point of feeling that he actually looks
out through all other eyes, becoming

172

literally omniscient, but rather that his
individual consciousness and existence
is a point of view temporarily adopted
by someone immeasurably greater than
himself.
(Watts, 1973, p. 28)

So, we have captured in this picture a momentary glimpse of connection with the ox, with the True Self, and it is, in Christian terms, "salvific" and important. We need these moments to go on, for there is suffering behind and ahead. Peter Berger (1970), in his book *A Rumor of Angels,* calls these unitive experiences tastes of an ultimate, more lasting, liberating wholeness for which the hearts of human beings everywhere have yearned. Ingram (1997) uses this picture as an opportunity to reflect on the unity of all living creatures, on the need for all of us to become conscious of our oneness with nature, an opening to the current environmental movement (p. 130).

Figure 7
The Ox Forgotten, Leaving the Man Alone

Riding on the ox, he is at last back in his home,
When lo! the ox is no more; the man alone sits serenely.
Though the red sun is high up in the sky,
he is still quietly dreaming;
Under a straw-thatched roof his whip and rope are idly lying.

The seventh picture marks a crucial stage along the spiritual path. The herder stops and pauses, reflecting on his liberation. And in so doing, he may well realize that the liberation of any one being is linked to the liberation of all. In our modern culture, the liberation of women comes to mind as unfinished business. Ingram (1997), in writing about this ox-herding picture, alerts us to the fact that all contemporary expressions of humanity's religious traditions, both Western and Asian, continue to maintain an unrelenting androcentrism. While there is a mix of gender and nongender identities among deities of different traditions, the structure and social framework of most traditions remain patriarchal. To achieve the appropriate balance in society and to reflect more accurately the inherent truth beneath all traditions, feminist scholars have set out to create a more accurate and useful record. They seek to frame a history that includes events important to women, and a theology that is no longer patriarchal. So it is worth pausing along the way of the Ten Pictures and reflecting on the liberation of women, seeking to incorporate such liberation in our institutions of higher education structurally as well as academically.

Judith Plaskow (1990), the well-respected feminist Jewish theologian, points to the fact that women's experience—the daily, lived, conscious events, thoughts, and feelings that constitute women's daily reality—is pluralistic, both in a single tradition and among the traditions. There are no accounts by women of Jewish history, or of most of humanity's religious ways, except for some tribal traditions. This is true in many religious traditions, and we are indebted to the women, historians and theologians alike, who have taken on the task of deconstructing and reconstructing their religious traditions. (Ingram cites Paula Cooey with reference to Christianity, Plaskow for Judaism, Rita Gross for Hinduism, and

Lina Gupta for Buddhism). In sum, it is important in finding a personal True Self to realize and recognize the universal presence of the Holy One in all creatures and to revere that presence

Revisioning Mission participants can reflect on liberation on their respective campuses. How free are members of either sex to be themselves fully on this campus? What about students? Are students encouraged to be their best selves, regardless of sex or race or orientation?

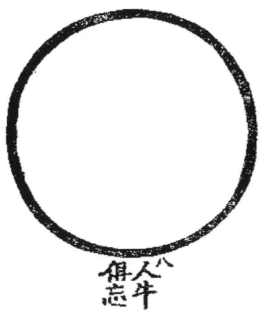

Figure 8
The Ox and the Man Both Gone Out of Sight

All is empty—the whip, the rope, the man and the ox;
Who can survey the infinity of heaven?
Over a furnace burning hot, not a flake of snow can fall;
When emptiness is experienced,
manifest is the spirit of the ancient masters.

This eighth picture brings us to the culmination of the spiritual journey, but certainly not the end. It's a little like Nirvana, heaven, peace on earth. We all have little glimpses of the Beyond along life's path; many of them keep us going. I think of William Blake's "To see a world in a grain of sand / And a heaven in a wild flower, / Hold infinity in the palm of your hand / And eternity in an hour."

Merton (1966) writes of this stage, where man and ox are both out of sight as *le point vierge* [the virgin point]:

> At the center of our being is a point of nothingness which is untouched by sin and by illusion, a point of pure truth, a point or spark which belongs entirely to God, which is never at our disposal, from which God disposes of our lives, which is inaccessible to the fantasies of our own mind or the brutalities of our own will. This little point of nothingness and of *absolute poverty* is the pure glory of God in us ...
> (p. 142)

Where are the gates of heaven on this campus? Where are the points of opening to Mystery here? If Merton is right, and the *point vierge* is where poverty meets the invisible light of heaven, what are our points of intersection? Reflection is called for here, and time for gratitude.

In the ancient version of the Ox-Herding Pictures, the Chinese Zen artist closes his series with this eighth picture; only later were pictures nine and ten added, probably to ground the series in real life. The spiritual person, after having come to know the True Self, returns to everyday life filled with goodness for people in need, with light to help others.

Figure 9
Returning to the Origin

Returning to the Origin, returning to the Source—already a
false step!
Far better to remain at home, blind and deaf,
and without much ado;
Sitting in the hut, the man takes no notice of things outside.
Behold the streams flowing—whither nobody knows; and the
flowers vividly red—for whom are they?

Home for all of us is the planet Earth. In our lifetime, we have
seen Earth from outer space and from the moon, and we marvel anew at the gift and the responsibility that is our home. Brian
Swimme and others invite us to contemplate the revolution in
thinking that we have witnessed in our time, a revolution akin to
that provided by Copernicus in 1543 when he proved that the earth
revolved around the sun. Our current moment of "breakdown and
creativity" is caused by the discovery that our universe came into
existence 13.7 billion years ago and "is so biased toward complexi-

fication that life and intelligence are now seen to be a newly inevitable construction of evolutionary dynamics."[3] In an interview with *EnlightenNext* magazine regarding the contribution to evolutionary consciousness of Teilhard de Chardin, Brian Swimme points out the important thinking of the Jesuit scientist. Living as we do in an evolving universe, we need to take new and deep levels of responsibility for our planet. Our motivation comes from contemplating the marvels of our mysterious universe: the Milky Way on a starry night, the Green Blob first seen by the Hubble telescope recently and thought to produce stars, the magic of a beach or a forest or a bird. On the one hand, we are radically amazed (Cannato, 2006). On the other hand, we are driven to action, seeking solutions to prevent the environmental disasters that seem increasingly common. Our spiritual journey takes place on an Earth that calls out for reverence and respect. Environmental sustainability can be a campus-wide theme that taps into a spirituality based on deep reverence for the earth. I'm impressed with initiatives taken by colleges and universities nationwide. Take a look at what is being done at the University of Northern Iowa: a sustainability coordinator, solar panel study rooms, attention to the budget spent on local and organic food, a commitment to working with the local community on farmers' markets, recycling and conservation, use of renewable energy, weatherization initiatives, even ozone-reducing local transportation. Indeed, it looks like what a contemplative in action does to show reverence for the earth and commitment to the Holy One's presence in our midst.

Figure 10
Entering the City with Bliss-Bestowing Hands

Bare-chested and bare-footed,
he comes out into the marketplace;
Daubed with mud and ashes, how broadly he smiles;
There is no need for the miraculous power of the gods;
For he touches all, and behold, the dead trees are in full bloom.

Back in the marketplace, down from the mountain, deep in the hurly-burly of daily life—here it is that our journey is tested. "How do we spin out of the tight cycle of the self?" asks Tillie Olsen, an American feminist of the 1930s who took up the plight of poor women. In her talk, Sister Mara Faulkner, a Benedictine nun who spoke at St. John's University in Collegeville, Minnesota, in 2010, quoted Tillie and presented a remarkable documentary of relevant images. Her pictures told the story: images of devoted women working side by side with peasant girls from developing countries, older nuns providing food in poverty-stricken neighborhoods, monastics praying for the disenfranchised. Her talk was a wake-up call for the room full of contemplatives, alerting all to the danger of the inward journey. And her talk led many to rethink their journey, to reexamine the trajectory of its spin, to recall again the world of needy folk hungry for the compassionate heart of prayerful people. Although Stanislavski, the Russian dramatist and thinker, reminds us that "the longest and most exciting journey is the journey inwards," Dorothee Sölle (2001), in her book *The Silent Cry*, calls our attention to another form of excitement. Going deep, she tells us, we touch the heart of mankind and join the silent cry on behalf of oppressed people everywhere.

The test of the spiritual journey, the indicator of success in finding the True Self, is said to lie in the way we live our lives. The key to finding and living in communion with the True Self comes, says Beatrice Bruteau (2004), from living with consciousness, keeping our sense of the deep self in the Divine Eternity, realizing that the Wholeness of Reality is the source of our being. And that Source of Being becomes the energy impelling us outward to be of service. Wisdom and compassion are the fruit of meditation, and on the college campus, many opportunities present themselves to put these into practice. We could start with a study of the many exemplary figures that have gone before us: Mother Teresa, Mahatma Gandhi, John Woolman, Martin Luther King, Anne Frank, Etty Hillesum, Bede Griffiths, Thomas Merton, James Luther Adams, and Dorothy Day. What do they have in common?   They were all deep thinkers, avid persons of prayer, and passionate advocates for the oppressed of the world. The Tibetan Buddhists talk about the inner marriage of wisdom (*prajna*) and compassion (*karuna*). This is the love of wisdom and the wisdom of love. This is worth striving for. The spiritual journey of each one leads to compassion for all. Our walk along the Camino de Vida—the road/way for life—takes many years, and those of us in higher education have the privilege of bringing others along the road with us.

We need to reflect on service opportunities on the campus and in the local neighborhood, on fostering such opportunities, and on participating in them. The work of higher education, particularly Catholic higher education, can only be enriched by continuing service, fostered with enthusiasm among alumni, faculty, and students alike.

Questions for Discussion

- Think again about "weaving a seamless connection between one's inner and outer life." What are the significant elements of each for you? How connected or disconnected do they seem to be for you?
- Think about life on this campus (and on those in your past) during your years of education and teaching and review. What has been your sense of the spiritual on campus?
- What has been your experience with religion and/or spirituality, whether consciously or unconsciously?
- How is your role as college professor or staff member a response to a vocational call? When did you experience this call and how do you live it out? (Remember, a vocational call does not have to have religious meaning or connotations.)
- Reflecting on the Ox-Herding Pictures and Story, what have been some of the decisions you've made or crossroads you've taken on your path? What were the benchmarks for: (1) setting out (making the decision, choosing a path); (2) liminality (that vague uncomfortable period after making a decision or choosing a path); and (3) coming home: returning, with a new identity?
- Picture 1: Searching for the Ox. Parker Palmer writes of his annual trip to Minnesota and a kind of retreat where he finds "a hidden wholeness." How would you describe a place where your personal wholeness can be knit together for your peers?
- Picture 2: Seeing the Traces. Where do you most regularly see "traces of the holy" in your life? How would you describe striking examples of "seeing the traces"?

- Picture 3: Seeing the Ox. In what activities or events have you glimpsed your True Self, the essence of who you are? What do you think is the essence of who you are: your unique gift to be lived out and offered to others—your family, community, colleagues, and students?
- Pictures 4 and 5: Catching and Taming the Ox. What current practices do you use to nurture your True Self? What kinds of opportunities, sponsored by your institution, would help to nurture your True Self? If you were doing the planning, what would you institute?
- Picture 6: Riding the Ox Home. How would you describe ways in which you feel at home and in touch with your True Self? In which areas are you still searching for understanding?
- Picture 7: The Ox Forgotten. How does your sense of the Holy One pervade your worldview? Your connection with others? Your respect for persons of different gender or religious preference?
- Picture 8: The Ox and the Man Both Out of Sight. What have been your "glimpses of heaven"? When? Where? How have they changed your view of life? Your sense of yourself? Of others? Of your work in higher education?
- Picture 9: Returning to the Origin. In what ways does your campus (and your family) engage in practices connecting reverence for the earth with devotion to the Holy One? How? What remains to be done?
- Picture 10: Entering the City with Bliss-Bestowing Hands. "The spiritual journey of each one leads to compassion for all." In what ways have you experienced and demonstrated compassion on campus?

References

Astin, A. W. (2004). Why spirituality deserves a central place in liberal education. *Liberal Education, 90*(2), 34–41.

Astin, A. W., Astin, H. S., & Higher Education Research Institute. (1999). *Meaning and spirituality in the lives of college faculty:*

A study of values, authenticity, and stress. Los Angeles, CA: Higher Education Research Institute, University of California, Los Angeles.

Astin, A. W., Astin, H. S., Lindholm, J. A., & Bryant, A. L. (2007). *Spirituality and the professoriate: A national study of faculty beliefs, attitudes, and behaviors.* Retrieved http://spirituality.ucla.edu/docs/results/faculty/spirit_professoriate.pdf

Astin, A. W., Astin, H. S., & Lindholm, J. A. (2011). *Cultivating the spirit: How college can enhance students' inner lives.* San Francisco, CA: Jossey-Bass.

Bennett, J. (2004). Academic spirituality. *Spirituality in Higher Education Newsletter, 1*(1), 1–7. Retrieved from http://spirituality.ucla.edu/docs/newsletters/1/Bennett.pdf

Berger, P. L. (1970). *A rumor of angels: Modern society and the rediscovery of the supernatural.* Garden City, NY: Anchor Books.

Bruteau, B. (2004). *Radical optimism: Practical spirituality in an uncertain world.* Boulder, CO: Sentient Publications.

Cannato, J. (2006). *Radical amazement: Contemplative lessons from black holes, supernovas, and other wonders of the universe.* Notre Dame, IN: Sorin Books.

Casey, M. (1996). *Sacred reading: The ancient art of lectio divina.* Liguori, MO: Triumph Books.

Cherry, C., DeBerg, B. A., & Porterfield, A. (2001). *Religion on campus.* Chapel Hill, NC: University of North Carolina Press.

Chickering, A. W., Dalton, J. C., & Auerbach, L. S. (2006). *Encouraging authenticity and spirituality in higher education.* San Francisco, CA: Jossey-Bass.

Corcoran, D. (2010). *Benedictine way of wisdom.* Address at the Monastic Institute, Collegeville, MN.

Dillard, C. B., Abdur-Rashid, D., & Tyson, C. A. (2000). My soul is a witness: Affirming pedagogies of the spirit. *International Journal of Qualitative Studies in Education, 13*(5), 447–462.

Dorff, F. (1988). *The art of passingover: An invitation to living creatively.* New York, NY: Paulist Press.

Dreyer, E. A., & Bennett, J. B. (2006). Higher education and a spirituality of everyday life. *Spirituality in Higher Education*

Newsletter, 3(1), 1–9. Retrieved from http://spirituality.ucla.edu/docs/newsletters/3/Dreyer_and_Bennett.pdf

Duerr, M. (2002). Survey of transformative and spiritual dimensions in higher education. Retrieved from http://www.contemplativemind.org/programs/academic/fetzer_report.pdf

Finley, J. (1978). *Merton's palace of nowhere: A search for God through awareness of the true self.* Notre Dame, IN: Ave Maria Press.

Fowler, J. W. (1996). *Stages of faith: The psychology of human development and the quest for meaning.* San Francisco, CA: Harper & Row.

Freke, T. (1998). *The illustrated book of Sacred Scriptures.* Wheaton, IL: Theosophical Publishing House.

Girard, R. (2001). *I see Satan fall like lightning.* Maryknoll, NY: Orbis Books.

Haughey, J. C. (2009). *Where is knowing going? The horizons of the knowing subject.* Washington, DC: Georgetown University Press.

Hixon, L. (1995). *Coming home: The experience of enlightenment in sacred traditions.* Burdett, NY: Published for the Paul Brunton Philosophic Foundation by Larson Publications.

Huston, P. (2010). Wake-up call: A midlife spiritual challenge. *The Christian Century, 127*(2), 30–33.

Ingram, P. O. (1997). *Wrestling with the ox: A theology of religious experience.* New York, NY: Continuum Publishing.

Lao-tzu, Feng, G., & English, J. (1997). *Tao te ching.* New York, NY: Vintage Books.

Lee, J. L., Matzkin, A., & Arthur, S. (2004). Understanding students' religious and spiritual pursuits: A case study at New York University. *Journal of College and Character, 5*(3). Retrieved from http://journals.naspa.org/jcc/vol5/iss3/1/

Lerner, M. (2000). *Spirit matters.* Charlottesville, VA: Hampton Roads Pub.

Lindholm, J. A. (2007). Spirituality in the academy: Reintegrating our lives and the lives of our students. *About Campus, 12*(4), 10–17.

Loori, J. D., & Marchaj, K. R. (2002). *Riding the ox home: Stages on the path of enlightenment.* Boston, MA: Shambhala.

Lowell, J. R. (1900). The first snow-fall. In E. C. Stedman (Ed.), *An American anthology, 1787–1900: Selections illustrating the editor's critical review of American poetry in the nineteenth century.* Retrieved from http://www.bartleby.com/248/351.html

Merton, T. (n.d.). When in the soul of the serene disciple. *Poetry Chaikhana: Sacred poetry from around the world.* Retrieved from http://www.poetry-chaikhana.com/M/MertonThomas/Wheninsoulof.htm

Merton, T. (1949). *Seeds of contemplation.* Norfolk, CT: New Directions.

Merton, T. (1966). *Conjectures of a guilty bystander.* Garden City, NY: Doubleday.

Merton, T. (1977). *The collected poems of Thomas Merton.* New York, NY: New Directions.

Merton, T. (2000). *Thomas Merton: Essential Writings.* (Introduction by Christine M Bochen). Maryknoll, New York, NY: Orbis Books.

Merton, T., & Leclercq, J. (1971). *Contemplation in a world of action.* Garden City, NY: Doubleday.

Merton, T., & Szabo, L. (2005). *In the dark before dawn: New selected poems of Thomas Merton.* New York, NY: New Directions.

Nhát Hanh, T. (1991). *Peace is every step: The path of mindfulness in everyday life.* New York, NY: Bantam Books.

Norris, K. (1998). *The quotidian mysteries: Laundry, liturgy, and "women's work".* New York, NY: Paulist Press.

Palmer, P. J. (2004). *A hidden wholeness: The journey toward an undivided life: Welcoming the soul and weaving community in a wounded world.* San Francisco, CA: Jossey-Bass.

Palmer, P. J. (2007). *The courage to teach: Exploring the inner landscape of a teacher's life.* San Francisco, CA: Jossey-Bass.

Peck, K., & Stick, S. (2008). Catholic and Jesuit Identity in Higher Education. *Christian Higher Education, 7*(3), 200–225.

Plaskow, J. (1990). *Standing again at Sinai: Judaism from a feminist perspective.* San Francisco, CA: Harper & Row.

Plotkin, B. (2003). *Soulcraft: Crossing into the mysteries of nature and psyche.* Novato, CA: New World Library.

Plotkin, B. (2008). *Nature and the human soul: Cultivating wholeness and community in a fragmented world.* Novato, CA: New World Library.

Rohr, R. (2009). Fr. Richard Rohr: Seeing with God's eyes, part 1 of 3. Audio podcast. *National Catholic Reporter.* Retrieved from http://ncronline.org/news/podcasts/fr-richard-rohr-seeing-gods-eyes-part-1-3

Rice, E. R. (2007). Faculty priorities: Where does faith fit. *Spirituality in Higher Education Newsletter.* Retrieved from http://spirituality.ucla.edu/docs/newsletters/3/Rice_Article.pdf

Rolheiser, R. (1999). *The holy longing: The search for a Christian spirituality.* New York, NY: Doubleday.

Shahjahan, R. (2009). The role of spirituality in the anti-oppressive higher-education classroom. *Teaching in Higher Education, 14*(2), 121–131.

Sölle, D. (2001). *The silent cry: Mysticism and resistance.* Minneapolis, MN: Fortress Press.

Tisdell, E. J. (2003). *Exploring spirituality and culture in adult and higher education.* San Francisco, CA: Jossey-Bass.

Watts, A. (1973). *This is it, and other essays on Zen and spiritual experience.* New York, NY: Vintage Books.

Wilber, K. (2010). *Actual self, false self, real self: What are states of consciousness?* Video file. Retrieved from http://integrallife.com/node/60735

Yinger, M. J. (1946). *Religion in the struggle for power: A study in the Sociology of Religion.* Durham, North Carolina: Duke University Press.

Recommended Reading

Cannato, J. (2006). *Radical amazement: Contemplative lessons from black holes, supernovas, and other wonders of the universe.* Notre Dame, IN: Sorin Books..

Chopra, D. (2007). *Buddha: A story of enlightenment.* New York, NY: Harper.

Edwards, T. (1995). *Living in the presence: Spiritual exercises to open your life to the awareness of God.* San Francisco, CA: HarperSanFrancisco.

Finley, J. (2004). *Christian meditation: Experiencing the presence of God.* San Francisco, CA: HarperSanFrancisco.

Forest, J. (2007). *The road to Emmaus: Pilgrimage as a way of life.* Maryknoll, NY: Orbis Books.

Keating, T. (2002). *Foundations for centering prayer and the Christian contemplative life.* New York, NY: Continuum.

Kelly, T. R., & Steere, D. V. (1941). *A testament of devotion.* New York, NY: Harper & Brothers.

Lao-tzu, Feng, G., & English, J. (1997). *Tao te ching.* New York, NY: Vintage Books.

May, G. G. (1982). *Will and spirit: A contemplative psychology.* San Francisco, CA: Harper & Row.

O'Murchu, D. (1997). *Reclaiming spirituality: A new spiritual framework for today's world.* Dublin: Gill & Macmillan.

Plaskow, J. (1990). *Standing again at Sinai: Judaism from a feminist perspective.* San Francisco, CA: Harper & Row.

Sölle, D. (2001). *The silent cry: Mysticism and resistance.* Minneapolis, MN: Fortress Press.

Tolle, E. (1999). *The power of now: A guide to spiritual enlightenment.* Novato, CA: New World Library

Wilber, K. (2007). *The integral vision: A very short introduction to the revolutionary integral approach to life, God, the universe, and everything.* Boston, MA: Shambhala.

Notes

[1] The HERI studies of faculty and spirituality in the academy reveal a wide range of attitudes including discomfort with the spiritual, distance from their particular discipline and the spiritual, and desire for more connection between personal life and academic calling.

[2] Two books address *lectio divina*, the careful reading of Scripture in detail and with loving guidance toward practice: Wiederkehr,

M. (1995). *The song of the seed: A monastic way of tending the soul.* San Francisco, CA: HarperSanFrancisco; Hall, T. (1988); *Too deep for words: Rediscovering lectio divina.* New York, NY: Paulist Press.

[3] Brian Swimme, in an interview with *EnlightenNext* magazine regarding the influence on his thinking of Pierre Teilhard de Chardin, available online at www.enlightennext.org/magazine/j19/teilhard.asp

Essay Four

The Catholic Intellectual Life: A Worldview for the Curriculum

One of the values of the notion of catholicity (wholeness) is that it gives direction to both faith and reason without requiring that they become conjoined. There will always be, in every human being, a drive for meaning and wholeness anyway; what both faith and reason contribute to this drive is an orientation to, and a relationship with, the known unknown that we call Mystery. (Haughey, 2009, p. 56)

Introduction: Catholic Epistemology

This essay introduces the reader to a "way of knowing" (an epistemology) that is at the core of the Catholic intellectual life. It then indicates the areas of learning that provide the subject matter for this way of understanding human creativity and achievement.[1] Such a rich intellectual life arose because of the relational epistemology at the core of the Catholic worldview. The analysis of Parker Palmer, Arthur Zajonc and Megan Scribner (2010) in *The Heart of Higher Education*, presented in the essay on faculty learning communities, provides insight into the Catholic intellectual life. In this essay, an analysis of John C. Haughey's *Where Is Knowing Going? The Horizons of the Knowing Subject*

(2009) will complement the discussion of Palmer and Zajonc's epistemology. Haughey offers a theological grounding for their epistemology, thereby enhancing an understanding of the term "Catholic" when discussing the intellectual life. In Haughey's view, a transcendent epistemological horizon and the doctrine of the Incarnation lay the theological foundation of the Catholic intellectual life.

The Catholic intellectual life is an essential dimension of Catholic university culture. For example, you could say it is a way of interpreting scientific research, but not necessarily part of the research project itself. On the one hand, it should infuse the curriculum and student cocurricular activities and become a way of seeing the world as a result of the undergraduate experience. On the other hand, a number of challenges need to be met if infusion is to take place across university life in its entirety. As a core element of the Catholic university's culture and curriculum, academic deans and faculty are the primary instruments of bringing the Catholic intellectual life into the curriculum. Such infusion will surely be a source of contention among a religiously and ethnically heterogeneous administration and faculty.

While a school of arts may see the Catholic intellectual life as the sine qua non of its academic core and disciplinary fields, other schools will need convincing because they do not necessarily perceive an integral connection between their diverse disciplines and the Catholic approach to the intellectual life. Furthermore, I take it for granted that virtually all new faculty will claim insufficient knowledge of what the Catholic intellectual life is. Especially for those outside the humanities, but even within them, relating this way of thinking to their disciplines requires a great deal of preparation and education. Giving a role to Catholic thought and its worldview or epistemology will not sit well with many administrators and faculty, not only because it is an unknown body of knowledge and way of seeing the world, but also because it is a pedagogical puzzle. Finally, the question will surely arise: "Isn't this a restorationist move, a return to a very parochial education characteristic of the Catholic university prior to the 1960s?" Hopefully, this essay will bring understanding to the Catholic way of thinking and its impact in virtually all areas of university education and Western civilization in both the Old World and the New. Once the epistemological puzzle is understood, suspicion should be greatly assuaged.

As has been noted frequently in this book, the essays are not only resources for the RM program; each one stands alone and will assist all academics in better understanding Catholic higher education, especially its culture and intellectual life. While this essay is directed at new hires, it will prove helpful in a number of university academic and cocurricular venues.

A discussion of Catholic intellectual life provides entrée into a distinctive way of thinking. Contemporaneous with the first century of Christianity and with roots in Israelite religious history and the Hebrew Scriptures, it represents continuity and change in the search for truth and meaning. Catholic intellectual life has much in common with that of the Anglican Communion and to a lesser extent with Protestant denominations, but it is a distinctive and distinguishing attribute that draws many faculty and students to Catholic education. As insightful as a study of Catholic thought can prove to be, it does not stand alone or unchallenged in the contemporary Catholic university. The latter has been profoundly influenced by the Enlightenment project and secularism, both of which are guided by the scientific paradigm of objectivism and opposed to any hint of affective learning.

Analysis of Catholic intellectual life complements the previous discussion of Catholic culture and will be a rewarding experience for new faculty members because they will understand in more depth the worldview or epistemology of Catholic education. This knowledge will also assist the new teacher in bringing to bear Catholic thought on aspects of relevant curricula and on research in fields such as art, music, history, biology, economics, education, ethics, European cultural studies, global studies, history, literature, philosophy, political science, sociology, and theology. Needless to say, each discipline or field of study has an impact on the Catholic intellectual life. It is a two-way street. The Catholic imagination is also brought to bear on and influenced by the hard sciences such as astronomy, biology, chemistry, ecology, engineering, and physics, as well as by the applied and social sciences such as business, anthropology, architecture, psychology, and social work. For new hires in many of these disciplines, the Catholic intellectual life opens areas of curriculum development and research that may have been untouched or overlooked in previous work.

Awareness of this stream of thought is the birthright of Catholics, an "open-source" treasure for all civilizations, not covert indoctrination. These two facets of classroom and campus—culture and intellectual life—differentiate Catholic education from culture and intellectual life in other institutions of higher learning. They offer a rich understanding of and an affective connection to Catholicism itself.

Another characteristic of Catholic intellectual life is a two-thousand-year heritage or legacy. Other than Jewish universities, no Western university can claim such an enduring and highly respected intellectual life within the academic community and among Catholic public intellectuals in the larger society.

Questions for Discussion

- What does the term "Catholic" mean to you when used to describe intellectual life? What place do you think the Catholic intellectual life deserves in the curriculum?
- What is the core element in this intellectual life that clearly distinguishes it from other ways of thinking?
- How would you differentiate a Catholic novelist from a novelist who is Catholic?
- How would a biologist incorporate the Catholic intellectual life into the curriculum?
- How would Catholic thought inform the study of English literature in the Romantic period?

Terminology

Before going further, it is important to clarify terms. I intention-ally use the term "Catholic intellectual life," of which heritage is an integral part. I do not use the term "Catholic intellectual tradi-tion" as a synonym for "Catholic intellectual life." "Intellectual life" conveys a living reality with a memory (the heritage of which the tradition is a part), an active, critical, imaginative mind, shaped, for example, by the Incarnation, hope, the present times, and the coming Kingdom of God, whereas "tradition" is more commonly thought of as the past or that which is handed down.[2] Although tra-dition presents the image of a stand-alone, time-bound set of philo-sophical and theological systems, or canons of art and literature, in reality these texts, the tradition, are a vital part of the Catholic intellectual heritage. Most importantly, the Hebrew Scriptures and the New Testament are fundamental to the tradition. Along with the teachings of the Catholic Church, they guide Catholic thought in all ages as they are brought to bear on contemporary life. The Catholic imagination is not restrained in discussing the Catholic intellectual heritage and its tradition. The opposite would be the case if one were focused on the intellectual tradition alone, but that focus would never satisfy the analogical imagination of the sacramental, incarnational mind—a keystone of Catholicism itself.

"Heritage" suggests a group's expansive legacy that, once received and in conversation with its tradition, is constantly exam-ined, criticized, made relevant and newly vibrant, becoming a gift to future generations, all of which constitutes the Catholic intel-lectual life. The Catholic intellectual heritage is a library of reli-gious writing, such as the Scriptures and their commentaries, the lives of the saints, theological texts, and literary, artistic, musical, and philosophical systems, as well as architectural masterpieces. These elements, spanning two thousand years, are shared in vary-ing degrees with other Christians, and with Jews and Muslims, who are also monotheistic. It is a heritage that is at one and the same time burnished with age, malleable through the centuries, and vitally alive as it shapes contemporary Catholic thought, especially social justice theory and practice. In sum, it is an inheritance for our own creativity and that of future generations of humanity, not only of Catholics.

Because of the Incarnation, a sacramental or "analogical" imagination informs the intellectual life and gives rise to "seeing God in all things." A brief excursion through the history and content of this way of thinking will give the new hire an understanding of the heritage and contemporary expressions of the Catholic intellectual life. Moreover, we will discuss relational epistemology in contrast to the postmodern social-construction-of-reality worldview. Finally, we will assess the impact of *Ex corde Ecclesiae* on the Catholic intellectual life and academic freedom in particular (John Paul II, 1990). Taken together, this essay, and that on Catholic culture, give substance and grounding to the distinctiveness of the Catholic university.

Question for Discussion

How do you interpret this statement: "Intellect, imagination, and heritage have the potential of being an explosive mixture when brought together in the Catholic intellectual life"?

Epistemology: Relational Knowledge, the Analogical Imagination, and Sacramentality

Individuals and societies are informed by an epistemology: a way of imagining, thinking about, understanding, and interpreting the world. The Catholic intellectual life is also informed by an epistemology, the outcome of the belief that since God created all that exists, and that which God created is good, creation itself reflects the glory of God and bodies forth the divine presence. Creation is the sacrament (or sign) of the divine presence—in particular, but by no means exclusively, in the human person, to whom an inalienable dignity attaches because the person is created in "the image and likeness of God" (Genesis 1:26). Influenced by the Gospel message of the inbreaking of the Kingdom of God, the Catholic worldview is bounded by a transcendent horizon, an endpoint—or, in theological language, an eschatology—that directs the believer to the full realization of God's reign. All human activity is seen and evaluated through this way of thinking and its transcendent horizon.

This theologically grounded epistemology is the result of an "analogical imagination," the great sacramental principle that gives rise to this Catholic interpretive lens and is the driving force of the Catholic intellectual life (Hellwig, 2000, pp. 1–18). As Anne M. Clifford (2008) notes: "Thus, Catholicism provides the visible reminders of the true possibilities of life and invites the raising of our spirits through the visual arts, architecture, music, poetry, and the stories of those who have lived bravely and deeply" (p. 368). Mark Massa (2008) reflects on the centrality of this epistemology: "'[T]he analogical imagination' [is] embraced by Catholicism— centered on a *sacramental* worldview that celebrates the material world as good, and a *mediated* understanding of God that is suspicious of religious individualism and untrammeled freedom" (p. 26).

Monika Hellwig is insightful on the uses of the analogical imagination: memory takes hold of the complex story of Catholicism, but it is imagination that interprets or gives meaning to the story. "The purpose of [building on religious memory] is to shape the memories and the imagination of succeeding generations of believers so that they will interpret all their experiences in terms of the pervasive presence of the sacred and in terms of a history of salvation" (Hellwig, 2000, p. 10). For example, since God is totally present to and separate from the finite, we know something of God through creation by analogy. The intellect tells us something of the mystery of God through the imagination's ability to make analogies. The seeming infinity of the heavens likewise reveals, to a degree, God's infinity. The comparison is always qualified because analogy is not equality. In the case of God, every analogy is only a finite indicator of the awesomeness of God.

Thus, an appreciation for this imagination and its legacy comes about from immersion in examples: reading novels, poetry, plays, philosophy, and theology as well as appreciating art, music, and architecture written or created within this dynamic, living heritage.

Moreover, Catholic epistemology and imagination bring insight and critique to bear on science and its application in technology (e.g. the development of nuclear weapons or the use of fetal stem cells). Understanding the worldview or epistemology responsible for the diverse manifestations of the intellectual life will enable us to understand better the framework within which it developed and continues to grow.

The Second Vatican Council, an ecumenical or general council of the Catholic Church[3], affirmed this distinctive epistemology in a seminal document, the *Pastoral Constitution on the Church in the Modern World* (*Gaudium et Spes*, henceforth GS).[4] Among its many affirmations, two are of note here (Vatican Council, 1965):

> The joys and the hopes, the griefs and
> the anxieties of the men [*sic*] of this
> age, especially those who are poor or
> in any way afflicted, these are the joys
> and hopes, the griefs and anxieties of
> the followers of Christ. Indeed, nothing
> genuinely human fails to raise an echo
> in their hearts. (para. 1)
> Thus, far from thinking that works
> produced by man's own talent and
> energy are in opposition to God's
> power, and that the rational creature
> exists as a kind of rival to the Creator,
> Christians are convinced that the
> triumphs of the human race are a sign
> of God's grace and the flowering of His
> own mysterious design.
> (para. 34)

This Catholic imagination receives nurture from the community, communal piety, and the intellectual life. Because of this nurture, we now see, through the historical lens of some forty years, the limitations of GS in terms of its focus on "the triumphs of the human race." Reference is made to the shadow side of these triumphs, as in paragraphs 79–81 on war and nuclear weapons. But GS, viewed from the second decade of the twenty-first century, is lopsidedly anthropocentric. There is virtually no mention of responsibility for the rest of God's creation. Even though ecological awareness was evolving in many parts of the world at the time of the Council, the bishops did not understand its importance or see it as an aspect of "the signs of the times" (French, 2006, pp. 196–207). The richness of the sacramental principle has brought Catholics to a fuller understanding of the analogical imagination through the ecological movement and has replaced the anthropocentric worldview with one that embraces all of God's creation and understands the human person within and responsible for that creation.

Thus, there is what Hellwig calls a "Catholic approach to knowledge," a method of reflection and critical thinking that is the pathway to human flourishing. Anthony Godzieba (2008) elaborates: "It is the way of envisioning reality through the eyes of faith that recognizes that the finite can indeed mediate the infinite, that all aspects of created being can mediate grace" (p. 16). Benedictines speak of this as "finding God in the ordinary, the quotidian," while Jesuits "seek God in all things."

The aspiration to human flourishing is also an interreligious aspiration, a belief that human life has meaning and that the meaning can be known. Consequently, a commonly held belief is that there is a normative standard of right and wrong that is not of human invention but that can be deduced by humans. "Beyond this we hold in common with all religious traditions the deliberately fostered yearning for communion with the ultimately transcendent, and the understanding that in some way this is connected with the way we relate to one another" (Hellwig, 2000, p. 6). The sacramental imagination is, for Godzieba, "the Catholic construal of reality." This construal affirms "the sacramentality of creation." As a result, "the crucial claim is that material 'stuff' has the potential to be a channel of grace, that creation necessarily mediates the presence of God that enables our participation in divine life, on God's initiative" (2008, p. 16).

Godzieba (2008) notes that the definition comes easier than a description of God's grandeur because the latter is all of reality and an inherent mystery: "the fundamental graced nature of created being as a mediation of divine presence, affirmed in Genesis 1–2; the intensification of this mediation in the incarnation of Christ; and its confirmation in Christ's resurrection" (p. 17). Sacramentality is the retina of the eye of faith. God's ineffability is manifest in God's "handiwork," as Gerard Manley Hopkins (1975) writes: "The world is charged with the grandeur of God. It will flame out, like shining from shook foil; it gathers to greatness, like the ooze of oil crushed."

Immersion in the ordinary events of life presents humankind with the transcendence and immanence of God understood through the eyes of faith. This immersion is even more complex because God's "sacramentality is both the *structure* of creation and a *process*, our active encounter with creation by which we relate to reality with every aspect of our being as made in the image and likeness of God (Gen 1:26–27)" (Godzieba, 2008, p. 17).Very much in tune with Palmer and Zajonc's relational epistemology, Godzieba concludes that God's creation is "a performance to be experienced," and of equal importance, "a praxis demanding our participation."

A performance experienced and a participative praxis? Are there standards of discrimination, criteria for the beholder of creation and the practitioner of deeds in this world? How does one evaluate knowing and doing? "In other words, how are we to discriminate among the new possibilities for existence called forth by the imagination so that we might discern which are eventually productive and which are destructive" (Godzieba, 2008, p. 21)? Joining the postmodern embrace of the "other" is in itself nondiscriminatory; or, as Godzieba (2008) notes, "A simple appeal to alterity and the 'call of the other' is too thin to provide the criteria for discernment" (p. 21). Fundamental normative questions beg inquiry: What affirms or denies human flourishing? And in response to this query, reflection on the discriminating character of religion is invaluable, "for the religions have always claimed to provide standards to judge a meaningful human life: in order to be fully human, one must be aware of humanity's finitude and its rootedness in the divine" (Godzieba, 2008, p. 21). In revealing the sacred, religion at the same time reveals the finitude and partiality or brokenness of the world and human creativity in all dimensions of life, but today especially in the world of science, technology, and business. Not only is limitation revealed, religion demonstrates the dependence of the profane on the sacred if the former aspires to transcendence. In this domain, Catholic intellectual life, especially its moral framework and social analysis, brings faith and reason to bear on this era of cultural, economic, and political turbulence, as well as on the dissolution of ethical norms demonstrated in contemporary environmental depredation, world hunger, genocide, ethnic warfare, and violence against the most vulnerable.

Godzieba speaks of materiality and the particular revealed in the centerpiece of the sacramental imagination, the Incarnation of Christ, wherein the finite Jesus mediates the infinite Logos. "The sacramental imagination's intentionality, grounded in the body but at the same time exceeding its material-empirical constraints, is a hint, a clue, a symbol of the fittingness of embodiment to function as the access-point of divine revelation—not simply revelation-as-information, but revelation-as-participation" (2008, p. 24). Furthermore, it is the criteriological character of the Incarnation that presents a power of discrimination. The normative nature of the Incarnation empowers the Catholic "to discern which imaginative refigurations are life-affirming and life-enhancing and which are life-denying." Otherwise, Godzieba concludes, "we have little to guide us in discerning which choices will play out in a humanizing or dehumanizing way" (2008, p. 24). Because we have access to the superabundance of the transcendent through the Incarnation, the sacramentality of the Catholic imagination give us a norm to steer clear of the materialistic reductionism of an objectivist epistemology and the relativism of postmodernity.

The Incarnation thus becomes the foundation for the relational epistemology that drives Catholic intellectual life.

Questions for Discussion

- What does this statement mean to you: "A 'mediated' understanding of God would be suspicious of religious individualism and untrammeled freedom"?
- Note: Discussion of this essay will be strengthened by examples of the Catholic intellectual life, especially in literature and the arts. *Babette's Feast*, a film set in nineteenth-century Denmark, is a classic example of the sacramental imagination. Screening might take place following the meal after this session.

Analogy—To What End? The Allure of a Transcendent Horizon

In the essay on the faculty learning community, we discussed the centrality of the professorial relationship to subject matter, to colleagues, and to the students. Palmer, Zajonc, and Scribner's "call to renewal and transformation" in higher education is an invitation to "collegial conversations in small communities of vision and practice." I would also characterize their relational epistemology and pedagogy as a collegial conversation with the subject matter of the academic disciplines. These conversations take place when the professor enters into an "I-Thou" encounter, generating a passionate love affair with knowledge. The educator brings this relational epistemology to bear on all teaching, aspiring to draw colleagues, but especially students, into this way of being and knowing. A transformation in knowing such as this is akin to enchantment. Both other people and the world itself are in the knower, and the knower is in others and all else.

John Haughey presents a theological perspective that takes Palmer, Zajonc, and Scribner's vision of a relational epistemology to a new level. He asks: "Where is this type of knowing going?" Knowing is not simply instrumental. "To what ends?" is the question that preoccupies Haughey. One can rephrase the question as

"What is the good you seek?" Haughey finds the good to be a whole-ness that is intentionally sought by the faculty member. "There is an appetite for wholes that is built into human consciousness. . . It is an appetite that is never satisfied" (2009, p. 5).

With regard to "wholes," Haughey (2009) speaks elsewhere of the individual's intentionality and the Catholic intellectual life as having "a heuristic character that tends toward a whole-ness that is more future than past, more unknown than known, more implicit than explicit" (p. xii). He also notes that the per-son and the intellectual life "seek a better grasp on reality than is already attained." The "better grasp" is the desire for the deep presence in an "I-Thou" relationship with knowledge and other people, the desire to make sense of where "knowing is going." This is the search for wholes. In a series of interviews, Haughey found a pattern among disparate faculty: "The good these six people are doing is to link different elements, forming wholes that would oth-erwise remain disconnected: Muslims and non-Muslims, first- and third-world medical teams, prisoners and the free, philosophy and God, nursing students and the inner city, the words of literature and the Word" (Haughey, 2009, p. 3).

All too often, however, we suffer from "poverty of insight." In fact, "[t]here seems to be an almost universal inability to see that the source of a persevering intention about the good is not self-evident. The conviction that the finite good comes from infinite goodness can neither be proven nor argued to, but it has been attested to for centuries" (Haughey, 2009, p. 6). Given this type of response, Haughey (2009), the theologian, asked faculty whom he led in workshops about how their faith was connected to their work. The question stems from his own theological presupposi-tion "that an ongoing, self-giving action on behalf of the good is inexplicable if God is not its cause" (p. 6). His move is to a theo-logical position for positing the conscious or unconscious source of the educator's search for "wholes" or the "good." He also refers to Karl Rahner's insight "that humans are the species that operates or exists from our present 'now' towards our future" (Haughey, 2009, p. 11).

Again, the question "To what ends?" intrudes. Bernard Loner-gan notes that "[w]ithout faith the originating value is man and the terminal value is the human good man brings about" (Haughey, 2009, p. 13). The second horizon of value for Longergan is rooted in faith: "[T]he originating value is divine light and love, while the terminal value is the whole universe. So, here the human good becomes absorbed in the all-encompassing good" (Haughey, 2009, p. 14). We have already seen that there is a universal human "drive for meaning and wholeness." "What both faith and reason contrib-ute to this drive is an orientation to, and a relationship with, the known unknown that we call Mystery" (Haughey, 2009, p. 56).

In short, the foundation of the Catholic intellectual life is the unity of faith and reason. Haughey observes that the latter cannot be located in one place, in one mind, in a membership, in a book, or even in the magisterium. "Rather, this tradition consists in the totality of all those instances in which a higher viewpoint has been sought and achieved, either by those who identify themselves with the Sacred Tradition or by those who don't . . . This tradition is formed by all those who have been prompted to seek an intelli-gible whole and have succeeded in doing so" (Haughey, 2009, p. 75), whether they are Catholic or not.

Palmer and Zajonc's insight into relational knowledge and the liberation from the bondage of Cartesian objectivism and instru-mentalism is further broadened by the transcendent horizon that is the vision sustaining the Catholic intellectual life. "But once we have a sense of the unlimited horizons of our minds, we should be able to appreciate the limitlessness of our capacities for knowing, while simultaneously realizing how little we know" (Haughey, 2009, p. 80).

Questions for Discussion

- How do you understand the following concepts: "transcendent horizon," the "Kingdom of God," "analogical imagination"? How do these terms apply to your discipline?
- Analogical imagination is not a religious concept, while sacramental imagination clearly is. The latter flows from

the theology of the Incarnation, which construes all of creation as imaging God, because God became human in the person of Christ. How might a discussion of the analogical and sacramental imaginations find a place in the curriculum?

- Haughey holds that "self-giving action on behalf of the good is inexplicable if God is not its cause." How would you defend or argue against this statement?

- The ultimate foundation of the Catholic intellectual life is the unity of faith and reason. How might this fact exclude Catholic thought in a twenty-first-century university setting from equal standing with disciplines founded on reason alone?

- What is the relationship between Palmer and Zajonc's "relational knowledge" and Haughey's "transcendent horizon"? In what ways are they complementary? In what ways are they different?

A Case in Point: The Sacramental Imagination and Human Welfare in Catholic Social Teaching

> The joys and the hopes, the griefs and
> the anxieties of the men [*sic*] of this age,
> especially those who are poor or in any
> way afflicted these are the joys and hopes,
> the griefs and anxieties of the followers
> of Christ. Indeed, nothing genuinely
> human fails to raise an echo in their
> hearts. (Vatican Council, 1965, para. 1)

These words, quoted once more from the opening paragraph of *Gaudium et Spes,* are of fundamental significance for Catholic social teaching. Not only is celebration rooted in the Catholic worldview, love of God's neglected ones is rooted there as well. God is related to us and calls us to acknowledge and act on our relationship with all peoples. With regard to those on the fringes of society, Catholicism makes "a fundamental option for the poor,"[5] especially for the welfare of the most vulnerable. The goal of compassion in action is that of human flourishing,[6] thus becoming the source of celebration.

The first social encyclical, *Rerum Novarum* (1891), analyzed the "social condition of labor," those systemic economic ideologies and political systems that objectified the person and reified community. Leo XIII's 1891 encyclical, considered the keystone of modern Catholic social thought, initiated openness to the political and social sciences, an openness that grew more pronounced throughout the twentieth and into the twenty-first centuries. However, social concern is no newcomer to the Catholic worldview. It evolved from Catholicism's two-thousand-year-old moral tradition—not always fully acknowledged or practiced by the Church itself—of caring for the sick, the indigent, the hungry, slaves, and captives.[7]

Catholic moral teaching stands steadfast against the amoral evaluation and application of scientific discoveries and technological and medical innovations. Many individuals and communities turn their backs on the moral teachings, regarding them as authoritarian and outmoded systems of thought. Catholic social thought, however, is deeply rooted in human reason, and it is attractive to other Christians, Jews, and Muslims because its foundation is the Scriptures. Because of the emphasis on human reason, it is also welcomed by Buddhists, Hindus, followers of other religions, and secular humanists.

The encyclical *Peace on Earth* (*Pacem in Terris*, henceforth PT) promulgated by John XXIII on April 11, 1963, is an extraordinary example of Catholic social thinking and its global appeal, demonstrated in the warm reception accorded the document by the international community. Openness to PT can be traced to its central thesis concerning politics: "The backbone of the document is its teaching on human rights. Morality, political authority, international relations, and the world community are all interpreted in light of the rights of human beings" (Christiansen, 2005, p. 223).

The Pope (1963) also appeals to an understanding of the human conscience, an understanding that transcends strictly religious belief: "But the creator of the world has imprinted in man's heart an order which his conscience reveals to him and enjoins him to obey" (para. 5).

While Catholicism is often viewed as a monolithic institution with absolute teaching authority, the reality is quite otherwise. There is much discussion, debate, and tension within the Catholic Church on many aspects of moral teaching, and especially on its appropriate application. Nevertheless, the ethical heritage of Catholicism is, in the minds of Catholics and of those of other religious persuasions or of no religious faith, one of the great normative religious traditions that hold fast to the complementarity of religiously revealed truths and human reason in its critique of contemporary society.

Questions for Discussion

- In what ways does the statement from *Gaudium et Spes* ("The joys and the hopes, the griefs and the anxieties of the men of this age") help you to understand the nature of Catholic social teaching?
- What evidence have you seen at this institution that Catholic social teaching shapes and influences its vision, mission, and practices?

Origins of Catholic Thought: A Crucial Meeting and Cultural Shift

The wellspring of the Catholic intellectual life is found in the Christian Scriptures, Acts 15, wherein "There follows a report of what may be judged the most important meeting ever held in the history of Christianity, for implicitly the Jerusalem conference (Acts 15:4–29) decided that the following of Jesus would soon move beyond Judaism and become a separate religion reaching to the ends of the earth" (Brown, 1997, p. 308). In their apostolic letter, leaders of the community state:

The apostles and elders, your brothers,
send greetings to the brothers of
pagan birth in Antioch, Syria and
Cilicia. We hear that some of our
members have disturbed you with their
demands and have unsettled your
minds. It has been decided by the Holy
Spirit and by ourselves not to saddle
you with any burden beyond these
essentials: you are to abstain from food
sacrificed to idols, from blood, from
the meat of strangled animals and
from fornication. Avoid these, and you
will do what is right.
(Acts 15:24, 28, 29)

Preaching to the ends of the earth eventually meant a decisive split with Judaism. "Even though the Savior of the Gentiles was a Jew born under the Law, Christianity would soon be looked on as a Gentile religion quite alien to Judaism for which the Law would become ever more important once the Temple was destroyed" (Brown, 1997, p. 308). There was no turning back. This is the foundational context of and impetus for the Catholic intellectual life: the blending of the Semitic and early Christian religious thought and worldview with the Gentile Hellenistic world and its culture. Inevitably, this blend meshed two cultures and gave rise to consequences, both good and bad, that are apparent today in every part of the world in which Catholicism or Christianity more generally has been preached.

Question for Discussion

What are examples in literature, philosophy, or religion that illustrate the blending of Semitic and Hellenistic thought? What are the implications of this blending for your discipline?

The Turn to the Gentiles and Its Consequences for the Catholic Intellectual Life

It was inevitable, then, that by the second century, if not earlier, those who today would be termed "theologians," as well as other Christian thinkers, were rubbing elbows with Greek intellectuals who shared the patrimony of Greek philosophy and culture as well as similar religious sensibilities with their Greek or Hellenistic Christian colleagues (Johnson, 2009). The latter group declared that the Spirit of God influenced not only Judaism but also Greek culture. "Thus in addition to telling them about what God has done in Jesus, it would be prudent for us to listen to and learn from the thought of these non-Christians. Significantly, this is not just a ploy to convert them but an effort to hear the Spirit as it speaks in their experience—the experience of those who are not Christian" (Cahoy, 2003, para. 33).

By the time of the first ecumenical council at Nicaea (325 CE), the turn to Greek philosophical categories appeared in creedal statements, thereby integrating Hellenistic thought into theological discourse. The wedding of Semitic and Greco-Roman Christianity is aptly symbolized in the Christian symbol *Chi-Rho*, used on the shields of Constantine's troops at the battle of the Milvian Bridge in 312 CE, *chi* and *rho* being the first two letters of Christ's name in Greek. "This striking device, with no precedent in scripture or early Christian tradition, was now to become an all-pervasive symbol of an imperial Christianity" (MacCulloch, 2010, p. 189). It was also a symbol of the melding of Semitic and Greek culture, philosophies, and theologies.

As in the early church, changes in contemporary cultural climates lead to new insights and questions about the Catholic intellectual life. The latter is not frozen in time. William Cahoy (2003) concludes that "[w]e need to listen to those outside the church to hear what God might be speaking through them" (para. 35). This two-thousand-year heritage of being open to others, or the "other," has had its golden moments mingled with decades, if not centuries, of parochialism, prejudice, and persecution. The culture of Catholicism is experiencing more of a golden moment today within Catholic higher education, wherein an interest in diverse perspectives leads to a deep respect for all points of view. It is not just an interest: "Quite the contrary, it is *required* if we would be truly Catholic . . . Turning in upon ourselves in parochialism or sectarianism, is *a failure to live up to our ideals as a church.* In the end it is a failure to be Catholic, not merely a failure to be humane, relevant or politically correct" (Cahoy, 2003, para. 62).

Questions for Discussion

- What is the irony in the fact that the first two letters of the appellation "Christ" were affixed to the shields of Constantine's troops?
- Some Catholics would say that Constantine's toleration of Christianity was a triumph for the faith, while others consider it a curse. What is your perspective on Constantine's act?

Catholic Intellectual Life: The Content

The Catholic intellectual life as described above is best understood as a rich mix of the fine and liberal arts as well as the hard, applied, and social sciences. These categories are among many examples of human thought and creativity to be found in the heritage of past millennia and in the vitality of the present moment. Heterogeneity of and within subject areas distinguishes the content of Catholic intellectual life for, as *Gaudium et Spes* notes, "Indeed, nothing genuinely human fails to raise an echo in their hearts [those of the followers of Christ]" (Vatican Council, 1965, para. 1).

Sacred Scripture

The Catholic worldview, or "sacramental epistemology," is evident in Catholic thought emanating from this distinctive way of knowing the world. The foundational texts of the heritage are the sacred Hebrew and Christian Scriptures (and commentaries on them), followed by the magisterium in its fullness, the lives of the saints, theological texts, literary, artistic, musical, and architectural masterpieces, and philosophical systems, among other fields. These elements are one part of the Catholic patrimony, spanning close to three thousand years and shared in varying degrees with other Christians as well as with Jews and Muslims. It is a heritage that is, at one and the same time, burnished with age but malleable through the centuries. The Scriptures, or the "Book," possesses common texts for the monotheistic religions and demonstrates perennial vitality in response to new questions asked of it. In a word, the Sacred Scriptures influence contemporary Catholic thought in many areas of life, especially (but not only) in the public square through social justice theory and practice. Catholic spirituality also draws its wisdom from these sacred writings.

Fundamental to the content of the intellectual life is our ability to remember and to imagine. "An insight that Catholics inherited from their Jewish or Hebrew past is that this is the way a people shapes its culture, and likewise the way the culture shapes the people" (Hellwig, 2000, p. 9). As Palmer says, "ways of knowing become ways of living." Palmer and Hellwig both would agree that these ways must always be subject to critical reflection in dialogue with the Church's teaching and in relation to the Catholic intellectual life and contemporary culture.

Because Catholics, like their Jewish forebears, are "People of the Book," the Bible itself is the foundational text of the Catholic intellectual life. The early Mothers (*ammas*) and Fathers (*abbas*) who wrote in the post–New Testament "Patristic" period include Sarah, Theodora, Syncletica and Saints Justin (layperson), Ephrem (deacon), and Jerome (priest). The three women cited here "are specifically designated *ammas* and their apophthegms (or wise sayings) are found in the alphabetical collection of *The Sayings of the Desert Fathers* . . . [T]hese women exercised a spiritual maternity on a par with the spiritual paternity of the *abbas*; thus they could transmit spiritual doctrine with the same right as monks" (Forman, 2005, p. 4).

The Doctors of the Church (thirty-three in number), whose lives span two millennia, from the fourth to the nineteenth centuries (e.g. Saints Jerome, Augustine, Athanasius, Basil, John Chrysostom, Thomas Aquinas, Catherine of Siena, John of the Cross,

Teresa of Avila, and Theresa of the Child Jesus), wrote commentaries on the Hebrew and Christian Scriptures as well as texts on theology and spirituality. Thus, the Catholic intellectual life has always been bound up with the sacred texts and related sermons, essays, and commentaries, using the various literary genres of the early Common Era. The writings by or about the Desert Mothers and Fathers, the Doctors of the Church, and many others are part and parcel of the Catholic intellectual life, making it at once vivid, contextualized, and, most importantly, human. Their stories "come out of the memory and understanding of generations of believers who resonated with their lives, actions, or teachings" (Hellwig, 2000, p. 9).

Question for Discussion

Catholic thought, as described above, is primarily religious. While it can be approached from a "religious studies" point of view, that is, phenomenologically, this reading maintains a certain distance from the text and uses the tools of natural and applied science to understand it. How might this do justice or injustice to the text?

The Rule of Benedict

An explicit example of early literary flourishing can be traced to the foundational document of Western monasticism, the *Rule of Benedict*, written almost fifteen hundred years ago (c. 530 CE). To this day Benedictine monks spend a good part of their lives engaged in *lectio divina* (divine or holy reading),[8] a practice first described by Benedict in Rule 48. It is a practice still present and growing in the Catholic and other Christian churches. However, this "holy reading" reaches no end point or concluding essay. The primary text was and still is the Scriptures, the reading of a section in a quiet space, slowly and reflectively, not once but many times. Using exegetical commentaries on the chosen text may precede *lectio* but is not necessary, as a sophisticated intellectual understanding of the text goes beyond the aim of *lectio*. The intent of the practice is to let the passage itself speak to the reader's heart, to allow oneself to become one with the reading, thereby transforming the reader's life.[9]

Benedict's rule was, as Abbot Patrick Barry (2004) notes, saturated with the Word of God: "St. Benedict's message reflects Scripture so vividly that it is itself to a great extent timeless" (p. 4). But even this ancient text was not merely petrified writing from antiquity, a curiosity of the Catholic intellectual life at the time. The Scriptures and the rule are prime examples of the vitality within the heritage, a vitality seen in the development of religious life and thought. The Catholic brings new questions to ancient texts such as the Scriptures or Benedict's rule: "As those, who through the ages have lived by [Benedict's rule], have been changed by catastrophe or enriched by development, so has the text acquired new depth, new resonances, new real life. There are things in it that have become irrelevant and others that have acquired meanings never imagined before" (Barry, 2004, pp. 8–9). And so it is with many foundational documents of the Catholic intellectual life.

These texts and others engaged readers in the early Christian centuries, and they do the same in the twenty-first century, primarily because of an epistemology of relatedness and community. Engagement, however, is not only reflection. The latter prompts a meditative response in texts on spirituality and in all the arts: biography, literature, music, painting, poetry, sculpture. A commentary on the Rule of Benedict by an anonymous ninth-century monk would be quite different from one written by Esther de Waal, a twenty-first-century spiritual writer and Anglican priest. While the writing may be explicitly religious, such as Augustine's *Confessions*, a profoundly Catholic sensibility may inform a modern novel such as Ron Hansen's *Atticus*, which depicts, for all intents and purposes, a classic father-son conflict.

Historical Writing

The writing of history likewise demonstrates the epistemology of the heritage. The writing flourished in monastic communities but had an "edifying character," according to Jean Leclercq. "This historiography is edifying in intention, in method, and in subject matter.

Its purpose is not purely scientific or intellectual, as if knowledge of the past were an end in itself. Its purpose was a practical one: to instruct, in order to do good" (Leclercq, 1982, p. 158). Good would be accomplished if the reader praised God and imitated the good that is exemplified and avoided the evil that was described. While a scientific aspect characterized this writing of history, the monks certainly did not have the critical methods employed by twenty-first-century historians. Credulousness, observes Leclercq (1982), rather than skepticism evolved in the twelfth century: "Yet, in every period the monk-historians gave proof of the scientific spirit" (p. 160).

Questions for Discussion

- Benedictines are often credited with saving Western civilization. Where have you come across this idea before? What do you think it means? How would you respond to this comment?
- Jean Leclercq wrote that the "love of learning and the desire for God" are closely related. How would you evaluate this statement?

The Liturgy

The liturgy of the hours or "the public worship of the Church . . . including hymns, psalms, readings, and prayers that are to be recited at various hours of the day" (Ford, 2006, p. 111) and the celebration of the Eucharist (Ford, 2006, p. 32)[10] truly embodied the monk's love of learning and the desire for God. As Leclercq further notes, the liturgy served as both stimulus and outcome of monastic culture and was linked to the entirety of monastic life. Testimony to this is the fact that the liturgy prompted the greatest number of monastic texts, written for chanting, not reading. Many works in this monastic legacy constitute the great poetry and music of the Middle Ages and come down to us today as Gregorian chant. The Benedictines, inspired by the Scriptures and the works of the patristic period, "marshaled all of the resources of their literary culture. This culture had shaped and set free talents which could henceforth realize their full potential and fulfill their highest ambitions. . . . [T]hey always made every effort to use in the divine service everything they knew about literature" (Leclercq, 1982, pp. 243–244). Moreover, literary composition for the liturgical celebrations went hand in hand with musical creation. "[I]f the composer knew beforehand that his text was to be chanted, and in what manner and at what moment in the liturgy, it was his duty to cast it in a literary form that made this possible" (Leclercq, 1982, pp. 244–245). Leclercq further notes that musical theorists worked with metrical experts, bringing the knowledge of music into the monastery and expanding it through their expertise. Furthermore, "neither arithmetic nor astronomy was studied for its own sake. Through the *Computus*, those disciplines which served to determine the dates of coming feasts became auxiliary sciences for the liturgy" (Leclercq, 1982, p. 245).

Monastic Culture

Monastic epistemology, wherein God was found in all things, both sublime and ordinary, led to the creation of monastic culture. That culture is best understood through the literary and musical creativity that produced poetry, hymns, and chant, all of which have occupied a significant place in the Catholic intellectual life:

> Just as the cathedrals of the thirteenth century have been compared to theological summas, monastic writings of the Romanesque period may be likened to the abbey churches of the period: the same simplicity, the same solidity, the same vivacity of biblical imagination . . . . What [the Abbé] Suger did in the field of architecture and the decorative arts, others did in the realm of literature; all tried to use the

> resources of culture in the service of
> prayer and divine praise.
> (Leclercq, 1982, pp. 245)
> It was the liturgy that ignited the
> monastic renewal in the Carolingian
> period (800–1000 CE):
> During the following centuries, it is in
> the atmosphere of the liturgy and amid
> the poems composed for it, *in hymnis et
> canticis*, that the synthesis of all the *artes*
> was effected, of the literary techniques,
> religious reflection, and all sources of
> information whether biblical, patristic,
> or classical. In the liturgy, all of these
> resources fully attained their final
> potentiality; they were restored to God
> in a homage which recognized that they
> had come from Him. (Leclercq, 1982,
> pp. 243–244)

Mystery and miracle plays, polyphonic music both secular and liturgical, sculpture and architecture, painting and stained glass, all flow from the headwaters of monastic culture wherein the love of learning and the desire for God were the deep currents of Catholic intellectual life. The following categories, discussed below, summarize the immensity of the intellectual life: classic texts; reflections on those texts; major figures in the heritage; the arts; memoirs; autobiographies; poetry; stories; the sciences; and technology (Hellwig, 2000).

Question for Discussion

While not idealizing the Middle Ages, it is important to realize that all aspects of intellectual life came together in the liturgy developed by monastic communities. The liturgy, the monasteries, and the cathedrals became centers of community life, thereby giving Europe a profound spiritual base for civilization. From this perspective, how did Catholicism help to shape the fabric of European life? How important is it to understand Christianity's role in Western history in order to understand that history?

Classic Texts: Touchstone for the Intellectual Life

As Hellwig (2000) notes, "certain formulations became classic, not to prevent later developments but to form a touchstone against which later developments were to be seen and judged" (p. 4). These classics (*tradition*), handed down over the centuries as part of the intellectual heritage, include among others the Scriptures, commentaries, creedal formulations, catechesis, theology, conciliar documents, rules, and spiritualities of religious communities.

Literature, Art, Architecture, Music

Literature in the heritage reflects closely the history and evolution of Catholicism, from mystery plays based on the events of Easter or the life of Christ, and morality plays such as *Everyman* or *The Murder of Abel*, to timeless masterpieces such as Dante's *The Divine Comedy* or Chaucer's *The Canterbury Tales*, to contemporary literature such as T. S. Eliot's *Murder in the Cathedral* and *Four Quartets*, and Robert Bolt's *A Man for All Seasons*, or the novels of Isak Dinesen (Karen Blixen), Graham Greene, C. S. Lewis (Anglican), Alice McDermott, Flannery O'Connor, J. D. Powers, or J.R.R. Tolkien.

Christian consciousness or epistemology is explicitly expressed in art and architecture, especially in the cathedrals and their upward thrust toward heaven. They were clearly sacred places. Of equal if not more importance is "the wider expression in decorative and representative arts, in the building of hospitals, pilgrim shelters, schools, and universities, in the structuring of cities, towns, and villages among believers, expressing their hierarchy of values and their vision of reality" (Hellwig, 2000, p. 5). This same consciousness is found in sacred and profane music from the symphony and opera, back to plainchant. I have stated my belief that Catholicism is at the root of Western civilization—a statement much contested in purportedly secular Europe. Hellwig's (2000) insight into the study of the Catholic intellectual life helps explain such denial: "By contemporary academic conventions it [art history and musicology] tends to be stripped of its religious relevance and studied only from a technical perspective" (p. 5). She further notes that "when these things are appreciated as part of the Christian intellectual heritage, they are studied in a way that tends to integrate the disciplines by relating everything to the meaning of human life in its relationship to the transcendent." Palmer would surely concur in this observation.

Science and Technology

While readers will usually assent to the review of the Catholic intellectual life developed thus far, many will wonder about Catholic thought in relation to the natural sciences and their technological application. Johannes Gutenberg's printing press gave rise to widespread dissemination of religious tracts and the Bible. His invention is in no small degree responsible for the Protestant Reformation. "The very notoriety and conflict generated by Galileo's demonstration of the Copernican hypothesis or Darwin's demonstration of the tenability of the evolutionary thesis testify to the relevance that the natural sciences have had to the integration of human life and knowledge with a spiritual focus" (Hellwig, 2000, p. 5).

The stunning breakthroughs in science and technology, such as in vitro fertilization, cloning through gene manipulation, and stem cell research (to name a few recent developments), are not stand-alone, contextless achievements. They demand interpretation, evaluation, and meaning within Catholic thought, as indicated earlier in this essay. In this regard, Christian ethics or Catholic moral theology affirms what Charles Curran, along with John Haughey, calls a "horizon" for reflecting on human activity. "The horizon forms the way in which the subject looks at reality and structures his own understanding of the world and reality" (Curran, 1976, p. 56). Not primarily content, horizon is "a formal structuring of the way in which the individual views reality." It is an epistemology. Thus Christian ethics "must view reality in terms of the Christian mysteries of creation, sin, incarnation, redemption, and resurrection destiny" (Curran, 1976, p. 56). The integration of these categories into Catholic intellectual life offers a balanced perspective on human activity.

The horizon of Catholic moral theology is a dynamic and inclusive stance. For instance, the emphasis on creation results in an affirmation of humankind's commonality and therefore the possibility of agreement on ethical issues within the Church and with other denominations or religions. Dialogue is the keystone. However, the doctrine of sin balances a tendency to be overly optimistic about the possibilities of achieving understanding, morality, and peace among humans. The reality of greed, egoism, and power tempers the Catholic assessment of science and technology, as well as economics. The empirical evidence of human sinfulness leads the Catholic thinker to ask about the purposes of scientific advancement or the effects of technological achievement and the global economy. Are these primarily for profit or human welfare? However, sin is not paralysis, nor should it lead to despair. Creation is basically good. At the same time, human sinfulness must be acknowledged in assessing the uses of science and technology.

Creation and sinfulness are complemented by other perspectives in the Catholic view of reality, one of which is the Incarnation of Jesus Christ. The latter is the essential manifestation of God's presence among us in and through creation, the source of the sacramental and analogical imagination. "The very fact that God has joined himself to humanity argues against any depreciation of the material, the corporeal and the worldly" (Curran, 1976, p. 75). Curran's last point concerning redemption and resurrection destiny highlights the tension between the present and that not yet achieved. "Redemption and resurrection destiny in the Christian ethical horizon serve to point to the danger of absolutizing any present structures, institutions or ideals. Resurrection destiny and the future serve as a negative critique on everything existing at the present time" (Curran, 1976, p. 78). Sin and the finitude of creation reinforce the relativizing dimension of the Christian horizon. Science and technology have improved the lot of many humans, disproportionately at best, but must never be enthroned as idols or amoral entities.

Question for Discussion

The impression many Catholics and Americans have is that Catholic moral theology is primarily focused on sexuality (birth control, homosexuality), with an approach that is negative and controlling. What is your view of Catholic moral thought as a result of reading this section? How might the Christian doctrine of original sin be relevant or irrelevant to the twenty-first century?

Relational Epistemology and the Postmodern Worldview

Twenty-first-century proponents of the Catholic intellectual life cannot take these apparent "givens" (Curran's Christian mysteries) for granted in a postmodern intellectual climate where such "taken-for-grantedness" is judged to be just one social construction of reality, "a first naïveté," a narrative of a time-bound culture that cannot claim a universal absolute, or ontological status, for any belief system. In other words, nothing can be taken for granted in a discussion of the intellectual life. As Terry Eagleton (2009) observes, "In post-Nietzschean spirit, the West appears to be busily undermining its own erstwhile metaphysical foundations with an unholy mélange of practical materialism, political pragmatism, moral and cultural relativism, and philosophical skepticism" (p. 9).

Because of the postmodern culture that pervades so much of academe, the Catholic university faces a subtle threat to its Catholic culture, intellectual life, and congregational heritage. The challenge parallels the privatization of religion in the United States. Freedom of religion is guaranteed but is in reality a passive or negative right assigned to individuals and their religious organizations. The state does not offer a role to religious groups either through financial support or by granting an official place in the public square. One should not conclude that the separation clause in the First Amendment should be revoked, but there is an interesting parallel "separation clause," as it were, in religiously affiliated universities.

Catholic universities have the right to express themselves as such without government interference—a negative right. However, the emphasis on the negative (or noninterference right in this case) creates the impression among a number of administrators and faculty that the Catholic culture and its manifestations indeed have a role to play. But the role is iconic, private, a legacy to be treated passively, to be looked on as part of the tradition from the founders, an artifact similar to the nostalgic, symbolic role of "Old Main" or the school song. In admissions work, the use of all evidence demonstrating the Catholic culture of the university can also play a utilitarian, "branding" role, marketing the institution to prospective parents and alums. These views mirror the prevailing American attitude toward religion in general: that it is private and personal. Thus, while there is near-total freedom for religion in the private sphere, there is a limited role for religion in the public square of the Catholic university world.

Another perspective on the passive/active commitment to Catholic culture, intellectual life, and religious heritage is the evolution of "Catholic" branding and branding associated with the founding religious community. There is value in a Catholic institution having a one-sentence descriptor that captures the mission of the university. For instance, graduates of Jesuit schools will most likely remember that their purpose in life is to be "a person for others." Graduates of Lasallian universities know that they "enter to learn and leave to serve." The university may have a pithy brand, but as with the passive/active issue, how many of the administrators or faculty are "branded"? In other words, do they internalize the values represented by the brand?

As a result of such differences regarding the university's stated mission and purpose, there are groups of administrators, faculty, and staff who think so differently about their university role that they have little in common with groups other than their own. Constituents of these groups will identify the university as Catholic and founded as Benedictine, or Ursuline, among other congregations. However, while one group views the Catholic culture and religious heritage as a badge of identity with a glorious past, others view the culture and heritage as "actionable," the present-day, life-giving, spiritual wellspring of the university's mission, without which the institution would lose its reason for being. These differences are noticeable in terms of how individuals self-identify their work: as a job, a career, a calling (vocation), or a ministry.

Perhaps the most challenging task, then, is moving members of these groups who may view affection for "all things Catholic" as nostalgia for a triumphalist Church to a more active, relational embrace. The future leaders of Catholic higher education must be intentionally nurtured for these roles, not only as individuals, but as communities of commitment. This hoped-for embrace is one of the intended outcomes of Revisioning Mission and constitutes more than a common understanding or a common appreciation of culture and heritage. Important as understanding and appreciation are, unless they evolve into a highly valued aspect of the individual's life, leading to active support of culture and heritage or, more fully, to commitment in the Mission Community, the most important affective goal of RM will not be attained.

Questions for Discussion

- How would you define "postmodern culture"? How would your definition differ from the description offered above?
- In what ways is religion a purely private affair and in what ways might it be a public matter?
- What type of separation should exist between religion and university life?
- It has been noted that some university faculty are more comfortable with the heritage of the founding congregation that with the "Catholic" aspect of its identity. What does this statement mean? What are the implications for life in the university?
- This question may surface many times during these sessions, but at this point, what do you think it means to be Catholic, both individually and collectively?
- What role do you believe that the Catholic intellectual life and the Catholic Church have in the public square?

Relational Epistemology: Ecumenical, Interreligious, and Pluralistic?

Catholic intellectual life acknowledges an ecumenical Christian approach to knowing, in which Jesus is the filter for interpreting life and meaning. This realization does not mitigate against those dimensions of the intellectual life that are uniquely and normatively Catholic and that provide the foundation for Catholic social teaching: "a commitment to the continuity between faith and reason; respect for the cumulative wisdom of the past; an anti-elitist bent; attention to the community dimension of all human behavior; concern for integration of goals and objectives; and keen awareness of the sacramental principle" (Hellwig, 2000, p. 7). One dimension that Hellwig lists does require some clarification: "concern for integration of goals and objectives." She explains this concern in a way similar to Palmer and Zajonc's relational epistemology.

Hellwig values the integration of "knowledge as a basis for true wisdom in the living of one's life." Her relational epistemology reinforces a critique of objectivist epistemology that values instrumental knowledge, the latter deleting questions of meaning and purpose because they are viewed as time-consuming or as individual matters of little import in the marketplace of ideas. And yet "the integration of learning in a coherent worldview or philosophy of life is a necessary basis for living a good, productive, well-directed life." (Hellwig, 2000, p. 7).

Pluralism is not an unalloyed value. Even more significant and dangerous for the public square in pluralistic liberal societies, according to Eagleton, is the fact that "lukewarmness about belief is likely to prove a handicap when one is confronted with a full-bloodedly metaphysical enemy. The very pluralism you view as an index of your spiritual strength may have a debilitating effect on your political authority, especially against zealots [both Christian and Islamic fundamentalists] who regard pluralism as a form of intellectual cowardice" (Eagleton, 2009, p. 10).

Pluralism may be the wolf in sheep's clothing, a cover for an epistemological objectivism that views each ethnic group or racial subdivision at arms length as a "quaint," colorful addition, constituents of the "rainbow coalition." As Eagleton notes, this is at once a too possessive and a too hands-off policy. Has any politician or cultural pluralist realized that a truly relational embrace of the "other" may lead to the crumbling of the ontological status granted to cultures on both sides? "A common culture in a more radical sense of the term is not one in which everyone believes the same thing, but one in which everyone has equal status in cooperatively determining a way of life in common" (Eagleton, 2009, p. 11).

Questions for Discussion

- What inherent contradictions follow from living in a pluralistic society?
- How does pluralism militate "against the integration of learning in a coherent worldview or philosophy of life"?
- What is the alternative to the "disintegration of ontological status" held by diverse groups that fully embrace one another?
- In our society, how is it possible for individuals and groups to have "equal status in cooperatively determining a way of life in common"?
- How does an individual profess belief in a religion as the "true" religion, yet fully embrace other groups on their own terms?

Ex Corde Ecclesiae: Impact on the Catholic Intellectual Life

In the eyes of the Catholic Church, the university "is born from the heart of the church" (John Paul II, 1990, para. 1). As a foremost repository of Catholic intellectual life, the Catholic university not only passes on the heritage of more than two millennia, it is also a wellspring of creativity for the present and future. While it is not the sole locus wherein Catholicism's intellectual life is found, the Catholic university serves as its institutional setting. Furthermore, the university serves as a magnet for Catholic historians, novelists, musicians, playwrights, poets, and public intellectuals.

In the discussion of Catholic culture, *Ex corde Ecclesiae* (ECE)[11] occupies an important place because it speaks to the character of Catholic education. However, here the role of academic freedom as discussed in ECE is addressed, since it is so closely related to the Catholic intellectual life. John Paul II in ECE states that "a Catholic university is distinguished by its free search for the whole truth about nature, man and God" (John Paul II, 1990, para. 4). It is a university "completely dedicated to the research of all aspects of truth in their essential connection with the supreme Truth, who is God" (John Paul II, 1990, para. 4). For John Paul II, "the search for the whole truth about nature, man and God" is not a feckless search. Note that he does not say "possessing the truth." It is a search similar to Catholic faith, in which the believer knows the fount of truth (Christ); but neither the Catholic nor those who are from other systems of belief possess the truth. John Paul II states, "Its Christian inspiration enables [the university] to include the moral, spiritual and religious dimension in its research and to evaluate the attainments of science and technology in the perspective of the totality of the human person" (John Paul II, 1990, para. 7). The scientific or other types of research would in themselves not be distinguishable as "Catholic," but "Christian inspiration" should guide the research in its effects on "the totality of the human person." A Catholic university, then, is about "meaning making."

Without question, the secular university would view "the search for truth and knowing the fount of truth" as absolutely antithetical to its mission; but the unity of searching for and yet knowing the truth is the wellspring of Catholic distinctiveness. This unity constitutes the theological foundation of its intellectual endeavors. How can these apparently opposite orders of reality be united?

"Knowing the fount of truth," who is Jesus Christ, must be understood in its scriptural and theological context. John 14:6 quotes Jesus as saying "I am the Way, the Truth, and the Life." In this sense, the believer knows Jesus, the "fount of truth." But this knowing is relational, the knowing of a Person who is yet a mystery, as is the unspoken quality in all human relationships. Likewise, the knowing of truth is always partial because of human finitude and intellectual finiteness. Thus, knowing the truth is always a "search for the truth," a journey that is imbued with mystery. For the Catholic, knowing the fount of truth that is Jesus Christ provides the lens or interpretive frame for a Catholic epistemology: the exploration of "the mysteries of humanity and of the world in the light of revelation." In this sense, the search for truth is carried out in the context of a personal and ecclesial relationship with Christ as fount of truth. To emphasize a point already made, even from a purely relational perspective, knowing the fount of truth is itself a mystery, never fully fathomable, even as every human relationship—indeed all of creation—is a mystery and never fully disclosing of the other.

The Introduction to *Ex Corde* stresses the search for truth, a search that serves "the dignity of man and the good of the church" (John Paul II, 1990, para. 4). There is a profound conviction on the Pope's part "that truth is the real ally of the church and that knowledge and reason are sure ministers to faith" (John Paul II, 1990, para. 4). He expresses a deep confidence in this search because of Christ, the Logos, described in John 14:6 (above). "The Logos . . . enables the human person with his or her own intelligence to find the ultimate reality of which he [the Logos] is the source and end" (John Paul II, 1990, para. 4). It is the Logos "who alone is capable of giving fully that wisdom without which the future of the world would be in danger" (John Paul II, 1990, para. 4).

While the Catholic university makes use of the objectivist epistemology, it also utilizes a relational epistemology by which scientific and technological breakthroughs are evaluated according to their impact on persons. For instance, religious studies and theology departments analyzed the refrain, "What does the economy do *for* people? What does it do *to* people? And how do people *participate* in it?" (National Conference of Catholic Bishops, 1986, p. 1) These departments studied its source in *Economic Justice for All: A Pastoral Letter on Catholic Social Teaching and the U.S. Economy*, promulgated by the American bishops in November 1986. Here is an exemplary ecclesial document championing a relational understanding of the economic system using the criteria of justice, compassion, and human flourishing. The pastoral letter has also become the centerpiece of curricula in social justice and economics courses. (The secular university all too often precludes itself from such a relational investigation.) The Pope concludes: "[B]y its Catholic character, a university is made more capable of conducting an impartial search for truth, a search that is neither subordinated to nor conditioned by particular interests of any kind" (John Paul II, 1990, para. 7). In other words, academic freedom appears to be even more of a value and operative principle in Catholic higher education than in secular institutions.

Ex Corde Ecclesiae and the American Association of University Professors

The Pope's concluding statement from *Ex Corde* presented immediately above offers an opportunity for further discussion of academic freedom. Notably, academic freedom is addressed in the initial paragraph of the first section of ECE, "The Identity of a Catholic University." The university "guarantees its members academic freedom" (John Paul II, 1990, para. 7). But there is a caveat: academic freedom, yes, "so long as the rights of the individual person and of the community are preserved within the confines of the truth and the common good" (John Paul II, 1990, para. 12).

The American Association of University Professors (2006) offers comments on entitlement "to full freedom in research and in the publication of results," and professorial entitlement "to freedom in the classroom in discussing their subject" (p. 3). However, the Association adds conditions that are similar to the ones in ECE (Nelson, 2010). "Institutions of higher education are conducted for the common good and not to further the interest of either the individual teacher or the institution as a whole. The common good depends upon the free search for truth and its free exposition" (AAUP, 2006, p. 3). Academic freedom is "subject to the adequate performance of [the teachers'] other academic duties."

Likewise, academic freedom pertains to teaching as well. The freedom applies "in discussing their subject." Again, the caveat: "but they should be careful not to introduce into their teaching controversial matter which has no relation to their subject" (AAUP, 2006, p. 3).

Guarantees of academic freedom and of tenure are significant privileges in any society, and they carry with them correlative responsibilities. These responsibilities are affirmed "in major policy statements, providing guidance to professors in their utterances as citizens, in the exercise of their responsibilities to the institution and to students, and in their conduct when resigning from their institution or when undertaking government-sponsored research" (AAUP, 2009, para. 1).[12]

For instance, the revised AAUP Statement on Professional Ethics (2009) stipulates quite clearly that "[faculty] accept the obligation to exercise critical self-discipline and judgment in using, extending, and transmitting knowledge" (AAUP, 2009, para. 1). Not only is intellectual honesty required, but faculty are obligated to protect the academic freedom of the students and respect their dignity as a person. Concern for the common good extends to colleagues, whom the professor must not "discriminate against or harass." In the Statement on Academic Rights and Responsibilities, published by the American Council on Education (2005) and endorsed by the AAUP, note is made of the need for "openness, tolerance and civility," especially in an environment of "intellectual pluralism and the free exchange of ideas" In conclusion, it appears that ECE, the AAUP, and ACE agree on the principles of academic freedom.

Questions for Discussion

- What do you understand the term "knowing the fount of truth" to mean? Some professors believe this position limits academic freedom. Why would you agree or disagree with them?
- What concerns do you have about academic freedom while teaching at a Catholic university?

- Some historians of American religion argue that anti-Catholicism is the last acceptable prejudice. What do you think about this statement? Why do you think this belief has developed? What prejudice against Catholicism have you experienced?
- Why would the study of a subject area in the light of faith have a right to academic standing? Why would it not have this right? What safeguards would be needed to insure that this type of study was academically rigorous?
- Do you agree or disagree that "ECE and the AAUP are in agreement concerning academic freedom"?

Conclusion

The legacy and continued creativity of Catholic intellectual life are not parochial possessions. The Catholic intellectual life is a gift for all peoples and all ages, though not a substitute for the heritage of diverse civilizations and religions in the twenty-first-century global society. Cultural sensitivity and a long history of religious imperialism should lead those most influenced by the Catholic intellectual life to develop a sense of modesty in discussing it with faculty from diverse ethnic backgrounds, especially with those from countries with a history of Western colonial control.

For new faculty, a deeper understanding of the Catholic intellectual life will bring a fresh perspective to their understanding of the Catholic university, presenting them with the worldview, methodology, and substance of this two-thousand-year-old way of embracing the world. The present essay provides further insight into the Catholic culture of the university (Essay One), a culture in which faculty are immersed and which is a locus for the Catholic intellectual life. Together, these essays on Catholic culture and Catholic intellectual life will facilitate greater understanding of the university mission and the goals of the curriculum, especially the general education or core requirements. They will also assist new faculty in developing syllabi in their own disciplines and in understanding those of colleagues in other fields of study. It is my hope that new faculty will gain from these two essays and ensuing discussions a robust picture of the distinctive religious character of the Catholic university and a clear understanding of the Catholic intellectual life that embraces the world and the diversity of peoples and beliefs in it.

While the Catholic culture and intellectual life provide sure footing on the journey through early academic life, the essay on the founding religious congregation (Essay Five) will present the context for understanding the importance of the final essay in the program: the Mission Community, the new living endowment of a Catholic university (Essay Six)

References

American Association of University Professors (AAUP). (2006). *1940 statement of principles on academic freedom and tenure: With 1970 interpretive comments.* (Policy documents & reports.) Washington, D.C.: American Association of University Professors. Retrieved from http://www.aaup.org/NR/rdonlyres/ EBB1B330-33D3-4A51-B534-CEE0C7A90DAB/0/1940StatementofPrinciplesonAcademicFreedomandTenure.pdf.

American Association of University Professors (AAUP). (2009). *Statement on professional ethics.* Retrieved from http://www.aaup.org/AAUP/pubsres/policydocs/contents/statementonprofessionalethics.

American Council on Education. (2005). *Statement on academic rights and responsibilities.* Retrieved from http://www.acenet.edu/AM/Template.cfm?Section=Search&section=Statements_and_Testimony1&template=/CM/ContentDisplay.cfm&ContentFileID=2078.

Barry, P. (2004). *Saint Benedict's rule.* Mahwah, NJ: HiddenSpring.

Brown, R. E. (1997). *An introduction to the New Testament.* New York, NY: Doubleday.

Cahoy, W. (2003). *The Catholic intellectual tradition: What is it? Why should I care?* Retrieved from http://www1.csbsju.edu/ catholicidentity/values/billcahoy.htm.

Christiansen, D. (2005). Commentary on *Pacem in Terris.* In K. R. Himes & L. S. Cahill (Eds.), *Modern Catholic social teaching:*

Commentaries and interpretations. Washington, D.C.: Georgetown University Press.

Clifford, A. M. (2008). Identity and vision at Catholic colleges and universities. *Horizons: The Journal of the College Theology Society, 35*(2), pp. 355–370.

Curran, C. E. (1976). *New perspectives in moral theology.* Notre Dame, IN: University of Notre Dame Press.

Eagleton, T. (2009). Culture and Barbarism: Metaphysics in a Time of Terrorism. *Commonweal, 136*(6), 9–14.

Ford, J. T. (2006). *Saint Mary's Press glossary of theological terms.* Winona, MN: Saint Mary's Press.

Forman, M. (2005). *Praying with the Desert Mothers.* Collegeville, MN: Liturgical Press.

French, W. (2006). Greening "Gaudium et Spes." In W. Madges (Ed.), *Vatican II: Forty years later* (pp. 196–207). Maryknoll, NY: Orbis Books.

Godzieba, A. J. (2008). The Catholic sacramental imagination and the access/excess of grace. *New Theology Review, 21*(3) 14-26.

Haughey, J. C. (2009). *Where is knowing going? The horizons of the knowing subject.* Washington, D.C.: Georgetown University Press.

Hellwig, M. K. (2000). The Catholic intellectual tradition in the Catholic university. In Anthony J. C. & O. J. Morgan (Eds.), *Examining the Catholic intellectual tradition* (pp. 1–18). Fairfield, CT: Sacred Heart University Press.

Hopkins, G. M. (1975). God's Grandeur. *The divine office: The liturgy of the hours according to the Roman rite.* London: Collins.

John XXIII (1963). *Pacem in Terris: Peace on earth; encyclical letter of His Holiness Pope John XXIII* (W. J. Gibbons, Ed.). New York, NY: Paulist Press.

John Paul II (1990). *Apostolic constitution of the supreme pontiff John Paul II on Catholic universities* commonly known as *Ex corde ecclesiae* (ECE). Retrieved from http://www.vatican. va/holy_father/john_paul_ii/apost_constitutions/documents/hf_jp-ii_apc_15081990_ex-corde-ecclesiae_en.html.

Johnson, L. T. (2009). *Among the gentiles: Greco-Roman religion and Christianity.* New Haven, CT: Yale University Press.

Leclercq, J. (1982). *The love of learning and the desire for God: A study of monastic culture.* New York, NY: Fordham University Press.

MacCulloch, D. (2010). *Christianity: The first three thousand years.* New York, NY: Viking.

Massa, M. S. (2008). Myth Buster. *Commonweal, 135*(14), 25–26.

National Conference of Catholic Bishops. (1986). *Economic justice for all: Pastoral letter on Catholic social teaching and the U.S. economy.* Retrieved from http://www.usccb.org/upload/economic_justice_for_all.pdf.

Nelson, C. (2010). Defining Academic Freedom. *Inside Higher Ed.* Retrieved from http://www.insidehighered.com/views/2010/12/21/nelson_on_academic_freedom.

Palmer, P. J. (1987) Community, conflict, and ways of knowing: Ways to deepen our educational agenda. *Change, 19*(5), 20–25.

Palmer, P. J., Zajonc, A., & Scribner, M. (2010). *The heart of higher education: A call to renewal.* San Francisco, CA: Jossey-Bass.

Soanes, C., & Stevenson, A. (2005). *Oxford dictionary of English.* Oxford: Oxford University Press.

Vatican Council. (1965). *Pastoral constitution on the Church in the modern world (Gaudium et spes); Promulgated by His Holiness Pope Paul VI.* Retrieved from http://www.vatican.va/archive/hist_councils/ii_vatican_council/documents/vat-ii_const_19651207_gaudium-et-spes_en.html.

Recommended Reading

Morey, M. M., & Piderit, J. J. (2006). *Catholic higher education: A culture in crisis.* New York, NY: Oxford University Press.

Notes

[1] As the RM team reads through this essay, the members might discuss the advisability of having experts on different aspects of the Catholic intellectual life participate.

[2] "That which is thus handed down; a statement, belief, or practice transmitted (esp. orally) from generation to generation." In

Soanes, C., & Stevenson, A. (2005). *Oxford dictionary of English.* Oxford: Oxford University Press.

[3] "An ecumenical or general council is a gathering of bishops and other Church leaders from around the world to discuss and resolve pressing issues in the Church" (Ford, 2006, p. 52). More specifically, the Second Vatican Council, or Vatican II (1962–65), "provided for an aggiornamento (updating) of Roman Catholic teaching and practice, especially in such areas as liturgy, ministry, religious liberty, ecumenism, and interreligious dialogue" (Ford, 2006, p. 192).

[4] Catholic teaching such as this Pastoral Constitution and Papal Encyclicals are often identified by the first few words of the document as written in Latin. Thus, "The joys and the hopes," translated as *Gaudium et Spes,* is commonly used as the name of this Constitution.

[5] For further discussion of the "fundamental option for the poor," see *Economic Justice for All,* no. 87, and other resources at the Office for Social Justice Web site, http://www.osjspm.org/economic_justice_for_all.aspx.

[6] "Flourishing" may be equated by some with the Greek term for "happiness," *eudaimonia.* However, this meant in pagan intellectual circles "a well-lived life." Semitic thought expressed happiness in the more robust term *shalom.* "The biblical writers understand flourishing as the life that is not only lived well but goes well; that is what constitutes *shalom.*" Job lived his life well, but his life certainly did not go well. It did not flourish or demonstrate the fullness of life associated with the Hebraic understanding of *shalom,* that is, fullness, peace, or justice. I am indebted for this insight to Nicholas Wolterstorff. Wolterstorff, N. (2007). Human flourishing. *Culture, 1*(2), 17. Retrieved from http://www.iasc-culture.org/culture/CultureFall07.pdf.

[7] The term "moral theology" is generally used within Catholic theology to categorize the moral heritage. As already explained, I use

the term "heritage" rather than "tradition." That is not necessarily the case with the authors to whom I refer in this and other essays. "Moral theology . . . refers to the branch of theology that is concerned with the values, principles, and norms of morally acceptable human conduct" (Ford, 2006, p. 125). At times, "Christian ethics" is used in place of "moral theology." Slightly more nuanced, "Christian ethics" is more of an ecumenical term and makes significant use of the social and behavioral sciences in its analysis of human acts.

[8] "This term . . . refers to the practice of reading a text, such as the Bible or other spiritual writing, slowly and reflectively until some aspect of the text speaks to the reader's heart" (Ford, 2006, p. 109).

[9] On the Rule and *lectio divina,* see *Saint Benedict's Rule,* translated and with an introduction by Patrick Barry, OSB (2004). Mahwah, NJ: HiddenSpring. A similar contemporary approach to textual reading is taken by Parker Palmer (1987) in his analysis of texts, reader, and epistemology in the article cited above: "I argue," Palmer says, "that the relation established between the knower and the known . . . tends to become the relation of the living person to the world itself" (p. 22).

[10] "This word (from the Greek *eucharistia,* meaning "thanksgiving" or "gratitude") sometimes refers to the celebration of the entire Mass and sometimes specifically to the consecrated bread and wine that have become the body and blood of Christ" (Ford, 2006, p. 72).

[11] As a matter of course I would use the English translation of the document's name. However, in this case, the document is generally recognized by its Latin name, which I will use throughout, in long or short form. All quotations are cited by paragraph location.

[12] On academic freedom and responsibility see American Council on Education. (2005). *Statement on Academic Rights and Responsibilities.* Retrieved from http://www.acenet.edu/AM/Template.cfm?Section=Search&section=Statements_and_Testimony1&template=/CM/ContentDisplay.cfm&ContentFileID=2078.

Essay Five

The Founding Religious Congregation: a Living Endowment

The founding congregations play a crucial role in Catholic education. With a few exceptions, religious congregations founded most Catholic universities, and in many ways, the founding congregations have served as living endowments for these institutions. In fact, during the 1920s and for several years into the 1930s, the North Central Association of Colleges and Schools equated this living endowment with a monetary one, because Catholic institutions at the time had very limited financial resources. Philip Gleason (1995) describes the living endowment as "the contributed services provided by priests, sisters, and brothers who taught at Catholic colleges without being paid regular salaries" (p. 185). Today the congregation may still provide this living endowment, although it may not be listed as a financial asset in the university's portfolio.

For many Catholic universities, the founding congregation has maintained a religious and pedagogical heritage embedded in Catholic culture. This heritage is responsible for distinguishing the university from its secular private and public counterparts. Within the world of Catholic education, the founders also endowed the institution with a distinctiveness that sets it apart from other universities.

Challenges to Catholic Higher Education Today

Catholic higher education today faces a number of challenges, many of them involving the ecclesial context in which the universities function. Among these challenges are:

Erosion of Catholic culture supporting Catholic religion

In his preface to *American Catholic: The Saints and Sinners Who Built America's Most Powerful Church,* Charles R. Morris (1997) notes that the Catholic Church has been a culture and a religion "*in* and *for* America, but never quite *of* America" (p. vii). He goes on to note that at the high point of its role as religion and culture, "the Catholic Church constructed a virtual state-within-a state so Catholics could live almost their entire lives within a thick cocoon of Catholic institutions" (Morris, 1997, p. vii). That culture no longer has the power it once possessed. Furthermore, this erosion of culture is presently occurring in tandem with an institutional crisis, namely, clerical sex abuse and cover-up by church officials and the attrition of lay Catholics.

> Morris's (1997) thesis, then, is:
> Most of the Church's much publicized recent problems—the financial, sexual, and other scandals that are blazoned across the front pages—can be understood as the floundering of an institution suddenly forced to make it way solely as a religion, shorn of the cultural supports that had been the source of its strength.
> (p. vii)

The challenge of this cultural erosion is, at the same time, an opportunity for renewal of the Church's self-understanding in its threefold role of priest, prophet, and teacher.

234

Growing tension in Catholicism as church and institution

Six years after Morris's book appeared, Peter Steinfels echoed Morris's thesis. Steinfels (2003) notes: "The Catholic Church can succeed as an institution while failing as a church. But it cannot succeed as a church while failing as an institution" (p. 14). He offers four points that support this premise:

- *The Church is at risk.* He suggests that a "review of church attendance rates, ratios of priests to people, knowledge of the faith, and financial contortions" offer clear evidence of the risk.
- *There are significant problems not covered by the media.* "The standard topics—sex, gender, priest shortage, papal authority—must be supplemented, even framed, by other concerns, especially questions of worship and spiritual life, of religious education and formation, and above all, of leadership" (Steinfels, 2003, p. 10).
- *Responses to the Second Vatican Council are frozen in time.* "Liberals and conservatives raise the same fears, make the same complaints, [and] offer the same arguments as they did twenty years ago . . . The time has come for analyses and recommendations that freely cross liberal-conservative party lines—and that also seek insight in the experiences of other religious groups" (Steinfels, 2003, p. 10).
- *This is a critical period for the Church.* "American Catholicism must be seen as entering a crucial window of opportunity—a decade or so during which this thirty years' war between competing visions is likely to be resolved, fixed in one direction or another or in some sort of compromise for at least a good part of the twenty-first century" (Steinfels, 2003, p. 10).

Understanding Religious Congregations

It is against this background of cultural erosion and growing tensions that I offer the following assessment of religious life and higher education. I will also use a case study to exemplify "Revisioning Mission" in one religious congregation. Taking this approach will lead to a fuller appreciation of what I will call "the new living endowment." As a result, I will:

- Examine two archetypes (the monk and the householder) as well as the *humanum*, a term referring to the fullness of personhood, and then apply the archetypes more specifically to the religious congregation.
- Review the religious heritage of founding congregations, using as the example the heritage of the De La Salle Christian Brothers (also known as the Brothers of the Christian Schools), founded by Saint John Baptist de La Salle, honored by the Catholic Church as the patron saint of teachers.
- Discuss the physical presence of the Brothers in relationship to the use of sponsorship covenants to ensure continuity, along with an analysis of the characteristics of a Lasallian university.
- Highlight charism and Catholicity in Lasallian higher education seen in terms of internal and external opportunities and challenges. Each Catholic university had its own founding congregation, so implications must be drawn from this one example; the issues presented here will not be the same or even similar for all congregations, but they will provide a foundation for understanding the unique gifts each congregation brought to its universities.

Questions for Discussion

- Which members of this university's founding congregation still have active roles on campus? What positions do they hold?
- What experience have you had with members of Catholic religious congregations? What have you taken away from these experiences?

236

- What is your understanding of Roman Catholic religious life? What attitudes or opinions do you have about the men and women who have chosen the religious life? Are you aware of the congregation's founding story and its influence on the campus?

- How might the rapid decline in the number of men and women in religious congregations affect the future of Catholic higher education?

- What issues would you add to the list of challenges facing the Catholic Church today? In your view, how should the Church address them? How do you think these challenges have affected Catholic education?

The Religious Congregation and Their Lay Colleagues: More in Common than Meets the Eye

While much of this essay is devoted to the religious congregation, it is important to note the overlap between the religious and laypersons. In the Mission Community (the subject of the next essay), there will be members of the congregation as well as laypeople. The present essay will help new faculty understand the commonality between the religious and lay members in the Mission Community. Though one group may be described as homogeneous and the other heterogeneous, they are not like oil and water.

Some forty or fifty years ago, the university was virtually homogeneous, with administration and faculty drawn from the religious congregation to educate a fairly homogeneous student body. Religious congregations are homogeneous single-sex groups living in community and professing the canonical vows of poverty, chastity, and obedience. In Catholic higher education today they administer and teach alongside a majority population of lay men and women who are heterogeneous in terms of ethnic background, religious diversity, and sexual orientation: some married, some single, many with children, and some wealthier than others. The fact that there is this diverse lay group on campus may come as a surprise to those with little knowledge of Catholic universities.

In the past, the diversity of the university community has been evolutionary and utilitarian. Today, however, there is intentionality in hiring this cosmopolitan population. The search for truth, a characteristic of Catholic education, would be hampered without a pluralism of perspectives and discussion partners. Diversity among the student body gives vitality to peer interaction and the personal quest for meaning. Ecumenical and interreligious dialogue between the student and faculty populations has brought a richness to Catholicism and Catholic thought generally, a quality that would be absent if homogeneity reigned. In contrast, a homogeneous Catholic administration, faculty, and student body would be very challenging to recruit, and this strategy would run counter to the realities of American society from which the students come and to which they will return upon graduation.

Thus, we have intentional heterogeneity among administration, faculty, and student body. Aside from the vows and communal living, there are significant overlapping characteristics of congregational members and laypersons. The foregoing essays on faculty and on adult spirituality have touched on aspects of this overlap. The following section on archetypes presents other dimensions of commonality.

Question for Discussion

By this point in the academic year, you are well aware of the university's expectations concerning the role of faculty in preserving and enhancing the Catholic character and the religious heritage of the founders. What are these expectations? What is your reaction to them? How do they go beyond or build upon the usual expectations of teaching, research, and service?

The Archetypes of Householder and Monk, and the Humanum: Differentiating and Uniting the Members of the Mission Community

Archetypes shed light on the commonalities of religious and lay life. In this discussion, I follow Raimundo Panikkar's usage of archetypes, which he attributes in part to Carl Gustav Jung's popularization of a word with a long history. Jung (1875–1961) believed that "an inherited idea or mode of thought . . . is derived from the experience of the race and is present in the unconscious of the individual."[1] Panikkar (1982) elaborates: "Archetype for me represents literally a fundamental type, i.e., a basic constituent or relatively permanent cast; in our case of human life . . . it represents a basis upon which at least a part of our life is built" (p. 25). He also views the archetype as a paradigm "which becomes for you the center of your myth. And myth is that in which you believe without believing that you believe in it. This is why we can only speak about other people's myths" (Panikkar, 1982, p. 25). However, laypeople and congregational members have much in common in relationship to two archetypes.

The Householder Archetype

As a group, newly hired faculty fit into the archetype of the "householder," described as follows: He or she juggles multiple personal and economic responsibilities, among which are: relationships; marriage; rearing children; fulfilling obligations to parents or other members of the immediate or extended family; finding adequate housing, and good child care and schooling; securing spousal employment if necessary; and searching for meaning in life. Accomplishing these tasks on a single or joint salary can be anxiety-provoking no matter the location of the university. Their work as professionals, "professors," also adds the stresses of work life to their role as householder. Achieving tenure and advancement in rank are fundamental rites of passage and the source of economic security for the professor householder, but they are demanding even beyond achieving the rank of full professor. While research and writing are in constant play throughout the process, they continue to be present throughout one's work life and present their own challenges.

Some observers of Catholic higher education have said that, in all honesty, many of the laypeople face more challenging economic issues than congregational members ever confront, even with their vow of poverty. It is true that community life and sharing goods in common would shield the individual religious from many householder obligations. However, religious life does have its share of challenges. Although goods are communally held, the members feel the challenges personally, and a number have a direct responsibility for addressing these issues, just as the lay householder does. Among the issues are raising funds to support the retired and elderly, as well as those members who require assisted living or nursing home care. There is also the anxiety of seeing membership continue to decline, with a significant number of years between the age of the youngest senior religious and that of the few entering ones, making it more difficult to retain younger newcomers. New members, few in number, have a variety of ministries to choose from and will not necessarily choose higher education. There is also the discouraging attrition of elementary and secondary Catholic education. The grieving and mourning that accompany the withering away of a religious group and its legacy in Catholic education and of other ministries is mostly hidden from lay colleagues. The grief is real and can be profoundly upsetting for the remaining members, including those in higher education. Some religious, as well as the lay staff, also have significant "householder" responsibilities toward the university, such as in senior administration, admissions, finance, or the physical plant.

Religious do not follow a rigid daily schedule as they did before Vatican II, and this adaptation provides much-needed flexibility. However, the deleterious influence of American individualism, consumerism, and secularism can affect the quality of community life. Even if this does not occur, living the common life presents many interpersonal challenges similar to those experienced by married couples. Religious members of the university teaching staff also face the same employment challenges that lay faculty face: namely, the earning of tenure and advancement in rank, which provide economic security for the individual and for the local congregational community. Lastly, in the present unsettled economic and cultural period, some vowed individuals question whether religious life is for them. One might call this a "lifestyle" issue, but the lay householder may face similar questions related to the vocation of teaching, or the demands of relationships and marriage.

It is easier to describe the concrete challenges that the congregational members and the lay faculty share. We must also remember the positive side of their lives, a side that is often taken for granted. The overall quality and satisfaction in both ways of life imbue them with a vitality and dynamism responsible for a long-term commitment. There is deep joy, fulfillment, and sense of purpose in religious life as an individual and as a member of community in which there is mutual support and shared values. Likewise, married life has similar positive characteristics. Neither should the single lay life be discounted as a "personal misfortune." It is also a way of life with its own deep joy, fulfillment, and sense of purpose.

The overlapping householder characteristics of the lay faculty member and the congregational member are graphic illustrations of how much both have in common. In working to assure the future of Catholic education, together they form a group with a common ground.

The Monk Archetype

We will now look at another archetype: that of the monk. Common sense may mistakenly lead the new hire to view this archetype as exclusive to congregational members. Although the universal archetype of the monk represents humankind's striving for meaning and transcendence, members of religious congregations institutionalize the striving by their vows of poverty, chastity, and obedience within community. However, they share this archetype with all people who are drawn to the spiritual search for meaning and ultimacy in life. Just as the archetype of the householder helps us understand the complex life of lay people and religious, the archetype of the monk will shine light on the commonalities of the spiritual search of lay and religious individuals.

Within consecrated life (another name for religious life), community is the primary relational context of the individual religious. According to Luke Salm:

The canonical vows are a juridical and historical requirement but do not in reality define the identity of the "religious." The distinctive element is a consecration beyond that of baptism, usually but not necessarily expressed by vows, e.g., of association, where the primary relational context is the religious community in a celibate lifestyle.

(Personal communication, April 29, 2004.)[2]

In one sense, then, vowed religious associate together because of a compelling, transcendent call, grounded in a shared mission for which the congregation was founded. They share this call with lay people, a "fundamental dis-ease . . . an unquenchable fire that renders us incapable, in this life, of ever coming to full peace" (Rolheiser, 1999, p. 3). Spirituality is how individuals respond to this "holy longing," whether one is a consecrated religious or a layperson, a devout Muslim or a convinced atheist. It is from the human psyche that the archetype of the monk is born. Because this fire within us all is primordial, spirituality is fundamental to our identity. "It is about being integrated or falling apart, about being within community or being lonely, about being in harmony with Mother Earth or being alienated from her . . . What shapes our actions is our spirituality" (Panikkar, 1982, p. 7).

The "archetypical" search for fullness may sound like just a nice theory when described, but it is a flesh-and-blood reality for me and many readers. Much depends on where each person is in life's journey. The spiritual dimension may come to consciousness when viewing the sunset or a starry night, or during sexual intercourse; sometimes in an intimate conversation, and often when tragedy confronts us. It is a primal characteristic of what we might call our spiritual DNA. Thus when Panikkar (1982) defends the thesis "that the monk is the expression of an archetype which is a constitutive dimension of human life" (p. 11), he is speaking of what is most profound and life-giving for each one of us. What is this dimension? Panikkar (1982) describe it as "the result of an urge, the fruit of an experience that eventually leads him [and her] to change . . . for the sake of that 'thing' which encompasses or transcends everything (the pearl, Brahman, peace, shama, moksa, liberation, God, satori, enlightenment . . .)" (p. 11). The urge requires a conversion—in lay terms, a paradigm shift, or a fundamental change in one's worldview.

Kyle T. Kramer (2008) graphically expresses the complementarity of the archetype of the monk with the archetype of the householder in *Blessed Interruptions*: "God can be found in the moments that upset our rhythms." In this essay he describes balancing a rich spiritual life with the life of a farmer in Indiana and of a husband, the father of three young children, and the director of lay degree programs at Saint Meinrad School of Theology in Saint Meinrad, Indiana. Religious and lay faculty share "the moments that upset our rhythms," and both can find God in those moments. Although the religious is not a householder in the full sense that the lay faculty member is, he shares the challenge Kramer describes above.

The Humanum

"Monkhood," for both vowed religious and laypersons, is one dimension of the fully human. "Monkhood is a dimension that has to be integrated with other dimensions of human life in order to fulfill the *humanum*" (Panikkar, 1982, p. 14). The latter has many dimensions, one of which is, for most people (as already noted), the householder. In other words, the new faculty hires, and all other persons at a Catholic university, fall not only under the archetype of the householder but also that of the monk as they all seek human flourishing or the fullness of the *humanum*. The *humanum*, applicable to all persons, embraces the above archetypes in the search for human flourishing in the realms of the affective, communal, economic, intellectual, and spiritual, among others. "The *humanum* is multidimensional [including sexuality, sociability, playfulness, artistic expression, etc.], and no single dimension can encompass the complexity of human life" (Panikkar, 1982, p. 15). The archetype of the monk leads each human to develop "the deepest core of our humanness." As a result, the archetype has universal appeal. As we shall see in the next section, charism is an important response to the search for fullness or transcendence at the core of the archetype of the monk.

Questions for Discussion

- Is there an inevitable mismatch between the actual population of the Catholic university and the emphasis on the Catholicity and religious congregational heritage that are the bedrock elements of the mission? Whether or not you agree, what can we expect from the administrators and faculty who guide and teach these young men and women?
- What surprises you about the commonalities shared by congregational members and laypersons?
- While you may easily identify with the archetype of the householder, in what ways would you identity with the archetype of the monk?
- Both archetypes are subsumed within the *humanum*, the aggregate of all qualities that make for a full life or human flourishing. What are some of the qualities of the *humanum* that make for a full life or human flourishing, especially at a Catholic university?

Charism: The Deep Story Renewed

"Charism" is a value-laden term of great importance to Catholic education, and therefore it requires careful analysis. In Christian theological terms, Ford (2006) describes it as "a spiritual gift or grace given by the Holy Spirit to persons for their own spiritual improvement as well as for the benefit of the Christian community" (p. 41). It is understood within the history of religious congregations as a grace or gift from God to a founder or reformer, but it is never for the individual alone. The charism is a realization on the founder or reformer's part that there is a significant need within the community that requires a new congregation or the reform of one already in existence. Prior to discussing the term, however, it should be clear that the charism of Ignatius Loyola, founder of the Jesuits, or the charism of any Catholic institution of higher education, cannot be separated from Catholicity (Steinfels, 2004, p. 22). At times, Catholic universities will emphasize the founding congregation over the Catholic context that is central to the group's own identity. David O'Brien (1994) notes the importance of the integral connection between the two, as does the Apostolic Constitution of John Paul II (1990) on Catholic higher education. At the same time, the charism is compelling to those who are not Catholic and attracts them to the mission, if not to Catholicism itself.

"Charism," Bernard Lee (2004) notes, "is a radically historicized social phenomenon" (p. 16). Duplication is not possible.

> Yet the quest for charism is not
> misplaced for those who understand
> that it can only be re-invented, posited,
> in a new socio-historical setting, but
> never simply reenacted. Charism is
> always and only timely and present. It is
> never a potency awaiting actualization.
> It is a finite creature born in its own age.
> (Lee, 2004, p. 16)

Religious congregations are organizations that, for the most part, respond to a need in the Church at a particular moment in its history. It is a charismatic moment, but this "founding charism" is particular to a time, culture, and need. In Greek, two terms better differentiate between ordinary time and the charismatic moment. Ordinary time is *chronos*, as in clock time or chronology. The moment of charism is *kairos*, extraordinary time, during which a person or movement gifted with a charism appears. *Kairos*, as with charism, is always embedded in the particularities of *chronos.* Thus, charism is rooted in both *kairos* and *chronos.* "When [charism] makes a community re-live again with power, it is a reinvented (not a retrieved) charism" (Lee, 2004, p. 18).

> What I am suggesting is that the founding of religious orders is charismatic in character and that sociologically we are justified in speaking of a founding charism. However, the survival of charism with profound animation and relevance requires later moments that are equally charismatic in character. Subsequent charismatic moments differ dynamically, socially, and historically from the founding charismatic moment.
> (Lee, 2004, p. 24)

Charism is thus historically grounded in a particular person, and the followers are drawn to that person. For example, think of Saint John Baptist de La Salle and the early Brothers of the Christian Schools with their concern for the salvation of the poor boys of Rheims, both in this world and in the next. Their passion welled up from the deep story of God's creation, redemption, and sanctification of the world. It also welled up out of a social context and was a powerful response to a need in that context or era, a response that was recognized by those who became De La Salle's disciples and by the larger society of seventeenth- and eighteenth-century France. A reinvented charism flows from the meta-narrative of the community, what Lee calls "the deep story" or the community's culture.

Culture and charism, however, require some clarification. In their analysis of organizational culture, John P. Kotter and James L. Heskett (1992) define culture in relation to the visibility of and resistance to change:

> At the deeper and less visible level,
> culture refers to values that are shared
> by the people in a group and that tend
> to persist over time even when the
> group membership changes . . . At this
> level culture can be extremely difficult
> to change, in part because group
> members are often unaware [Lee's deep
> story] of many of the values that bind
> them together.
> (p. 4)

Culture, Lee (2004) says, has a style. "While a style might be mimicked, even effectively, it only shapes the heart and mind and body of one who grows up in it, or spends sufficient time in it to get its drift" (p. 19). Kotter and Heskett (1992) make a similar point:

> At the more visible level, culture
> represents the behavior patterns or style
> of an organization that new employees
> are automatically encouraged to follow
> by their fellow employees . . . Culture, in
> this sense, is still tough to change, but
> not nearly as difficult as at the level of
> basic values.
> (p. 4)[3]

Thus we are put on alert that the development of a Mission Community—in a sense, the charism renewed—is a significant challenge. The renewal of charism is actually a rebirth of a religious congregation institutionalized with values of which the members may not be aware. While the core values of the Mission Community will be the same, the visible values embedded in a specific homogeneous lifestyle of the congregation will be those of one group within the Mission Community. No longer equating charism with congregation may meet stiff resistance from within because the deep story, culture, and styles appear to be recast and no longer under the full control of the founding congregation. In reality, community for mission has been broadened. It includes the congregation with its deep story, culture, and styles, and a community of laypeople with its own deep story derived from the congregation but with a different culture and style. In any case, the overlap for both groups will be significant.

Lee (2004) concludes: "Although I do not mean this in a technical psychological sense, I have a feeling that a deep story is sort of midway between a collective unconscious and a collective conscious" (p. 23). The deep story affirms a sense of self in terms of a relationship to God and an apostolate (religious mission) to preach the Good News. In this sense, religious congregations make explicit the deep story of an individual in a unique communitarian way. Understanding affirmation of the self as more than a psychological term now leads us to a discussion of the "universal call to holiness."

Questions for Discussion

- What is the charism of the founding congregation at your university? How has the charism shaped the beliefs, values, and practices of the institution? If you do not know, how might you find out?
- In what ways, if any, has the charism of your university been reinvented?

The Universal Call to Holiness: Charism and the Centrality of the Archetype of the Monk

> Through this holy synod [the Second Vatican Council], the Lord renews His invitation to all the laity to come closer to Him every day, recognizing that what is His is also their own (Phil. 2:5), to

> associate themselves with Him in His
> saving mission. Once again He sends
> them into every town and place where
> He will come (cf. Luke 10:1) so that
> they may show that they are co-workers
> in the various forms and modes of the
> one apostolate of the Church, which
> must be constantly adapted to the new
> needs of our times.
> (Vatican Council, 1965a, para. 33)

This key statement in the 1965 Vatican Council *Decree on the Apostolate of the Laity*[4] foreshadows lay partnering. Association or partnering with the religious community is taking place in virtually all religious congregations as they adapt "to the new needs of the times." There is passing reference as well to "the Church's one apostolate." In order to understand that apostolate, one must return to an earlier conciliar document, the *Dogmatic Constitution on the Church* (*Light of the Nations* or *Lumen Gentium*, 1964): "By her relationship with Christ, the Church is a kind of sacrament or sign of intimate union with God, and of the unity of all mankind. She is also an instrument for the achievement of such union and unity" (Vatican Council, 1965a, para. 1). The Church's mission flows from its "sacramentality," a term used analogously with the seven sacraments, whereby Christ acts through the Church (Vatican Council, 1965a, para. 1). "The nature and encompassing mission of the Church" consists in "bringing all men to full union with Christ" (Vatican Council, 1965a, para. 1). The mission is brought to fulfillment by those in holy orders, in the religious state, and by the laity (O'Malley, 2008, p. 310).

> These faithful [the laity] are by baptism
> made one body with Christ and are
> constituted among the People of God;
> they are in their own way made sharers
> in the priestly, prophetical, and kingly

> functions of Christ; and they carry out
> for their own part the mission of the
> whole Christian people in the Church
> and in the world.
> (Vatican Council, 1965b, para. 31)

Thus, the laity are called; they have a vocation just as the clergy and religious have one. "[A]ll the faithful, whatever their condition or state, are called by the Lord, each in his own way, to that perfect holiness whereby the Father Himself is perfect" (Vatican Council, 1965b, para. 11). The call to holiness is also apostolic. Lay people, too, work for the sanctification of the world, but from within the world.

> Therefore, the chosen People of God
> is one: "one Lord, one faith, one
> baptism"; sharing a common dignity
> as members from their regeneration
> in Christ, having the same filial grace
> and the same vocation to perfection ...
> All [clergy, religious, and laity] share a
> true equality with regard to the dignity
> and to the activity common to all the
> faithful for the building up of the Body
> of Christ.
> (Vatican Council, 1965b, para. 32)

There is little doubt that at this point those who are not Catholic wonder where they fit in. Rightfully so, but remember the above statement: "[T]he Church's one apostolate . . . must be constantly adapted to the new needs of the times." Today in Catholic higher education, the warm hospitality of an ecumenical and interreligious embrace and profound respect for the religious or individual search of others pervade its institutions. This means that the search for fullness and transcendence, the archetype of the monk in each administrator, faculty member, staff person, and student, is an integral part of the mission and culture of the Catholic university. Evidence for this is found in the high number of administrators, faculty, staff, and students who are not Catholic but who are attracted to work or study in these universities in the United States and around the world. This is so because each person is free to respond to the archetype of the monk on his or her own terms.

Question for Discussion

What are some of the ways you might respond to the archetype of the monk, and how would these responses affect your work?

Response to a Fundamental Human Paradigm

Within the religious congregation, the call to holiness or personal sanctification is embedded in its deep story, or in what Panikkar (1982) calls *mythos*. However, as we have seen, studying the archetype of the monk includes not only studying the tradition of monasticism, it means studying "the accumulation of human experiences still ongoing, [and] brings us to observe the signs of our times and directs us to the future" (Panikkar, 1982, p. 8). In virtually all religions, there is a group called "monks." They seek holiness, fullness, or the transcendent. This group embodies the universal aspiration to similar goals that come to consciousness at different times in life, as described above. The monk himself is not the archetype; "[y]et it is in and through this (monastic) way that we may gain access to the universal archetype" (Panikkar, 1982, p. 8). For Panikkar (1982), then, monkhood "is something so very much human that it is ultimately claimed to be the vocation of every human being, what everybody should be or is called upon to be—in some way or other, sooner or later" (p. 9).

Humanum is the term Panikkar (1982) uses to define the core of the human being or the perfection of each person, realized in multiplicity and diversity. "The endeavor of every religion is to give a concrete scope and possibility through which the human being (individually or collectively) may achieve the *humanum*. . . . Religion is a path to the *humanum*, be it called salvation, liberation, or another generic name" (p. 13). Yet religion means something other than achieving one aspect of the individual's *humanum*, such as becoming a writer, intellectual, or statesperson. Religion, the individual search pursued in common with others on the same path, is closely related to the archetype of monkhood, embodied in the individual search for an ultimacy that demands a conversion. This is a deeper, subtler approach to "the universal call to holiness." "And in fact there does seem to be something in the *humanum*, as we have defined it," says Panikkar (1982), "that transcends mere humanity and points to another degree of reality not to be found on the merely 'natural' level" (p. 14).

Religions may be characterized as a search for the transcendent dimension or fullness of the *humanum*, a search of the person—a social animal—within a community. As already noted, Panikkar (1982) goes so far as to say "Monkhood is a dimension that has to be integrated with other dimensions of human life in order to fulfill the *humanum*" (p. 14). Going it alone, as it were, without the wisdom and support from any religious community, is a significant challenge. Thus, monkhood is the search for the one thing necessary, or as Panikkar prefers, the search for the center, a term congenial to both Western and Eastern thought.

> If we look for oneness on the periphery
> we cannot reach that equanimity, that
> *shama*, that peace peculiar to the monk;
> we cannot have that holy indifference
> toward everything because we are not
> equidistant from everything. Monkhood
> represents the search for the center.
> (Panikkar, 1982, p. 15)

Question for Discussion

Panikkar views life as reaching its fullness in realizing the *humanum*. How do you assess his approach in view of your own life? How is it possible for an individual to realize the *humanum* without other persons being involved in the realization?

The De La Salle Christian Brothers in Higher Education

The Christian Brothers provide an interesting case study of the role of a religious congregation in this new era for Catholic higher education. There are two presuppositions governing their universities. One is the continued presence of the Brothers in Lasallian universities. The other presupposition is the commitment on the part of both Brothers and lay associates to charism and Catholicity through a new form of community. The presence and commitment of the Brothers will facilitate continuity and evolution. Their ongoing commitment but physical absence will challenge, but not make impossible, the viability of this continuity and evolution. In either case, but most especially in the Brothers' likely absence in a significant way from American Catholic higher education in the foreseeable future, charism and Catholicity will only endure through pluralistic lay-partner communities in each college. (I take it as a given that the founding congregation, even if no longer a campus presence, would have representation in these communities.) The congregation is, after all, together with the partners, the guardian of the Catholic culture and religious heritage of the institution.

Why does the presence of the De La Salle Christian Brothers reinforce the Catholic identity of Manhattan College or any of the other six Lasallian institutions of higher learning in the United States?[5] On the absence of the religious community, George Dennis O'Brien (2002) is insightful:

> A first problem for the university,
> then, might be legitimating the very
> *idea* of life commitment. One clear
> virtue of Catholic universities in the
> past was the presence within the life of
> the institution of life commitment. In
> former days this reality of commitment
> was conveyed by the presence of
> the sponsoring religious order.
> Michael Harrington mentions in an
> autobiographical writing how he was

affected by the presence of the Jesuits
at the College of the Holy Cross. They
represented commitment to a way of life
... The people who sponsored the place
had, it seemed, faced "the real" and
chosen a way. The university's "owners"
did not *live* in the ivory tower.
(p. 121)

The Sponsorship Covenant: Strengthening Continuity

As the Brothers move into new forms of mission and their numbers continue to decrease, a Sponsorship Covenant between the board and the Brothers has evolved as a means of continuing the Lasallian Catholic mission and culture of the institution. One example of sponsorship is the case of Manhattan College.

On December 17, 2002, the New York District of the Brothers of the Christian Schools (now the District of Eastern North America) and the Board of Trustees of Manhattan College entered into a Sponsorship Covenant. The latter arose out of "the strong desire of both parties to continue and to enhance this relationship [of an intertwined history and mutually beneficial collaboration of the Brothers and Board since 1853], and the benefits accruing to each, as we move into the 21st century" (Manhattan College, 2008b, p. 41).

Exemplifying O'Brien's emphasis on the presence of a group of religious, visibly committed to the real, that is, to life decisions, the Sponsorship Covenant states:

This relationship [between the Brothers
and the Board] gives Manhattan
its distinctive identity through the
actualization of its Catholic identity;
the clear definition of its Mission; the
ongoing inspiration of its educational
philosophy; the values and ethos
that underpin our caring campus
community; the exceptional quality

of teaching; the commitment to
scholarship; [and] the remarkable
record of service to students and
alumni, most especially, those who were
the first generation of college students
in their family.
(Manhattan College, 2008a, p. 41)

Given De La Salle's commitment to elementary education, what is the role of "Lasallian higher education" in the Lasallian Education Movement today? This is not the place for a discussion of the evolution of Lasallian colleges in the United States or internationally. Suffice it to say that the American institutions were founded mainly in response to the spiritual and practical needs of "first generation" Catholics, beginning, but not exclusively, with the sons of nineteenth-century Catholic immigrants. In that sense, they were an extension of the founder's vision of a new social context based on a reading of the historical situation at the time.

What are the unique characteristics of these institutions[6], characteristics that not only make them different from secular public or private higher education in the United States, but also differentiate them from other Catholic colleges and universities? A clear response to this question will provide guidance in the transition from religious to lay leadership in Lasallian education.

Two decades ago, Brother Luke Salm (1983), FSC, answered that question in a brief one-page document, "The Brothers' School," incorporated into a booklet describing Christian Brothers' colleges in the United States and Toronto Region (p. 11).[7] The six characteristics are a set of guidelines for all Lasallian education programs. Since they are broadly conceived, I have taken the liberty of using Salm's document and focusing the characteristics as they apply to Lasallian higher education.

Question for Discussion

Is there a Sponsorship Covenant between the board and the founding congregation at your university? If so, what does it say? How does it influence and guide the work of the university? How will it affect you as a member of the university? What are the most important aspects of the covenant?

Six Characteristics of a Lasallian University

1. Sensitivity to Social Issues
2. The Importance of Religious Education
3. Commitment to Excellence in Teaching
4. Accent on Quality Education
5. An Education Emphasizing the Practical
6. Independent Distance from Church Authority

The importance of taking these six elements together cannot be stressed enough. There is a synergy among them, and as a result, the whole is greater than the sum of its parts, even though, while virtually all Catholic universities do embrace the above elements, they may express them in different ways. It should also be noted that the characteristics listed here are in the abstract. While not having the approbation of the General Council or American region of the De La Salle Christian Brothers, the six, taken together, are grounded in a specific 330-year-old Lasallian heritage and culture. Distinctiveness is in the concrete example of specific universities. A further specification of distinctiveness will be found as well in the individual Lasallian university with its own particularity of culture and heritage. Benedictine universities, as well as universities sponsored by other congregations, embrace these characteristics, but they do so in a manner consistent with their own culture and heritage.

These elements provide a model or template for analyzing the characteristics of a Catholic university. The first characteristic—sensitivity to social issues, the one that gave rise to the religious congregation itself—will be discussed. Likewise, the second characteristic—the importance given to religious studies and theology—will be considered because these disciplines distinguish Lasallian universities. A study of these two characteristics in particular is important because the future of the Lasallian Educational Movement at the university level will depend on a thorough understanding of and commitment to these two characteristics by lay faculty. Moreover, the other characteristics logically flow from the first and second. Characteristics three through five are self-explanatory. However, the sixth characteristic, one that all Catholic universities must address, merits commentary as well.

Characteristic 1: Sensitivity to Social Issues

> [Sensitivity to social issues] is the reason that brought the Institute [Congregation] of the Brothers into being in the first place. If the social problems of today's world are no less acute than they were in the time of De La Salle, they are more complex and less susceptible to direct and easy solution. Nevertheless, the Brothers try to give priority to direct educational service to the poor where that is still possible. Where it is not, the Brothers, try in all of their educational endeavors to show special concern for the disadvantaged and to make education for social justice an important element in the curriculum and in extracurricular activities. That is what the Brothers mean when they take a special vow [make a promise] of "service to the poor through education." (Salm, 1983, p. 11)

The "commitment to social justice" in the Manhattan College mission statement, for example, receives specific acknowledgment in the college catalog:

> From its beginning, Manhattan
> College has paid particular attention
> to educating first-generation college
> students, and was an early proponent of
> access to minority students, establishing
> special scholarship funds for minority
> students as early as 1938. Currently, over
> 25% of the student body are from racial
> and ethnic minorities.
> (Manhattan College, 2010—12a)

Manhattan College would not be a viable economic institution if it were to translate its commitment to social justice and special service to the poor as solely a commitment to first-generation, disadvantaged minority students. Clarifying the nature of a commitment to the poor, Brother Alvaro Rodriquez Echeverria, Superior General, and the General Council of the Christian Brothers note in their 2010 Circular Letter:

> [I]t is critical to mention that from the
> beginning schools were established for
> many classes of people. The schools
> for wealthier students have always tried
> to be at the service of the schools in
> direct service of the poor . . . [A]n effort
> should be made to be more concerned
> that these centers are teaching a
> doctrine of social justice focused
> on systemic change and empirically
> offering all students an opportunity
> to "know" and serve the poor and
> marginalized. Nevertheless, serving

> the poor among the young should be a
> constant concern. (p. 25)

Salm also comments on outreach to the poor in contemporary society. The acute and complex global social problems of today do not lend themselves to easy solutions. For instance, the Lasallian Education Movement has a presence among students in the more affluent suburbs, who may still face challenges, such as dysfunctional families and single-parent homes. Such was the case in De La Salle's time. The young boys who were "far from salvation in this world and the next" were also starved for "attention, affection, and inspiration." However, the reader must keep in mind that "despite all the complexities and rationalization, the Lasallian enterprise could not lose its traditional sensitivity to the needs of the poor without losing its identity" (Salm, 1983, p. 11).

The foundation of the educational commitment to the poor is respect for the dignity of each person. While human rights may be considered the secular or philosophical analog to respect for the dignity of each person, the latter principle in Catholic social teaching flows from belief in the creation of the individual in the image and likeness of God, belief confirmed by the incarnation of Jesus Christ (O'Brien, 2002, p. 116). That same God wants all persons to know the truth and be saved. Thus, creation and redemption of the human race go hand in hand. De La Salle, however, was most concerned with those on the margin. These were the vulnerable young boys roaming the streets of urban France, who had no practical skills to give them economic stability and no religious sensitivity to lead them to salvation.

The imperative to address the needs of the poor also directs the Lasallian university to be more attentive to the discrimination and vulnerability that often accompany social, ethnic, and religious pluralism among administrators, faculty, staff, and students. Certainly, the culture of postmodernism has been an impetus in society and in higher education for respecting two important dimensions of pluralism: diversity and human rights. The Catholic institution of higher learning, while influenced in these areas by postmodernism, is, theologically rather than philosophically, motivated by the God-given inherent dignity of the individual as one created by God. Commitment to dialogue with diverse communities about "important matters" is one of the most important consequences of Vatican II.[8] This is so because God speaks through these communities. The latter are not to be simply tolerated, but rather embraced, because we are all children of God and part of the human community.

Furthermore, dialogue and the call to action are necessary because the "present situation" (e.g. north/south economic imbalance, nuclear weapons, world hunger) is not acceptable, is infected by sin, and demands systemic analysis and assumption of responsibility. Catholics and Catholic institutions of higher learning have no monopoly on this analysis and a call to action. To engage in the latter, the Lasallian university relies on the insights of its Catholic community and its diverse religious, secular, and ethnic communities, all of which constitute the whole of the Lasallian higher education community at each institution.

Question for Discussion

What is the university's commitment to the poor? How is this commitment lived out as part of the institution's mission and vision?

Characteristic 2: The Importance of Religious Education

A second but not secondary quality of the Brothers' school is the importance given to religious education. This, too, means something different than it did in seventeenth-century France. In the American context, respect for religious freedom leads the Brothers to a somewhat different approach to religious education, one that takes into account the varying needs and experiences of the student in order

to open them to Gospel values and
to bring to maturity their personal
faith commitment within the Catholic
tradition.
(Salm 1983, p. 11)

Teaching religion in a Lasallian institution such as Manhattan College is quite different from doing so in a Lasallian high school. The latter directly addresses questions of faith through a catechesis[9] that is relevant to American Catholic adolescents. In these schools, imparting theological understanding and nurturing religious faith go hand in hand. However, a Lasallian university is a reflection of American society: it is quite diverse in its population and varied in religious representation. Thus, "not all those who come to the Christian school are looking for an education that is explicitly Christian" (Brothers of the Christian Schools, 1997, para. 39).

Using Manhattan College as a case study, one finds, as with the majority of Catholic universities, that the ethnically diverse student population consists of adults (having reached their eighteenth birthday during the first year of college) who are religiously pluralistic. Approximately two-thirds of the students are from Catholic backgrounds, while the other students represent a variety of mostly Protestant traditions; there are also Muslim, Jewish, Hindu, and Buddhist students, as well as agnostics and atheists.

During the fall or spring semester of their first year at Manhattan College, students fulfill a curricular requirement, "The Nature and Experience of Religion." The instructor will generally find a great deal of unevenness in the knowledge base that the young men and women bring to the course. A significant number will have attended Catholic elementary and/or secondary school, but once again, the professor cannot presume a common knowledge base even among those students. Some of the Protestant students may represent the evangelical or Pentecostal branches and are frequently very knowledgeable in the area of Scripture. Students of other religious backgrounds likewise vary in the knowledge base they bring to the introductory course. In general, students bring an experiential perspective on religion based on attendance at services, participation in retreats, and a considerable amount of time viewing television. As presented in the essay on students, today there is more interest in spirituality than religion, especially organized religion. Finally, some students are indifferent or hostile to organized religion as a result of personal experience or based on a variety of informational sources that are not always accurate (Astin, Astin, & Lindholm, 2010).

The first-year course addresses this divergent group of men and women, who are asserting and experiencing an independence that is on a continuum of growth differing qualitatively from high school, but not necessarily advancing in a consistently upward movement toward greater maturity and responsibility. As children of postmodernity, the vast majority cannot conceive of an overarching meaning system that would be taken for granted in their culture. Given this student profile in an American context, the pedagogical approach of Lasallian educators to the introductory course respects their religious freedom and, as Salm notes above, "takes into account the varying needs and experiences of the student." The purpose, he continues, is "to open them to Gospel values and to bring to maturity their personal faith commitment within the Catholic tradition." These words were penned in 1983, written in view of all Lasallian educational programs, but they do not necessarily represent the contemporary mind-set of religious studies professors whether they are Catholic or of another or no religious belief.

Opening the minds of the students to the varieties of religion and the characteristics common to a number of traditions, the first-year course examines the history and motivations of diverse movements and groups, and the manner in which believers experience and practice religion. The curriculum of this course is such that it could be followed on any campus—public, private, denominational, or secular. Implicit in the course description is the faculty's hope that the course will bring about attitudes of tolerance and openness toward world religions, and that stereotypical perceptions and prejudices will be transformed into understanding.

The first-year course is representative of the transformation of the department itself at Manhattan and at many other universities. Reflecting the change in pedagogy and goals, "Religious Studies" replaced "Theology" as the department name in 1970. However, a previous change is the one that truly reflects the underlying shift in the self-understanding of the faculty. In 1958, the department was simply "Religion." The change to "Theology Department" emphasized that the courses were academic in character, without indoctrination or religious training, but still with an emphasis on Catholicism. "Religious Studies" is more encompassing, including theology and a study of other religions and contemporary problems.

In the 1970 transition, courses on Catholicism were no longer required. However, in 2012—13 the Religious Studies Web site indicates a curriculum revision that takes into account the current emphasis on the Catholic culture and religious heritage of the institution. On the School of Arts Web site, the Manhattan College Religious Studies Department describes its mission and its requirements in this way:

> **Introduction:** The mission of the Religious Studies Department fulfills the mission of Manhattan College by seeking to provide a contemporary, person-centered educational experience characterized by high academic standards, reflection on faith, values, and ethics, and lifelong career preparation. These goals are accomplished through our nine-credit requirement that includes 1) a course that introduces the study of religion as an academic discipline and global phenomenon, 2) a course that explores the riches of the Catholic

intellectual tradition, and 3) a course
that raises awareness of global and/
or contemporary issues. Our goals for
majors and minors include an ability
to critically read and analyze religious
texts, a facility with the methods of the
academic study of religion, a familiarity
with specific religious traditions, and
an understanding of the role that
religion plays in contemporary life.
The introductory course focuses on
a particular theme while introducing
students to some of the research tools
used in the academic study of religion.
A Roman Catholic concentration
is offered and a Roman Catholic
interdisciplinary minor, in cooperation
with other departments, may be elected.
In addition, students may write a six-
credit honors thesis for departmental
honors recognition.
(Manhattan College, 2010—12b)

While the Roman Catholic concentration has been offered
over the past three decades, the Roman Catholic interdisciplinary
minor is of relatively recent origin. The most striking change today,
however, is in the requirement to elect "a course that explores the
riches of the Catholic intellectual tradition."

In sum, religious education at Manhattan College, as well as at
other Catholic colleges in the United States, has many meanings.
In addressing this second characteristic of a Lasallian school, Salm
(1999) notes the following benefits accruing to the students:

It can help the student understand his
religious experience and commitment
at the deepest level of maturity and
freedom. Religious education reveals

264

the element of mystery in human
existence, the possibilities that
transcend the empirical order, and the
horizons that expand the meaning of
what it is to live and to die. Religious
education is value-centered education
and so concerned with all that relates
to life, love, trust, fidelity, freedom,
justice, brotherhood and sisterhood
in community. Religious education
raises doubts about limited perspectives
and unexamined presuppositions; it
raises questions that can lead from
agnosticism to faith. A religious
educator knows how to lead students
who no longer respond to traditional
doctrine and creeds, legal codes or
sacramental cult, to seek new words to
express what they doubt and what they
believe, to externalize their awe at a
transcendent mystery in sign and ritual
that they can relate to, to identify their
failure and to repent of sin, to live out
their commitment in justice and love.
(p. 2)

Questions for Discussion

- How do the curriculum and requirements at the university reflect the university's charism, mission, and vision?
- How are the university's charism, mission, and vision realized within your discipline?

Characteristic 6: Independent Distance from Church Authority

The sixth characteristic is the most
subtle of all, but something quite

265

distinctive and very real. Although
instinctively loyal to the Roman
Church, and respectful of the dignity
and functions of the priesthood, the
Brothers have managed to keep their
schools at a certain independent
distance from Church authority. By
definition Brothers are excluded from
the mainstream of ecclesiastical politics
and theological disputes. Thus, as
they lay religious, they can more easily
identify with their colleagues, students
and parents and so understand better
and support movements to give laymen
and laywomen a great role in the life of
the Church.
(Salm, 1999, p. 2)

This final characteristic, loyalty to and independent distance
from Church authority, allows the other characteristics to flourish.
Loyalty and independence, a "loose coupling" with the Church,
leaves the Brothers free to develop the school or university according to their vision without the imposition of parish or diocesan
authority. Salm also observes that "in a Lasallian school . . . there is
likely to be a more open and prophetic stance to some aspects of
Catholic tradition, piety, and observance" (Salm, 1999, p. 2). Com-
menting on another aspect, he states that "being laymen themselves, the Brothers understand and are in a position to support
movements to give laymen and laywomen more leadership roles
in the Church" (Salm, 1999, p. 2). As a result, this characteristic
facilitates the transformation of the schools and universities from
institutions of the "De La Salle Christian Brothers" to the "Lasallian Education Movement" composed of the Brothers and lay associates.

In his closing observations on this characteristic, Salm (1999)
notes that "there is a growing realization that brotherhood implies

sisterhood, that the brotherhood in the Lasallian education community includes a sisterhood, establishing an equal and equitable relationship between teachers who can call one another brothers and sisters" (p. 2).

Questions for Discussion

- Does the characteristic "Independent distance from church authority" strike you as surprising for a Catholic institution? Have you noticed any instances of this distance?
- Based on your experience since your arrival, what are the distinctive characteristics of your university? How do they compare to characteristics of a Lasallian university?
- differentiates your university from other Catholic universities and from secular private or public counterparts?

Charism and Catholicity in Catholic Higher Education

It is my conviction that the charism and Catholicity of the universities sponsored by the De La Salle Christian Brothers—as well as those sponsored by other religious congregations and dioceses—will continue, and will evolve, if a set of opportunities are seized and the corresponding challenges met. Four of these opportunities and challenges are internal, have been discussed in this essay, and are summarized below:

Need for stability

In a period of social and ecclesial change, there is a pressing need to continue the creative development of the congregational charism of each university for these turbulent times.

Presence of a committed cadre

Fidelity to the vision of the congregational founder will require the establishment of pluralistic congregational/lay communities, the members of which will have committed themselves to both charism and Catholicity. While all partners need not and should not be Catholic, there must be a core group of Catholics committed to the university's Catholic culture and congregational heritage.

Diversity of the cadre in a diverse world

A congregational/lay movement will call for the embrace of laypersons diverse in their religious or secular worldviews, yet supportive of charism and Catholicity. Embrace is warm and personal, never simply tolerance from a distance. Diversity must be an integral dimension of the community, not only because religious, cultural, and ethnic diversity is a reality among partners, but also because diversity is integral to Catholic higher education. A more subtle understanding of Catholic identity, important insights into the mystery of God and religious experience, and critical assessment of Catholicism comes with a diverse community, especially among the faculty.

The "catholic" nature of Catholicism

Through the lens of religious faith, those who are believers within an academic community come to an experiential understanding of how God acts in and through the intellectual and religious identity and commitment of diverse religionists, agnostics, and secular humanists. Likewise, through the lens of agnosticism and secular humanism, those who profess no religion also come to an experiential understanding of the effects of identity and commitment on religious persons (Wilcox & King, 2000, pp. xv–xxv). On these points, Peter Steinfels (1995) notes:

> Catholic identity must embrace
> scholars of other faiths and of no faith,
> not simply as admissible presences
> in Catholic higher education, but as
> essential to its purposes. It is clear
> that in many cases Protestants, Jews,
> adherents of other religions, and
> agnostics and atheists may bring critical

scholarly insight and good will to the
Catholic campus mission far beyond
what many Catholics offer.
(p. 16)

Higher Education Confronts the Ecclesial Opportunities and Challenges

Philip Gleason (1995) is graphic in describing the challenges facing the Church: "This clashing of the tectonic plates of culture [in an era of revolutionary change in America during the 1960s] produced nothing less than a spiritual earthquake in the American church" (p. 300). The impact of this experimentation and upheaval on Catholic higher education resulted, as we learned in Essay One, in the collapse of the overarching synthesis or worldview that provided the academic framework for American Catholic institutions and their intellectual life. This worldview had been swept away. Gleason (1995) concludes: "As institutions, most Catholic colleges and universities weathered the storm. But institutional survival in the midst of ideological collapse left them uncertain of their identity" (p. 305).

As Steinfels noted, the Catholic Church can succeed as an institution while failing to be Catholic, but it cannot succeed as Catholic while failing as an institution. The same observation could easily be made of the Catholic university; I think Gleason would agree. It is much easier to assess institutional success than to assess the success of maintaining and enhancing Catholic culture, the congregation heritage, and the outcomes the university seeks in this regard. Therein lies the challenge facing Catholic higher education.

The implications for Catholic leadership in higher education are important and are underscored by the proliferation, since the 1990s, of Offices of Mission and Identity on Catholic campuses. At the present time, the majority of Catholic universities have a mission officer. However, Gleason (1995) states:

> The task facing Catholic academics
> today is to forge from the philosophical
> and theological resources uncovered in

the past half-century a vision that will
provide what Neo-Scholasticism did for
so many years—a theoretical rationale
for the existence of Catholic colleges
and universities as a distinctive element
in American higher education.
(p. 305)

Note Gleason's use of the term "academics." He does not say "administrators" or "campus ministry team." Because departments play a critical role in most hiring decisions, the religious affiliation of candidates more than likely plays little role in who is hired. However, "the future of Catholic identity will ultimately rest in the hands of the laity and in the hands of the faculty . . . No vision can be implemented and perpetuated without the assent and support of a majority of faculty members" (Steinfels, 1995, p. 16). This is the heart of the matter and the driving force behind this book and its proposed orientation/formation program focused on the faculty and others at the university.

A transition to lay leadership in Catholic higher education began in the late 1960s. It proved to be a challenging and trying negotiation, one that is not over. The changeover was due in part to the conciliar emphasis on the laity in the church. More importantly, the rapid growth of Catholic educational institutions occurred at a time when the strict constitutional separation of church and state in higher education was breached. Catholic higher education anticipated the new possibility of public funding made possible through federally sponsored research, state funding, and student financial aid. Eligibility led to the intentional distancing of institutions from their religious identity, at times beyond government expectations.

Furthermore, there should be little doubt about the impact that the "Land o' Lakes Statement" had on lay hiring. The Statement was the outcome of a conference of Catholic university presidents, bishops, scholars, and congregational leaders in 1967 at Land o' Lakes, Wisconsin. The theme was "The Nature of the Contemporary Catholic University." There was a decided emphasis on academic freedom and institutional autonomy—clearly appealing elements to potential lay hires.

The document goes on to point out that "the Catholic university adds to the basic idea of a modern university distinctive characteristics which round out and fulfill that idea. The Catholic university must be an institution, a community of learners and of scholars, in which Catholicism is perceptibly present and effectively operative" (Gallin, 1992, p. 7). This institution, this community, has a clear mission today, given the commodification of human life in all its aspects. As Margaret O'Brien Steinfels (1995) observes: "That mission means keeping the human person at the center of our inquiry. The human person must be seen in his or her social context, where an implicit and shared understanding of the good can be found and expressed" (pp. 9–10). The social context is a community where "we are to love the Lord and love one another as he has loved us" (Steinfels, 1995, p. 16).

"Loving the Lord and loving one another," or even just "loving one another," goes to the heart of the problem in academe. Echoing Parker Palmer, Mark Schwehn (1993) puts it well: "The most authentic centers of knowledge in the future will have to be based upon a correlative conviction, namely, that there is a relationship between our love of learning and our love for one another, and that both of these loves are in turn, expressions of our desire for God" (p. 125). Catholic education, then, is the work of a community of believers, a community that embraces many others as well. Margaret O'Brien Steinfels (1995) concludes: "In our culture that is a suspect category, nowhere more so than in the university" (p. 10).

Conclusion

This essay has traced the development of religious congregations: the archetypes of the monk, the householder, and the *humanum*, as well as homogeneity and heterogeneity of religious congregations and lay partners respectively, both of whom share fundamental values and aspirations. In the second half of the essay, we discussed charism, institutionalization, and the case study of the De La Salle

271

Christian Brothers. The latter group is one example of a religious congregation that has evolved to the point where the congregation sees itself as part of the contemporary Lasallian Education Movement. "Together and by Association" (in a phrase previously synonymous with the Brothers' way of life and pedagogy but now also used to describe their relationship with lay partners), both entities bring the charism of Saint John Baptist de La Salle, reinvented, into the twenty-first century.

RM assumes a continued commitment to the pursuit of excellence in teaching, research, and service. Fundamental to these pursuits are the two distinctive mission characteristics of the Catholic university that likewise depend upon commitment: the Catholic culture and the congregational religious heritage. These are the unique aspects of an educational system that created the institution of higher education in Western civilization.

Why is it so important that these dimensions not only be preserved, but also be living, dynamic characteristics that giving meaning and direction to teaching, research, and service? If these characteristics were excluded or simply left to atrophy, the universities would cease to be Catholic and would lose their soul. Times do change, and so do universities. But in this case, such fundamental change would spell the end of these universities as we know them.

What is behind these "nonnegotiable characteristics," characteristics in which these institutions are heavily invested administratively, educationally, and financially, among other ways? The answer is at once simple, complex, personally challenging, and countercultural: The universities are Catholic and from "the heart of the Church." They are "the places were the Church does its thinking"—at least a good deal of it. Most importantly, these universities are, in many ways, the Church's last best chance to influence many future leaders in the United States and other societies, whether they are Catholic or profess other belief systems.

The cognitive hope is that the graduates will have a robust grasp of Catholicism as a global religion. It is a religion possessing a well-articulated system of social teachings that are universally appealing and applicable because they speak to the minds and hearts of all peoples. Catholic universities, moreover, challenge their students affectively by asking them questions of meaning, purpose, and ultimacy, while confidently assisting the students as they search for answers.

The expression "the Church's last best chance" may sound ominous to some. I see it as an opportunity to complement Catholic religious instruction that in most cases ends with confirmation in a parish or with senior year in Catholic secondary schools. The latter are in decline and parishes are burdened with financial and personnel issues. Furthermore, young adult formation has not been a strong suit in the Catholic Church, certainly in comparison to the same formation in the Protestant community. It is my belief that Catholic leadership in American society and the Church will be a crucial outcome for Catholic universities in the United States.

Furthermore, the Catholic university is brought to life and animated by the particularities and nuances of the founding religious congregation and its heritage. Through congregational members, new hires, and other faculty, administrators, and staff, all acting as partners in association forming a Mission Community, the religious heritage and the Catholic culture will be more than preserved; they will thrive. As described in the following essay, the Mission Community offers a means and a model to assist Catholic universities in making the Catholic culture and the religious heritage of the founding congregation more robust as these institutions move through the twenty-first century.

References

Astin, A. W., Astin, H. S., & Lindholm, J. A. (2010). *Cultivating the spirit: How college can enhance students' inner lives.* San Francisco, CA: Jossey-Bass.

Brothers of the Christian Schools (General Council). (2010). *Associated for the Lasallian Mission . . . an act of HOPE.* Retrieved from http://www.lasalle.org/media/pdf/circulares/461_circ_en.pdf

Brothers of the Christian Schools. *The brothers of the christian schools in the world today: A declaration.* (1997). Trans. Salm, L. Lincroft, NJ: La Salle Provincialate.

Ford, J. T. (2006). *Saint Mary's Press glossary of theological terms.* Winona, MN: Saint Mary's Press.

Gallin, A. (1992). *American Catholic higher education: Essential documents, 1967–1990.* Notre Dame, IN: University of Notre Dame Press.

Gleason, P. (1995). *Contending with modernity: Catholic higher education in the twentieth century.* New York, NY: Oxford University Press.

John Paul II (1990). *Apostolic constitution of the supreme pontiff John Paul II on Catholic universities* (commonly known as *Ex corde Ecclesiae* (ECE)). Retrieved from http://www.vatican.va/holy_father/john_paul_ii/apost_constitutions/documents/hf_jp-ii_apc_15081990_ex-corde-ecclesiae_en.html

Kotter, J. P., & Heskett, J. L. (1992). *Corporate culture and performance.* New York, NY: Free Press.

Kramer, K. T. (2008). Blessed interruptions: God can be found in the moments that upset our rhythms. *America, 199*(6). Retrieved from http://www.americamagazine.org/content/article.cfm?article_id=11013

Lee, B. J. (2004). *The beating of great wings: A worldly spirituality for active, apostolic communities.* Mystic, CT: Twenty-third Publications.

Manhattan College. (2008a). Sponsorship Covenant: Background. In *Manhattan College: An introduction to the Catholic culture and to our Lasallian heritage* (p. 41). New York, NY: Manhattan College.

Manhattan College. (2008b). Sponsorship Covenant: Rationale. In *Manhattan College: An introduction to the Catholic culture and to our Lasallian heritage* (p. 41). New York, NY: Manhattan College.

Manhattan College. (2010—12a). *Catalog,* Manhattan College mission and history: Historical note, p. 11. Retrieved from Manhattan College home page, "Quick Links" @ http://www.manhattan.edu/.

Manhattan College. (2010—12b). *Catalog,* Undergraduate, Religious Studies: Introduction, p. 278. Retrieved from Manhattan College home page, "Quick Links" @ http://www.manhattan.edu/.

Morris, C. R. (1997). *American Catholic: The saints and sinners who built America's most powerful church.* New York, NY: Times Books.

O'Brien, D. J. (1994). *From the heart of the American church: Catholic higher education and American culture.* Maryknoll, NY: Orbis Books.

O'Brien, D. (2002). *The idea of a Catholic university.* Chicago, IL: University of Chicago Press.

O'Malley, J. W. (2008). *What happened at Vatican II.* Cambridge, MA: Belknap Press of Harvard University Press.

Panikkar, R., & North American Board for East-West Dialog. (1982). *Blessed simplicity: The monk as universal archetype.* New York, NY: Seabury Press.

Rolheiser, R. (1999). *The holy longing: The search for a Christian spirituality.* New York, NY: Doubleday.

Salm, L. (1983). The Brothers' School. *The seven Christian Brothers colleges in the United States, 1983–1984.* New York, NY: Manhattan College.

Salm, L. (1999, January). Characteristics of Lasallian Schools in the USA. *Lasalliana*, 47-15-C-206, 1(2). Rome, Italy: Brothers of the Christian Schools.

Schneiders, S. M. (2000). *Finding the treasure: Locating Catholic religious life in a new ecclesial and cultural context.* New York, NY: Paulist Press.

Schwehn, M. R. (1993). *Exiles from Eden: Religion and the academic vocation in America.* New York, NY: Oxford University Press.

Steinfels, M. O'B., Association of Catholic Colleges and Universities, & University of St. Thomas (St. Paul, Minn.). (1995). *Catholic higher education: Practice and promise, diverse expressions of Catholic identity.* Washington, DC: Association of Catholic Colleges and Universities.

Steinfels, P. (2003). *A people adrift: The crisis of the Roman Catholic Church in America.* New York, NY: Simon & Schuster.

Steinfels, P. (2004, Spring). To the Jesuits: Don't forget you're Catholic. *Conversations on Jesuit Higher Education*, 25, 22.

Retrieved from http://epublications.marquette.edu/conversations/vol25/iss1/16

Vatican Council. (1965a). *Decree on the apostolate of the laity (Apostolicam Actuositatem)* promulgated by His Holiness Pope Paul VI on November 18, 1965. Retrieved from http://www.vatican.va/archive/hist_councils/ii_vatican_council/documents/vat-ii_decree_19651118_apostolicam-actuositatem_en.html

Vatican Council. (1965b). *Dogmatic constitution on the church (Lumen Gentium)* promulgated by His Holiness Pope Paul VI on November 21, 1965. Retrieved from http://www.vatican.va/archive/hist_councils/ii_vatican_council/documents/vat-ii_const_19641121_lumen-gentium_en.html

Recommended Reading

Vatican Council. (1965). *Pastoral constitution on the church in the modern world (Gaudium et spes)* promulgated by His Holiness Pope Paul VI on December 7, 1965. Retrieved from http://www.vatican.va/archive/hist_councils/ii_vatican_council/documents/vat-ii_const_19651207_gaudium-et-spes_en.html

Notes

[1] Archetype. (n.d.). Retrieved January 6, 2011, from http://www.merriam-webster.com/dictionary/archetype.

[2] In his emphasis on "the relational context of religious community," Salm follows Schneiders (2000), *Finding the Treasure.* Salm also observed, "I probably have fewer occasions to feel the pinch of poverty or the constraints of obedience than most laypersons. I am celibate by choice as are some laypersons and all Christians are called to be chaste according to their state. Biblical scholars no longer see the triad as 'evangelical counsels.' The sooner we can dispose of the myth of the traditional vows, the easier it will be to make sense out of what is somewhat inaccurately called the religious or the consecrated life. It is different all right but it needs a less triumphalist vocabulary" (L. Salm, personal communication, April 29, 2004).

[3] See also Schein, E. H. (1992). *Organizational culture and leadership.* San Francisco, CA: Jossey-Bass.

[4] *Apostolicam Actuositatem,* henceforth AA. There is no easily usable English translation from the Latin for the first words of the Decree.

[5] The others are Christian Brothers University (Memphis, TN), LaSalle University (Philadelphia, PA), Lewis University (Romeoville, IL), St. Mary's College (Moraga, CA), and Saint Mary's University (Winona, MN).

[6] The seven American Lasallian universities, in the order of their founding, are Manhattan College, Bronx, NY, 1853; La Salle University, Philadelphia, PA, 1863; St. Mary's College, Moraga, CA, 1868; Christian Brothers University, Memphis, TN, 1871; Saint Mary's University, Winona, MN, 1933; Lewis University, Romeoville, IL, 1960; and Bethlehem University, Bethlehem, Palestine, 1973. Sponsored by the Vatican, the latter is a member of the United States Lasallian Association of College and University Presidents.

[7] The seven colleges Salm lists include the College of Santa Fe (closed in 2010).

[8] See Abbott and Gallagher, *The Documents of Vatican II,* "Dogmatic Constitution on the Church" (*Lumen Gentium*), "Decree on Ecumenism" (*Unitatis Redintegratio*), "Pastoral Constitution on the Church in the Modern World" (*Gaudium et Spes*), "Declaration on the Relationship of the Church to Non-Christian Religions" (*Nostra Aetate*), and "Declaration on Religious Freedom" (*Dignitatis Humanae*).

[9] Catechesis: instruction in the Catholic faith and teaching for children and those entering the Church. "Catechetical teaching is usually given in preparation for receiving the sacraments of initiation: Baptism, Eucharist, and Confirmation" (Ford, 2006, p. 36).

ESSAY SIX

THE MISSION COMMUNITY: A NEW LIVING ENDOWMENT

> A truly lay spirituality must emerge
> from lay experience, be constructed on
> lay premises, develop lay leadership,
> and promote a kind of personal
> practice and ministerial involvement
> that is compatible with and truly
> transformative of lay life. If Religious
> congregations can meet this challenge
> to assist without taking over. . . we
> will have responded to the historical
> challenge brought to us by the
> people seeking association with us
> and we will have participated in what
> may be the most important renewal
> movement in the history of the Church,
> the emergence of a fully adult and
> responsible laity.
> Sandra M. Schneiders, *Finding the
> Treasure* (2000, pp. 97)

"The Mission Community: A New Living Endowment" is the culminating essay of *Revisioning Mission*. It is culminating in the sense that the theme of a Mission Community brings the other essays together and gives a structural locus for the individual topics discussed. This moves beyond being a "concluding essay" to one that points the way toward a genuinely lay spirituality, as described by Sandra Schneiders in the opening quotation. Moreover, the essay "The Spiritual Journey" (Essay Three) has served as a guidepost for the Faculty Learning Community throughout the Revisioning Mission program. It will also serve as an excellent resource for this essay and beyond. The Mission Community is both the culmination of a year-long formation process and another name for associative groups already established. It is a culmination, but also part of the ongoing process of moving into the future with the religious congregation and the laity "together and by association" in common pursuit of the university's mission.[1]

Education and Formation

While the congregational and lay members authenticate the religious heritage, it is the congregation itself and its leadership that provide the ultimate resource for the interpretation of the religious heritage and authentication of the Mission Community in a Catholic university. Of course, the board of trustees shares responsibility for nurturing the Catholic culture and religious heritage that are the foundation of the mission, in addition to their fiduciary responsibility for the financial health of the institution. This shared trusteeship of the culture and heritage of the Catholic university is the basis for a sponsorship agreement between the board and the religious congregation. One important role of the Mission Community, in conjunction with the Office of Mission, is to provide formation programs and resources for the board in its role as trustee of the university's mission. The MC should also be in dialogue with the board of trustees with regard to diverse interpretations of the mission and its foundational characteristics.

Because the terms "education" and "formation" are sometimes used interchangeably in pedagogical contexts, it is worth taking a moment to clarify the distinction between the two in the Revisioning Mission context. "Education" refers to informational sessions that explain Catholic higher education, as do the essays in this book. However, "formation" refers to the hope that program participants will take the education to heart, that is, that they will internalize the aspirations and values of the Catholic university. The summative outcomes of any program are twofold: education and formation. The first outcome sought is that all participants will have a clear, accurate understanding of what constitutes a Catholic university and that they will support the mission or, at the very least, not denigrate it. Beyond that, it is hoped that there will be participants who, through a formal or informal process of discernment, will commit themselves to an active leadership role in preserving, enhancing, and bringing the Catholic culture and the religious heritage of the founding congregation into the twenty-first century.

Association and Mission

Catholic universities almost universally recognize the importance of, and the debt they owe to, their founders. Some, if not all, are taking steps to continue the guidance of the founding community, even when no actual members of the community are available for campus work. They are doing this by developing "mission communities": groups of laypeople who have become "associates" of the religious communities in some way, whether formally or informally. One example of such a mission community, Brothers and Partners Associated for the Lasallian Mission, will be explored in greater detail in this essay, as will the history and reasons behind the associate movement. The insightful words of Sandra Schneiders above set the tone and direction for understanding the role of lay leadership in Catholic universities as a work in progress. Lay leadership embodied in the Mission Community (MC) represents a transformation in Catholic higher education. However, the transformation from a strict divide between the religious congregation and lay colleagues, to one of association or partnership, is in a developmental stage for the foreseeable future. My hope is that *Revisioning Mission* will provide a resource for those groups already in place.

In this essay, we explore in depth the Lasallian Education Mission and the evolution of religious-lay association in the congregation as ways of illustrating these new realities of university life. I have chosen the Christian Brothers for this illustration because of my close association with them over many years and my knowledge of their evolving concept of association. I believe that mission officers and the directors of an RM program will obtain important learnings in the quest for a dynamic Mission Community from studying this example. These learnings flow from the congregation's transformational understanding of "association," an idea that has given a contemporary vitality to De La Salle's vision and to the work of the Brothers and their partners. That sense of association will enhance the dynamism of an MC and present a model for the future vitality of Catholic universities.

Like most other religious communities engaged in Catholic higher education, the Christian Brothers are passionately committed to the mission of Christian education, especially among the most vulnerable persons on the fringes of all societies. But they see the mission from two unique perspectives, now embedded in their self-understanding and institutional structure. One perspective is that the Brothers and lay associates are the guardians of the Lasallian mission and heritage. From a second perspective, as laypeople themselves (in Catholic canon law, professed brothers and sisters are considered laypeople), they are on a mission to recruit other laypeople—men and women, married and single, Catholic and non-Catholic—to assume an equal role in their work. This expansion of mission initiatives has led to an extraordinary result: there are more mission foundations or schools in the twenty-first century than when the Lasallian Education Mission was composed primarily of Brothers, with very few laypeople from outside the congregation involved in the mission.

Of course, no one can predict the evolution of "Associated for the Lasallian Mission," or any other mission community, but as we shall see, the Brothers regard their efforts as "an act of hope" (Circular 461[2]). This reflects the attitude of their founder, De

La Salle, who never tried to predict what would happen next. As he said, "God led him step by step." What the Brothers are doing today is profoundly Lasallian and deeply rooted in a Christian spirituality motivated by trust in God's providence—and yet it is something profoundly new and different nonetheless. This trust is an act of faith in God's guidance and goes to the heart of De La Salle's own journey and work. His story is very similar to the stories of so many founders of religious congregations: They faced extraordinary obstacles, but they never gave up, because their trust in God's providence was bound up with their hope in God.

Questions for Discussion

- Why would there be a need for a Mission Community to continue the work of the founding congregation?
- This essay calls the participants to shoulder responsibility for the future of Catholic higher education. Practically speaking, what would this responsibility mean for you?

The Mission Community: An Active and Visible Force on Campus

A Mission Community has staying power, as well as continuity over a longer time span than do individual employees committed to the mission; and most importantly, it develops a communal memory concerning Catholic culture and the religious heritage of the founding congregation. As the communal memory, the MC assumes a prophetic role in the university enabling it to speak "truth to power."

Yet I also want to emphasize that the MC is collaborative, engaged with colleagues in all sectors of the university. The Mission Community is to the university what a religious congregation is to the Catholic Church. It should be "loosely coupled," or, as Luke Salm would say, having some distance and freedom provides an environment for assessing the authenticity of the mission.

An informal, inclusive group (no matter how it is organized), the MC should never be an elitist organization. It offers no inside track to tenure nor university-wide leverage and privilege. The adjectives "ecumenical," "interreligious," and "secular humanistic" may not even be adequate to characterize the diversity or pluralism of the membership; all are welcome, none are excluded. Realistically, however, not all members will join this group, and this for a variety of reasons: time commitment related to success on the tenure track, challenging research projects, significant administrative or staff responsibilities, and, for younger faculty, rearing a family, especially when both spouses work outside the home. Others may be more tentative with a "wait-and-see" caution or simply not interested in assuming this responsibility.

This "New Living Endowment" of religious and laypeople in a Mission Community will draw on the enduring strength of the university's Catholic culture and its congregational heritage, rendering them powerful enough to assist in the university's transition through this uncertain stage of history. The strength of this endowment will be founded on a confident optimism in the power of God's grace and the commitment of an ever-increasing number of laypeople in the United States and around the world. Belief in this forward movement requires a deep spirituality on the part of all members committed to a robust future for Catholic higher education. There are simply too many challenges to leave it to human effort alone, and they all require faith, hope, and love of God and one another. Those who are humanist likewise require a deep spiritual life grounded in a transcendent, hope-filled belief in the future of these universities.

Qualities of the Mission Community

Summarizing the salient characteristics of the Mission Community will be helpful at this point. The Mission Community is:

- Voluntary
- Diverse
- Grounded in prayer and spirituality
- Structured
- Loosely coupled to the Mission Office and other sectors of the university

- Locally developed
- Supported by all sectors of the university

Structure and organization require discipline and commitment to carry initiatives forward. The MC should not be thought of as a club for social networking. In fact, an intentional community such as this should be characterized by communal prayer, reflection, contemplation, discussion, and retreats, along with its many outreach activities. Launching the MC will not happen in one fell swoop, but a distinctive spiritual dimension will provide the wellspring of strength and perseverance for discerning the future of Catholic higher education at each university. Drawing on the wisdom of the Lasallian experience worldwide, MCs must be locally grown, with a structure that admits of evolution and responsiveness to changing times.

A president or a board of trustees cannot require employees to be members of a Mission Community. Participants join freely, intentionally embracing the group, an embrace that goes beyond the usual obligations of administrators, faculty, and staff. Group strength is evident in the social capital[3] that the members bring to this community and in the leadership role to which they commit themselves. The Mission Community can also rely on the social capital of many other individuals who work at the university but who for one reason or another cannot, or choose not to, be active members. Social capital, in one sense, flows from the MC itself because it has a moral authority based on its members' commitment to the bedrock of the university's mission: the Catholic culture and religious heritage of the founding congregation. In fact, moral authority is more powerful than legislated or mandated authority because its inherent values are self-evident. By this authority, the MC addresses the university about its heart and soul because the former has taken up a call to preserve and enhance the university as a Catholic institution. Moral authority would evaporate only if the board of trustees and the founding congregation agreed to disassociate the university from the sponsorship of the Catholic Church and the congregation's religious heritage.

Question for Discussion

What might be the role of a Mission Community in your university?

Concretely, Where Is This Going?

While moral authority and social capital are critical to vitality and influence, an administrator will want some hard facts about the Mission Community. After all, the MC would not exist without the hands-on support of the president and other administrators, even though its power comes from a mandate that transcends individuals and administrations. The president can turn to the MC for support of the university's vision and mission, but there are financial costs involved. These costs result from the type of collaboration on which the president and the MC agree, and such collaboration will require a budget. In most cases there will be committees that will shoulder responsibilities for awards, book discussions, convocations and education programs, founder's week activities, lecture series, prayer services, RM programs, retreats, and student education. For almost all these undertakings, monetary support will be necessary. Of course, the MC will work closely with the Mission Office, which generally sponsors many of the above programs.

Indeed, the genesis of RM and the evolution of the Mission Community usually, though not necessarily, begin in the Mission Office. As a result, the Mission Office is frequently the university's official link with the Mission Community. By virtue of its link to the university, the MC should report regularly to the president or board on its work and submit a yearly report of its activities and finances that would be part of the university's public record.

The creation and design of a Web site displaying the vision, mission, and schedule of activities will be one of the first orders of business. Invitations welcoming all university employees should be front and center on the home page and sent as a general email reminder on a regular basis. To reiterate a point made earlier, there should be no rush to develop internal guidelines for the Mission Community. The above list of suggested activities will dictate their own need for meetings. It is the wisdom and accumulated experience of the group that will be the most important resource for determining when the Mission Community meets for group prayer, reflection, retreats, or discussion of journal articles and church or congregational documents, as well as dialogues with the founding congregation and the university administration or groups of faculty and staff. Eventually, patterns will appear and more formal guidelines will develop.

A "Loosely Coupled" Mission Community: Vision and Action

The particular form the MC takes will arise from the culture and heritage of the institution. As should already be evident, this essay does not present a precise blueprint for the structure and activities of the MC. However, the term "loosely coupled" requires further discussion. The membership of the Mission Community is "loosely coupled" in that its membership is open-ended, requiring neither specific qualifications nor a need to fit into preconceived university committee categories. In this period of transition, there is a need for freedom to think big thoughts guided by a transformational vision. Thus, these loosely coupled structures (LCSs) are a necessary condition for a Mission Community to develop.

However, an LCS is not just a necessary condition; it is synonymous with the Mission Community. An LCS allows an organization (the university) to continue its day-to-day work while the LCS addresses the transitional challenges associated with the institution and the new lay leadership in Catholic education. "[I]t could be argued that loosely coupled systems preserve many independent sensing elements and therefore 'know' their environments better than is true for more tightly coupled systems which have fewer externally constrained, independent elements" (Weick, 1976, p. 6).

Another advantage of an LCS is the flexibility for "localized adaptation." An LCS such as the Mission Community "potentially can retain a greater number of mutations and novel solutions than would be the case with a tightly coupled system. A loosely coupled system could preserve more 'cultural insurance' to be drawn upon in times of radical change than is the case for more tightly coupled systems" (Weick, 1976, p. 7). Remember also Panikkar's critique of routinized or institutionalized charisma. The Mission Community is well situated to assess this ever-present challenge. However, I do not want to give the impression that the Mission Community is self-contained or isolationist. Although it has a close relationship with the Mission Office, there will be myriad opportunities for the MC to work with other groups and committees on campus.

The Mission Community provides nonjuridical leadership through education and engagement with the university population. There is no doubt in my mind that a university has a responsibility to provide such leadership rooted in its Catholic culture and religious heritage. Carrying out the responsibility by means of an MC will vary from campus to campus, but a velvet glove rather than a heavy hand will carry the day. Demonstrations of civil discourse, common ground, and shared values characterize a vibrant organization such as a university. They set an important tone and reinforce the moral argument of moving the Catholic university through the twenty-first century, faithful to its past but committed to the future.

Mention of the student body is noticeably absent from the discussion thus far. This omission requires comment, because the students are the raison d'être of Catholic universities. The MC will certainly plan programs for the students, but my concern is not so much with those initiatives. The latter have less of an impact than the daily engagement of faculty and academic administrators with students in the classroom, service learning, collaborative research, office appointments, and informal discussions. The same is true of the day-to-day presence of student-life staff in residence halls and campus ministry, on the playing fields, and in service learning programs. If the MC has a strong influence in shaping the campus culture by working with these divisions of the university, the impact on the students will be pervasive and enduring. At the same time, I would not exclude students from a role in working with the MC through a parallel student group. Such groups already exist in one form or another on a variety of Catholic campuses (e.g. Lasallian Collegians). It will frequently be a question of making the connections between those groups and the Mission Community.

As a result, a dynamic living endowment of the founding con-gregation and lay partners attracted by and freely committed to a Mission Community becomes the guarantor, along with the board of trustees, of Catholic higher education's continuity into the future and its impact on students. However, implementation of this action plan will be fully realized through support by all sectors of the institu-tion, from the president's office, the board of trustees, the provost, and the academic deans and faculty to the student life office and athletic division, as well as the entire administrative and support staff of the university. This embrace does not presume that all the indi-viduals in these sectors are of like mind, interest, or commitment. That is not the point, nor would it ever happen, or even be desirable.

Questions for Discussion

- What seems to be the purpose of the Mission Community? How do you see yourself participating in or interacting with such a community on your campus?
- What are the benefits and challenges inherent in a Mission Community?
- How might a Mission Community affect the workings of a university or the work of an individual faculty member in your discipline?

Achieving RM Goals

The first RM goal has been accomplished by the participation of new hires in this orientation program, which has focused on edu-cating faculty about the building blocks of a Catholic university, primarily a cognitive goal. The second goal—offering the invita-tion to become a member of the Mission Community—is the more affective goal of the program. Ideally, the new faculty member moves from understanding the university mission into willingness to take responsibility for helping to assure the university's continu-ity well into the twenty-first century.

By the conclusion of this essay, the reader will have a better understanding of the challenges involved. Regardless of a decision about membership, each will have completed a journey through RM, and they are to be congratulated. These individuals have achieved the first goal: understanding. This in itself is no small achievement, as it will have a lasting effect on their view of Catholic higher education, their relationship with students, and their sense of collegiality with others. They will, moreover, have understood the larger context of Catholic higher education and will realize that they are part of an international education movement that is relational and student-centered by nature, hallowing the dignity of each person by fully embracing ethnic diversity and religious/nonreligious pluralism, possessing a vibrant intellectual heritage and life, and striving to enhance a robust and distinctive culture driven by an intentional community open to all.

In the following sections of the essay, I will discuss three topics that bear directly on the formation of a Mission Community: community and corporation, the Association movement, and a case study: *Associated for the Lasallian Mission . . . an act of HOPE.*

Question for Discussion

How would you explain the reality that your department and university exist in the larger context of Catholic higher education in the United States and globally? What are the some of the implications of being in that context?

Community and Corporation

The tension between community (association based on personal ties) and society (association based on contractual relations) endures in any complex, bureaucratic, rational organization. All the more does this complexity characterize a Catholic university, led by the professoriate, a cadre that "professes" to transcendent goals of student cognitive and affective development for the individual and for the common good of society.

Understanding the difference between community and society will lead to a study of the evolution of associations (lay-congregational partnerships) in Catholic education later in this essay.

Associates, or lay partners, are neither substitutes for religious congregations that may no longer staff the university, nor are they understudies for these religious men and women. They are equal partners in an enterprise that transcends corporate status. To reiterate an earlier point, not everyone will be or should be expected to be a part of the Mission Community. Membership in the Mission Community is not exclusionary on the part of the university; the choice is made by the participants themselves. It should also be obvious that the Mission Community cannot be equated with what is often referred to as the "university community."

Presidents and provosts, whether at Catholic universities or elsewhere, often use the word "community" when they speak about all those who make up the university—they might refer to a "student community" or a "faculty community" or the "university community." This usage suggests warmth and relatedness among all participants. However, the university is at the same time a legal entity, an education corporation with nonprofit status. Assumptions of equivalence between community and corporation (aka society) inevitably create misunderstandings and tensions, often pitting human relations over and against contractual obligations. Think of delicate tenure decisions or sensitive termination-of-service letters. Members of the "community" have legal status and standing; they are all employees, each person having a contract with rights and responsibilities in this bureaucratic, rational, goal-oriented organization.

I know from experience that faculty members usually perceive impersonal words such as "employee," "bureaucratic," "rational," and "organization" as "corporate," which is not an endearing category for professors, who also do not respond well to calling students "customers." While this tension between the communal and the corporate is real, it generally does not become conscious until conflict arises.

The distinction between community and society that Ferdinand Tönnies draws is helpful for our understanding of a Mission Community. He describes community as "all intimate, private, and exclusive living together" (Tönnies & Loomis, 1957, p. 34). This association is a *Gemeinschaft*, or, in English, "community." "[T]he domestic *Gemeinschaft*, or home life with its immeasurable influence upon the human soul, has been felt by everyone who has ever shared it" (Tönnies & Loomis, 1957, p. 34). He clearly distinguishes "community" from a word that had been used synonymously for it in German: *Gesellschaft* (society). At times we also confuse "community" and "society" in English. A community is alive, a "living organism," whereas a society is a "mechanical aggregate and artifact" (Tönnies & Loomis, 1957, p. 35). A *Gesellschaft* is "the artificial construction of an aggregate of human beings which superficially resembles a *Gemeinschaft*" (Tönnies & Loomis, 1957, p. 64). In the former, they are separate individuals. In the latter, they are united. In the *Gesellschaft* "everyone is by himself and isolated, and there exists a condition of tension against all others" (Tönnies & Loomis, 1957, p. 65). Individuals are linked to the university contractually, but not necessarily to one another in a department, division, or school of the institution. Given this stark distinction, one cannot expect a contractual relationship between, for example, a faculty member and the university to evolve automatically into the much more personally demanding Mission Community. When planning the establishment of a Mission Community, the director of the RM program should explain to all university personnel how the term "Mission Community" is being used. This could be done by email, a formal memo, or a series of conversations around the topic.

Tönnies's distinction between community and society is sharply drawn, an "ideal type." However, the Catholic university certainly does not fit the ideal type of either *Gemeinschaft* or *Gesellschaft*. Contractual obligations on the part of the university and the employees give a legal, organizational foundation to the modern, complex university, and in this sense it is a corporation, albeit a nonprofit one (Tönnies's "society"). What differentiates the Catholic university from the business corporation or other secular, bureaucratic organizations is the conviction that the students are children of God, endowed with an inherent dignity and therefore the primary motive for or focus of all university activities, even research. It follows from this conviction that all who work at the university share this same dignity and, by extension, so do all peoples in the global "community." This perception is the differentiating motive distinguishing the Catholic university from all institutions that are not religiously based. I do not say this to disparage the latter, but simply to call attention to contrasting motives concerning institutional relations with students and employees.

It is that singular belief in the dignity of God's creation that modifies any understanding of university-as-society in Tönnies's definition. As we have seen, the heart of Catholic education is relational and, as John Haughey (2009) points out, the work is ideally done with a transcendent horizon in view. Professors and students have rights and obligations, to be sure, but the faculty and the young men and women they teach understand that there is more to the classroom culture than following requirements in a syllabus (Astin, Astin, & Lindholm, 2011). This element of "more" is, I believe, the intangible Catholic culture and religious heritage that are palpable to so many on campus. It is the Catholic "fine mist" often experienced by faculty across the departments and schools of the university. Many administrators, staff, and other employees will speak of the same reality. Margaret O'Brien Steinfels, in discussing the Catholic intellectual life, has put it succinctly: "[These are institutions] where the person is at the center of our inquiry in a community where we love one another" (Steinfels, 1995, pp. 9–10).

The distinctiveness of Catholic education is exemplified by Palmer and Zajonc's (2010) *Heart of Higher Education*. As we have seen, their thesis is that education should be relational, that the subject matter and the faculty should "hook" the students. But I do not want to drift into ideal types. We are all aware that Catholic universities have their own share of lapses when students, administrators, faculty, staff, and others who work at these institutions are not treated well or fail to treat others as they should be treated. From a Catholic perspective, the effects of original sin are quite empirical and ever present. It is my contention that the Mission Community can play a central role in ensuring a distinctive and distinguished future for Catholic higher education by remaining faithful to its founding principles.

Questions for Discussion

- Based on your experience over the past year, how would you assess the tension between community and society at your university?
- What are the characteristics of the community at your university? What are its strengths and weaknesses, opportunities and challenges?

The Evolution of Association or Lay Partnerships

The presence of partners or associates in university mission communities is not unique in American Catholicism. There is a broader movement by many lay Catholics to become associates of religious communities. They do not intend to become members of the religious communities, but they find in these groups a spiritual home and an anchor for work in ministry. In 2000, the North American Conference of Associates and Religious (NACAR) sponsored a study of the associate movement conducted by the Center for Applied Research in the Apostolate (CARA):

> An important finding from the Study records 92% of associates making a formal commitment to live the mission and charism of the religious congregation and 94% renewing that commitment. These percentages are even higher in the poll of associates reported in 2002. This fact points up the realization that associates are becoming a stable arm of the religious congregations to which they commit. (O'Connell, 1999, p. 19)[4]

Sister Ellen O'Connell notes another important finding in the CARA report: "As time goes by, associates deepen in their desire to put their spirituality in action through ministry. Nine out of ten associates report their desire to serve others in ministry has increased since becoming an associate" (O'Connell, 1999, p. 19). Sister Cathy Schwemer, former executive director of NACAR, estimates that in 2010 there were 45,000 to 50,000 associates of religious communities in the United States, Canada, and Mexico (C. Schwemer, personal communication, November 29, 2010). The phenomenal growth of the associate movement is clearly a sign of the times, to be read carefully by the Church and by the mission officers in Catholic higher education.

In 1996, Pope John Paul II issued an Apostolic Exhortation, *Vita Consecrata*, a document meant to assist religious communities in addressing the question of identity. While the Pope notes that there are only two states in the Church—lay and clerical—"within the Church's lived experience, there are three: the lay, clerical, and religious states" (John Paul II, 1996, para. 60; Sammon, 2002, p. 33). While the Pope's (1996) words were of great help in clarifying the nature of religious life as a lived experience in the Church, a state of life complete in itself (para. 60), he also made clear that there is a common bond between the laity and religious brothers and sisters: the lay state (paras. 54–56). As a result, religious men and women in the United States and elsewhere face a daunting challenge: a redefinition of their identity in terms of mission, community, and spirituality, and in terms of their relationship with the laypersons who work with them in ways never dreamed of only a few decades ago.

Sean Sammon, writing in 2002, noted that there were 50 percent fewer religious in the United States than there had been in 1966 (p. 1). The following statistical chart details the further downward trend since the 1960s in virtually all categories, except for the recent slight increase in the number of priestly ordinations and graduate level seminarians and the continuous increase in the number of permanent deacons. For our purposes, it is important to note the ongoing slide in the number of Catholic elementary and secondary schools as well as the drop in student numbers. Catholic secondary schools have traditionally been feeder schools to Catholic universities. As all of these schools and the number of students continue to decline, they are having a long-term impact on the number of Catholic students entering Catholic tertiary institutions.

Table 1
Frequently Requested Church Statistics[a]

Table 1

Frequently Requested Church Statistics[a]

	1965	1975	1985	1995	2000	2005	2010
Total priests	58,632	58,909	57,317	49,054	45,699	42,839	39,993
Diocesan priests	35,925	36,005	35,052	32,349	30,607	28,702	27,182
Religious priests	22,707	22,904	22,265	16,705	15,092	14,137	12,811
Priestly ordinations	994	771	533	511	442	454	459
Graduate level semi-narians	8,325	5,279	4,063	3,172	3,474	3,308	3,483
Permanent deacons	n/a	898	7,204	10,932	12,378	14,574	16,649
Religious brothers	12,271	8,625	7,544	6,535	5,662	5,451	4,690
Religious sisters	179,954	135,225	115,386	90,809	79,814	68,634	57,544
Parishes	17,637	18,515	19,244	19,331	19,236	18,891	17,958
Without a resident priest pastor	549	702	1,051	2,161	2,843	3,251	3,400+
Where a bishop has entrusted the pastoral care of the parish to a deacon, religious sister or brother, or other lay-person (Canon 517.2)	n/a	n/a	93	314	447	553	517+
Catholic population	45.6m	48.7m	52.3m	57.4m	59.9m	64.8m	65.6m

Continued

Percent of U.S. population	24%	23%	23%	23%	22%	23%	21%
Catholic elementary schools	—	8,414	7,764	6,964	6,793	6,122	5,889*
Students in Catholic elementary schools	—	2.557m	2.005m	1.815m	1.800m	1.559m	1.508m*
Catholic secondary schools	—	1,624	1,425	1,280	1,297	1,325	1,205*
Students in Catholic secondary schools	—	884,181	774,216	638,440	653,723	653,226	611,723*
Mass Attendance CARA Catholic Poll (CCP): Percentage of U.S. adult Catholics who say they attended Mass once a week or more (i.e., those attending *every* week). For more background information on measurement, see: *The Nuances of Accurately Measuring Mass Attendance.*	—	—	—	—	22%	23%	22%

*Most recent estimates of the National Catholic Educational Association (NCEA). School data for previous years are from the Vatican's *Annuarium Statisticum Ecclesiae* (ASE).

+Data are for 2009.

Note. Courtesy of the Center for Applied Research in the Apostolate: *Catholic data, Catholic statistics, Catholic research.* Retrieved from the Center for Applied Research in the Apostolate Web site, http://cara.georgetown.edu/caraservices/requestedchurchstats.html

[a] The chart displays comparative statistics from 1965 to 2010. Generally, these data reflect the situation at the beginning of the calendar year listed. The sources for this information include *The Official Catholic Directory* (OCD), the Vatican's *Annuarium Statisticum Ecclesiae* (ASE), and other CARA (Center for Applied Research in the Apostolate) research reports and databases. All data are cross-checked to the extent possible. For the U.S., the numbers reported here include only figures for those 195 dioceses or eparchies that belong to the U.S. Conference of Catholic Bishops. This includes the 50 states, the District of Columbia, the U.S. Virgin Islands, and all U.S. military personnel stationed overseas.

This steep decline in priests, brothers, and sisters may be attributed in part to the unintended consequences and inherent contradictions already enumerated and the quest for a new sense of identity on the part of religious men and women. Regardless of the reasons, religious congregations, in the United States and in Western cultures more generally, face a critical period in which survival for some groups or severe diminution for others march in lockstep with the impetus to redefine identity (Schneiders, 2000, pp. 78–90). Robert D. Putnam (2000), writing about the decrease in community in the broader American context, echoes what has already been said about religious communities:

> For the first two-thirds of the twentieth
> century a powerful tide bore Americans
> into ever-deeper engagement in the life
> of their communities, but a few decades
> ago—silently, without warning—that
> tide reversed and we were overtaken
> by a treacherous rip current. Without
> at first noticing, we have been pulled

apart from one another and from our
communities over the last third of the
century.
(p. 27)[5]

Some observers of religious life may conclude that the steep decline in numbers has been the primary driving force behind the association movement in the United States. There is no doubt that the dramatic change in numbers has been a factor, but the universal call to holiness presented in *Lumen Gentium* must not be forgotten as the most significant motivator driving the association movement. As a result of the Council and research into the origins of their congregations, these groups realize that the universal call to holiness includes all of the baptized, many of whom have become close colleagues of and partners with brothers, sisters, and clerical religious, both in the apostolic work of their communities and in their spirituality and prayer life (Rummery, 2008). In a word, lay partners are not simply "tolerated." They are recognized as equal partners exercising their baptismal right and call to ministry within the church, as are lay partners from other Christian denominations. Lay partners of other religious or no religious persuasion should be understood from within their own circle of belief as doing good, following a call, or living out the universal archetype of the monk, the latter applying to the humanist as well (Schneiders, 2000).[6]

The spiritual life and apostolic ministry of religious communities in the United States are a beacon of hope and meaning to lay colleagues and to many men and women who have contact with these groups, giving direction to the lives of many lay Catholics as well as to the lives of other Christians, Jews, Muslims, Hindus, Buddhists, and even more diverse religious believers, as well as those who are of no religious belief.

However, partnership does not mean the extinction of religious life. Statistics are not the only benchmark in measuring the viability of consecrated life. The Black Death, the Reformation, and the French Revolution, devastating as they were, did not destroy religious life in Europe. There is no reason to think that Western culture today will accomplish that destruction, even though the eroding forces of that culture have affected religious life more deeply than any previous threat, precisely because the threat is deep within the secularizing culture in which religious men and women live, work, and are influenced by contemporary media, no matter how hard they work to avoid it.

Speaking more generally about Western society, Alasdair MacIntyre's (1981) oft-repeated words aptly describe the challenge that consecrated religious face: "This time, however, the barbarians are not waiting beyond the frontiers; they have already been governing us for quite some time. And it is our lack of consciousness of this that constitutes part of our predicament" (MacIntyre, 1981, p. 245). The threat, then, is profoundly internal, while the Black Death and French Revolution were much more external threats. (The Reformation threat, too, was external, but it was internal as well.)

Another point that must be recognized is that the large number of men and women who entered religious life in the 1950s and 1960s was a historical aberration and should not be used as a benchmark for the viability of religious communities today. That demographic upturn of five to six decades ago presents a skewed picture of religious life. Viability cannot be equated with numbers.

While laity and religious have formed a new partnership in association, the work of the Holy Spirit in directing the future of Catholic Christianity is an ongoing process. Catholic spirituality teaches that a person must assuredly cooperate with God's grace, but confidence in God's providence should lead Catholics to believe, as noted by Sammon, that "a new day is dawning" for religious life as such, especially in the United States. To reiterate a point made earlier: lay associates are not "substitutes" or "understudies" for religious men and women. Laypeople are well along in the process of becoming partners with religious communities, partners in the mission and in the spirituality that gives vitality and meaning to the work of Catholic higher education.

Thus, one might see the "signs of the times" as follows: the future of consecrated life will be driven by mission, community, and spirituality, but it will be a life integrally related to the same drive for mission, community, and spirituality on the part of lay-persons.[7] At the same time, lay partners are not necessarily Catholic, although "they may spend a part of their life sharing in community experiences and contributing to the richness of this way of life" (Dooley, 2003, p. 6). As a result, religious communities offer what parishes are so often lacking: adult religious development: "Life and faith, to be lived with integrity, as a whole, requires the capacity to see the connections and to make meaning from life experiences, including ministry; to come to know the experience of God more deeply in one's life" (Dooley, 2003, p. 7).

Is it surprising that the spiritual bedrock of consecrated religious and associates is the same? Not at all, if one accepts Panikkar's interpretation of the monastic archetype. Remember Rolheiser's (1999) insight that there is a "fundamental dis-ease within us, an unquenchable fire that renders us incapable, in this life, of ever coming to full peace" (p. 3). Spirituality is how persons respond to this "holy longing," whether one is a consecrated religious or a layperson, a devout Muslim or convinced atheist. Thus, because this fire within is primordial, spirituality is fundamental to our identity. As Rolheiser (1999) noted in the previous essay: "It is about being integrated or falling apart, about being within community or being lonely, about being in harmony with Mother Earth or being alienated from her . . . What shapes our actions is our spirituality" (p. 7). As we have seen in Essay Five, archetypes provide a means of understanding the Mission Community composed of religious and lay colleagues. As heuristic tools, they assist us in understanding the tensions and convergences of these two significant groups.

Echoing Panikkar, Schneiders (2000) concludes that the archetype

is a universal pattern or psychic
paradigm of spirituality that informs
the struggle toward full humanity of all
serious human seekers, whether or not
they become monastics in the formal

> institutional sense, and it is not specific
> to or limited within any particular
> religion or religious tradition.
> (pp. 6–7)[8]

We see the universality of the archetype of the monk playing out in the process of a layperson becoming a partner. He or she responds to fundamental issues in every person's life: Who am I (personal identity)? What am I/we here for (mission)? Who will accompany me in my quest for fulfillment (community)? How do I achieve the deepest possible peace given my "holy longing" (spirituality bound up with mission and community)?

Parker Palmer gives us another perspective on the common bedrock shared by religious or monastics and lay partners. It is a perspective that reinforces Ronald Rolheiser's (1999) "holy longing" (p. 7). Palmer (2000) notes:

> Our deepest calling is to grow into our
> own authentic selfhood . . . As we do so,
> we will not only find the joy that every
> human seeks—we will also find our
> path of authentic service in the world.
> True vocation joins self and service, as
> Frederick Buechner asserts when he
> defines vocation as "the place where
> your deep gladness meets the world's
> deep need."
> (p. 119)

Maintaining a collective identity is a challenge to partners, since the charism and founding of a religious community, in its origins, gave rise to a clearly identifiable, homogeneous group, such as the Sisters of Mercy or the Dominican fathers, brothers, and sisters. However, to take the example of the De La Salle Christian Brothers, who have worked on the partnering issue since the 1960s, one sees the unfolding of heterogeneous lay partnering:

"As this is reinterpreted in the framework of the Church/Communion and even in the context of ecumenism, based on other life situations, it has given rise to diverse Lasallian identities, all of which are recognizable as coming from the same, common family stock" (Botana, 2003, p. 15). A "multi-Lasallian identity" is giving rise to a new charism emerging from the deep story of Lasallian origins. Substitute "Benedictine," "Franciscan," or "Jesuit" for "Lasallian" with the same results. Such an evolution is life-giving, but it is also anxiety-provoking, a movement into unchartered territory, much as Abraham faced in leaving Haran for the land to which God would lead him (Genesis 12). Remember De La Salle's startling revelation about himself:

> It was undoubtedly for this reason that
> God, who guides all things with wisdom
> and serenity, whose way it is not to force
> the inclinations of persons, willed to
> commit me entirely to the development
> of the schools. God did this in an
> imperceptible way and over a long
> period of time, so that one commitment
> led to another in a way I did not foresee
> in the beginning.
> (Blain & Arnandez, 2000, p. 80)

A Case in Point: *Associated for the Lasallian Mission . . . an act of HOPE*

Let us consider again the De La Salle Christian Brothers and their pioneering work in restructuring Lasallian higher education globally. The evolution of religious-lay partnership or association in the Christian Brothers has been developing for some fifty years, providing a case study for the associative or lay partnering movement in Catholic education.

We will give special attention to a landmark document that affirms and clarifies the Lasallian Education Movement's aspirations: *Associated for the Lasallian Mission . . . an act of HOPE* (ALM). This circular, written by the Superior and the General Council of the Christian Brothers (2010), is an important milestone in the evolution of the Lasallian associative movement, and a central concept in the meaning of "Lasallian."

I will use the circular ALM as a way to illustrate how other Catholic universities could proceed in their quest for continuity of culture and heritage. Of course, change in a university's or a community's foundational culture cannot occur quickly; implementing the essential concepts in the document will take many years of ongoing discernment, the never-ending process of seeking to understand what God is asking of each of us. There are also many contingent factors beyond the control of universities that will affect the future of ALM and similar movements aimed at continuity in Catholic education. Among these factors are American and global financial instability, the continuing downward trend in congregational membership in the United States, a steady reduction in the pool of students from Catholic secondary schools, an increase in students who are unchurched or have no religious affiliation, and tension between tuition increases and service to first-generation students, as well as leadership and faculty candidates with little background in Catholic higher education. However, collegial conversation on campus among all parties—administrators, faculty, staff, and the founding congregation—will keep the focus on continuity in bringing culture and heritage into the construction of the Mission Community.

ALM is but one example of the evolution of the Mission Community. This circular letter makes it even clearer that laypeople are the key to the continuity of robust Catholic higher education in the United States and elsewhere.

Circular number 461, *Associated for the Lasallian Mission . . . an act of HOPE,* addresses "what it means in today's world to serve 'together and by association' in the Lasallian educational mission of providing a human and Christian education to the young, especially those who are poor" (Brothers of the Christian Schools, 2010, para. 1.3). The following sections highlight significant points in the circular.

Association Guidelines: Not So Fast

Each university has much to learn from other institutions and their founding groups. The emphasis on association within the Christian Brothers is a case in point. They are in no hurry to prescribe a structure of association for lay colleagues, even though association is fundamental to the Lasallian charism. "We chose not to curtail but rather to fan into flame the work of the Spirit as new forms of association emerge and develop" (Brothers of the Christian Schools, 2010, para.1.3). This is the same methodology Saint John Baptist de La Salle used in the earliest years of the foundation. He was in no hurry to have his first followers become a religious congregation, which did not happen until 1725, more than four decades after the founding and six years after the De La Salle's death.

Institutionalization within the structure of the Catholic Church brought a great deal of conformity and supported the eventual routinization of the founding charism. Routinization is not the issue today. The De La Salle Christian Brothers and their lay colleagues view the heritage of John Baptist de La Salle as providing the impetus for a gradual evolution into many Lasallian Mission Communities. In this transformation of "together and by association" (Brothers and lay partners), Brother Alvero emphasizes "unity in diversity" and "response and flexibility." This emphasis reveals itself in respect for the dignity of each person, the foundation of Lasallian education. The results of such respect is evident in the local situation in eighty countries among the 79,000 multiethnic and multireligious lay partners, and a similar mix of more than 800,000 students on all levels of education (Brothers of the Christian Schools, 2010, para.1.12).

The principle of subsidiarity is another important criterion for developing association ((Brothers of the Christian Schools, 2010, para. 1.15.1). Subsidiarity "refers to the principle in Roman Catholic social teaching that favors decision making and responsible social action at the lowest feasible level" (Ford, 2006, p. 179).

The present essay began with a quote from Sandra Schneiders, of which the most important insight for our present purposes is: "A truly lay spirituality must emerge from lay experience, be constructed on lay premises, develop lay leadership, and promote a kind of personal practice and ministerial involvement that is compatible with and truly transformative of lay life." Brother John Johnston (2000), Superior, in his Pastoral Letter, expresses a similar point of view: "We need to welcome enthusiastically those who wish to become Lasallian Associates and help them create new ways of living the Lasallian charism. They themselves, however, must be the protagonists in this search" (p. 25). Once more, I refer the reader to Essay Three on the spiritual journey, which affirms that a deepening of personal and group spirituality comes about through stages of commitment, not all at once. It is a process of discernment, of seeking. Spirituality is developmental; progress comes, as De La Salle would say, "one step at a time."

Schneiders and Johnston both present significant challenges to laypersons who wish to collaborate with religious congregations. Authenticity must be the foundation for partnership. Will it be difficult to create these "new ways of living the Lasallian charism"? It would appear not, given Salm's understanding of the beginnings of the congregation: "The exclusively lay character of De La Salle's Institute demonstrates the authenticity and effectiveness of a lay ministry and a lay spirituality in the Church." Authenticity and effectiveness were also coupled with a worldview that is Lasallian to the core, centered on rereading reality:

> John Baptist de La Salle ingrained
> [rereading reality] in us and we find
> it continually throughout the last
> three centuries . . . [His] priestly
> concern developed within him a great
> attentiveness to situations and events
> and a pertinent imagination to carry out
> specific choices . . .
> (Brothers of the Christian Schools,
> 2002, p. 22)

The current enthusiasm for expanding association to include lay partnering has resulted in heightened sensitivity on the part of some Brothers concerning the very use of the term "association" in such a context. They have an institutional memory and heritage wherein "association" is "hallowed" because it is who they are and is, in fact, the first of the vows of religion that each Brother professes. Luke Salm offers an important insight as to whether this new usage of "association" is leading to a clear differentiation between the vowed life and that of lay associates. It is a differentiation that speaks to much that is in common among the Brothers and their brothers and sisters, all of whom are associated "for the mission of education in the service of the poor":

> It is not the "material content" of the vows that constitute identity. After all, many laypersons are poor and find it harder sometimes than the Brothers to make ends meet, some are celibate, and most live under structures of obedience in the workplace and in the home. If poverty, chastity, and obedience can be shared, so also can association for the Lasallian mission, Lasallian spirituality and even community on occasion. But the primary reference and lifestyle for the vowed Brothers lies in his association in community; for the lay associates, the primary referent remains the family or other such associations. (Salm, 2007, p. 4)

As the 43rd General Chapter (2000) clearly mandated, the Brothers of the Christian Schools have initiated a new phase in their apostolic work. This new phase is a comprehensive reinterpretation of their educational mission—a reinterpretation begun, to a great extent, as a result of the Second Vatican Council (1962–65). It was the Council that called all religious congregations to a renewal of identity and mission by rediscovering their founder's charism (Lundy, 2003).

Reaching a Tipping Point in Circular 461: *Associated for the Lasallian Mission . . . an act of HOPE*

Brother Antonio Botana notes that "the General Chapter [2000] suggests in Recommendation 4 that 'the formation of Brothers and Partners be a priority in the Institute over the next seven years'" (Brothers of the Christian Schools, 2000, p. 17). Botana (2003) also states that "at times of transition it is much more important to facilitate motivation and formation of persons—Brothers and laypeople—than to organize structures which 'give the impression' that everything is going well" (p. 11). The work must undoubtedly give rise to structures, but the latter must be built on the solid foundation of motivation and formation. As a result, there will be a good fit between the individuals and the structures they develop. Brother Michel Sauvage reinforces this tentativeness in his discussion of the 1691 vow of association and union, a vow that "outlined a precise plan but not a rigid one. It did not impose defined obligations that simply had to be observed; in this way it expressed fidelity as a search to be carried out rather than a heritage to be passed on" (Brothers of the Christian Schools, 2010, para. 1.6).

Consequently, in this work of moving into an unknown future, there are two passages. The first is from what Sauvage calls the "heritage" of the founding group to a new era. The new era, a liminal phase, is that of transition itself, one characterized by fidelity, but one in which uncertainty, tentativeness, experimentation, fluidity, even backtracking, are done in a spirit of discernment and trust in God. It is a trying period and not for the faint of heart. Yet "transition" clearly has biblical roots as seen in God's call to Abraham, to the prophets, and to Jesus' disciples. In this there are two tensions: uncertainty and trust.

The second passage is from transition to transformation. Still present, however, are the lack of certitude and the need for trust. This is so because I do not believe the second passage to transformation is ever fully completed in any finite work of God, except in the Resurrection of Christ and the realization of the kingdom in the Second Coming. Transformation to a new way of seeing, of acting, and being in community constitute a new charism built on the older one, but once transformation appears to be realized, the "routinization clock" begins ticking. Routinization, with its feelings of security, comfort, and amnesia about the profundity of transformation, results in a new "tradition" and calls for new passages of transition and transformation. Even though I have discussed heritage, transition, and transformation in theological language, I believe that the basic insight about never-ending trans- formation makes sense to individuals in higher education. In a secular institution as in a Catholic one, transformation is always a process, never fully concluded. The moment it is perceived as completed, the process of transition and transformation, built on the heritage, must begin again, because routinization begins to set in almost immediately.

While a permanent structure for lay leadership in Lasallian higher education has not yet been approved, associations of administrators, faculty, and staff are forming the current practice of association.[9] The core group is such that it seeks to expand its influence through widening circles of support among other com- mitted Catholics, Christians, Jews, Muslims, Hindus, and practic- ing adherents of other faiths or of humanism who are also sup- portive of the Lasallian Education Movement.

ALM further directs that warm relationships and good com- munication should be sought with those who are not strongly com- mitted to this vision but who are committed to higher education as more broadly conceived. At the same time, significant efforts must be made to communicate with those who are indifferent to this view of the future. ALM reiterates an early point that was made concerning those who take exception to a focus on mission. Great charity and openness should also characterize relationships with faculty who take exception to a Lasallian worldview or who are openly hostile to the creation of a Lasallian culture on campus. It is also necessary to maintain a clear relationship between the Lasallian Education Movement and Catholicism, its ecclesial foun- dation and spiritual wellspring.

Because it receives its mandate or mission from the Catholic Church, the Lasallian Education Movement is organically connected to it. However, in light of the Second Vatican Council and subsequent interpretations, Catholicism is understood in a new context. Thus, ALM, chapter 1, section 1.12, notes three important perspectives on the Church:

> 1. The Church is "the people of God," not "the perfect society" whose hierarchical functioning assures everything needed for subsisting and fulfilling its mission. The Church is a "communion," a "community of communities" (diocesan and local). The Church is a sign and a sacrament in human history of the loving and just relationships that Jesus Christ lives and prays for and that the Spirit endlessly inspires (see *Lumen Gentium*, Chapter 5, "The Universal Call to Holiness in the Church").
> 2. Everyone who is baptized in the Spirit has equal dignity and is called to holiness.
> 3. The Spirit invites all baptized people, according to their state of life and their personal vocation, to participate in the Church's evangelizing mission and bestows on them the charisms necessary to serve the common good.

Contemporaneous with this renewed understanding of the Church and its members, religious congregations and clergy began a downward demographic trend, yet the Lasallian Education movement has grown significantly.

> While the number of Brothers declines,
> the number of young people served
> by Lasallian educational institutions
> increases. For example, the total in
> 1966 was 16,824 Brothers and 737,112
> students, but in 2009, the statistics are
> 4,883 Brothers and 857,819 young
> people served. There are today 2,117
> Brothers actively involved in the mission
> along with 677 priests and other
> religious [and] 76,310 other Lasallians

> [of whom] 39,203 are women and
> 37,107 are men.
> (Brothers of the Christian Schools,
> 2010, para. 1.13)

What is especially of note is the number of women working in Lasallian schools. The circular highlights the important contribution they make, and not simply because many schools are now coeducational. Their participation is essential:

> [The women's] presence, undoubtedly,
> will help to construct a more humane
> and community-centered society; help
> to reexamine ways of thinking; help
> to situate the entire Lasallian world a
> bit differently in history; and help to
> organize social, political, economic and
> religious life in a way that can be more
> intuitive and relational. Once again the
> founding story continues to be lived out
> anew . . . continues to move from crisis
> to crossroads; from discouragement to
> hope.
> (Brothers of the Christian Schools,
> 2010, para. 1.14)

The reader will note that there is no explicit mention of persons committed to other faith traditions or of no religious faith in the three perspectives on the Church that ALM lists. Although the congregation itself is closely linked to the Church, this does not mean the mission is exclusively Catholic. After all, the 76,310 laypeople are not all Catholic, yet they are all integral to the congregation's mission. The entire document, the work of the Brothers, and the results of the Council make for a new and capacious understanding of the Lasallian Education Mission. Among the Council documents that collectively have influenced virtually all religious congregations are the *Decree on Ecumenism* (*Unitatis Redintegratio*, 1964), the *Decree on the Relation of the Church to Non-Christian Religions* (*Nostra Aetate*, 1965), the *Declaration on Religious Freedom* (*Dignitatis Humanae*, 1965), the *Decree on the Mission Activity of the Church* (*Ad Gentes*, 1965), and the *Pastoral Constitution on the Church in the Modern World* (*Gaudium et Spes*, 1965).[10] Their impact is evident throughout ALM.

"Association" is the term of choice to understand the evolution of the De La Salle Christian Brothers, but it is a term that applies to developments in many religious congregations. While not all those in Lasallian higher education participate in association as described in this book, it is imperative that there be "an attitude of respect, patience and constant invitation that encourages unity in diversity" (Brothers of the Christian Schools, 2010, para. 1.23).

"Constant invitation" requires some comment. No one likes to be hounded, and if continued invitation begins to be experienced as pressure, there will be a total disconnect on the part of the invitee. I am sure that ALM does not intend this type of welcome, but rather wishes to communicate in a sensitive way so that the administration, faculty, and staff know that there is "no secret door to knock on" or any preconditions—that all persons, from diverse ethnic and religious backgrounds or of humanist persuasion, are welcome as equals and bring a new perspective to Lasallian association.

The conviction that Lasallian Association is evolutionary can be seen in its five fundamental elements that "identify the experience of Lasallian association and promote unity in the ongoing, dynamic process of association across the Institute's Districts and Regions" (Brothers of the Christian Schools, 2010, para. 2.1).

1. **"Association exists for the mission."** Associating together has no other raison d'être than human and Christian education through evangelization of young people, especially the poor (Brothers of the Christian Schools, 2010, para. 2.2). At the same time, some Lasallians educate students from many classes of society, including the wealthy, but these teachers have obligations to the poor as well. "An effort should be made to be more concerned that these centers

are teaching a doctrine of social justice focused on systemic change and empirically offering all students an opportunity to 'know' and serve the poor and marginalized" (Brothers of the Christian Schools, 2010, para. 2.2.4).

2. **Association is concrete.** It means "being a member of a community for the mission" (Brothers of the Christian Schools, 2010, para. 2.3). Associates bring their own personal and community life experiences, and both are significant dimensions of the role they play in the lives of students. What speaks most loudly is their ethical behavior and the relationships they build with the students. All of this must take place in a culture of hospitality, peace, and radical respect for each person (Brothers of the Christian Schools, 2010, para. 2.3.1).

3. **Association is experiential, a dynamic journey.** "Association is a gift given and not a status attained." It is a "calling" that transcends a "job" or a "career." Calling could be understood as Rolheiser's "holy longing," but calling may also be a mystery coming from deep within the person and with no religious overtones. Once a person is called, formation and community are critical elements to bring the calling to full fruition (Brothers of the Christian Schools, 2010, para. 2.4.7).

4. **"Association stems from the awareness through faith** of receiving a vocation that combines personal and social aspects of the individual's own life" (Brothers of the Christian Schools, 2010, para. 2.5). Authentic calling is always for the common good, but not everyone understands calling "through faith," especially when Lasallian association casts a global net. Likewise, not everyone understands their work as "building the Kingdom of God." Some associates may be secular humanists motivated by a deep commitment to human rights and social justice and yet identify as Lasallians. Sensitivity is fundamental to any discussion of vocation, faith, and the Kingdom of God.

5. **"Association presupposes a freely made commitment** for a determined period of time, which might also include

a position of official responsibility for certain aspects of the mission" (Brothers of the Christian Schools, 2010, para. 2.6). Commitment is "one of the most challenged and affected concepts [in contemporary culture]" (Brothers of the Christian Schools, 2010, para. 2.7). Lasallian association presents an opportunity for an associate to personally address this issue.

Given the diverse membership of a mission community, non-residential forms of community offer another opportunity for the religious and lay members to associate for mission. These communities are central to any consideration of Mission Communities, regardless of the founding congregation. They have the following characteristics, which are applicable to a wide variety of universities, wherein these communities:

1. meet on a regular basis.
2. organize around the central Institute values of faith, service, and community.
3. act locally, "together and by association," while recognizing close ties with the District, the Region, and the Institute (Brothers of the Christian Schools, 2010, para. 6.10).

Reaffirming the faith of John Baptist de La Salle and his way of doing things, the circular notes "that these groups will evolve naturally and at their own pace" (Brothers of the Christian Schools, 2010, para. 6.10). Forward movement—"unity in diversity"—is the main concern. With regard to the formation of those interested in joining a Mission Community, the document notes that formation is absolutely necessary but does not in itself guarantee internalization. "Effective formation is rooted in the experience of a community of learners" (Brothers of the Christian Schools, 2010, para. 6.11). This is precisely the expectation discussed in the introductory essay on the Faculty Learning Community.

Brother Gerard Rummery, FSC, offers an important closing insight through his reflections on the importance that the first Brothers gave to the title "Brother," whereby they united community and mission as one reality:

When our great researcher Brother
Maurice-Auguste presented his
interpretation of HOW and WHY De
La Salle's first teachers chose to call
themselves "Brothers" . . . he would
always pause in his text to point out
that although the words Frere, Frater,
Friar, etc. were used in various religious
congregations to describe a form of
common membership, what was unique
about the choice of the word by DLS's
followers was the CONTENT which was
given: *brothers to one another* [like monks,
friars, etc.,] but also *brothers to the young
people confided to us* by God [something
completely new because it linked their
state and their mission inseparably].
Maurice would then say, *"This is the
anthropological cornerstone on which De La
Salle's vision is founded because it can be
realized only within a COMMUNITY"*...
My reflection on the fact that the
Lasallian vision of education today
has crossed boundaries of language,
religion, race, culture and gender is that
it has done so because its foundation is
anthropological.
(G. Rummery, personal communication,
June 28, 2011)

Building on Brother Maurice-Auguste's insight into the unity
of community and mission as "the anthropological cornerstone of
the founder's vision," I would extend the latter's vision of community to include the many lay partners whom the Christian Brothers
(vowed laypersons) relate to as their brothers and sisters. It is my
belief that the dynamic growth in the Lasallian Education Move-

ment has come about because its anthropological cornerstone is the same as the one on which De La Salle's vision is founded. In other words, the Lasallian Education Movement consists of brothers (some of whom are vowed) and sisters to one another and to young people. Mission and identity are united in community. Together and by association—in community—is the only way this group can function together and carry out its mission. In fact, teaching in and through community is the only way education will succeed. Lasallian education is dynamic and relevant because it has this anthropological cornerstone, *community*, a word with deep significance for this movement. I would venture that this cornerstone is one that is needed in Catholic higher education itself.

Questions for Discussion

- What is the relevance of *Associated for the Lasallian Mission* to you and to your university?
- For the Lasallian Brothers, community and mission are inseparably linked. What are the implications of uniting community and mission for lay partners? Will doing this give the Mission Community a greater or lesser chance for success? How does this idea of the Mission Community affect your role at this university?
- What interest does the Mission Community hold for you? Do you feel inclined to join it? Why have you come to that conclusion?
- After reading the section on ALM, what do you see as the opportunities and challenges in developing a Mission Community on your campus?

Conclusion

Ending this essay with an emphasis on formation should strike a chord with those who have participated in the RM program. They have experienced a type of formation by achieving the first goal of the program: cognitive understanding of Catholic higher education. Formation will continue for those who accept the invitation to join the Mission Community, but acceptance will be more of an ongoing process of reflection, discernment, and discussion with members of the founding congregation and other lay partners in the Mission Community. No doubt there will be future meetings, programs, and retreats during which the participants will learn more and have the opportunity for greater personal reflection. Personal reflection and effective formation, that which is "rooted in the experience of a community of learners," will, I believe, provide the best means of assuring a vibrant Mission Community and future for Catholic higher education.

References

Astin, A. W., Astin, H. S., & Lindholm, J. A. (2011). *Cultivating the spirit: How college can enhance students' inner lives.* San Francisco, CA: Jossey-Bass.

Benne, R. (2001). *Quality with soul: How six premier colleges and universities keep faith with their religious traditions.* Grand Rapids, MI: W. B. Eerdmans.

Blain, J. B., & Arnandez, R. (2000). *The life of John Baptist de La Salle, founder of the Brothers of the Christian Schools.* Romeoville, IL: Lasallian Publications.

Botana, A. (2003). Lasallian association: The ongoing story. *MEL Bulletin*, 2. Retrieved from http://www.lasalle2.org/English/Resources/Publications/PDF/Association/Botana-Lasallian%20Association-The%20Ongoing%20Story.rtf

Brothers of the Christian Schools. (2000). The documents of the 43rd general chapter. *Circular 447*. Rome, Italy: General Council of the Brothers of the Christian Schools. Retrieved from http://www.lasalle2.org/English/Resources/Publications/repu.php

Brothers of the Christian Schools. (2002). In view of 2006: The International Lasallian Educational Mission Assembly. *MEL Bulletin*, 1. Retrieved from http://www.lasalle.org/media/pdf/mel/cahier_mel/01cahier_mel_en.pdf

Brothers of the Christian Schools. (2010). *Associated for the Lasallian Mission . . . an act of HOPE* (ALM). Retrieved from http://www.lasalle.org/media/pdf/circulares/461_circ_en.pdf

Catholic Church, John Paul II, & United States Catholic Conference. (1996). *The consecrated life: Vita consecrata; post-synodal apostolic exhortation Vita Consecrata of the Holy Father John Paul II to the bishops and clergy, religious orders and congregations, societies of apostolic life, secular institutes and all the faithful on the consecrated life and its mission in the Church and in the world.* Boston, MA: Pauline Books & Media.

Dooley, A. (2003). Formation and lay partnership. *The Associate,* 8(1).

Ford, J. T. (2006). *Saint Mary's Press glossary of theological terms.* Winona, MN: Saint Mary's Press.

Haughey, J. C. (2009). *Where is knowing going? The horizons of the knowing subject.* Washington, DC: Georgetown University Press.

Johnston, John. (2000). The challenge: Live today our founding story. *Pastoral Letter.* Retrieved from http://www.lasalle2.org/English/Resources/Publications/CD.php

Lundy, D. (2003). How did St. John Baptist de La Salle see the vocation and mission of the Christian teacher? *Lasallian studies: A study guide to the educational and catechetical heritage.* Buttimer Institute, June 30–July 19, 90–93.

MacIntyre, A. C. (1981). *After virtue: A study in moral theory.* Notre Dame, IN: University of Notre Dame Press.

O'Connell, E. R. (1999). The North American Conference of Associates and Religious: A companion for the journey. *The Associate, 4*(1), 19.

Palmer, P. J. (2000). *Let your life speak: Listening for the voice of vocation.* San Francisco, CA: Jossey-Bass.

Palmer, P. J., Zajonc, A., & Scribner, M. (2010). *The heart of higher education: A call to renewal.* San Francisco, CA: Jossey-Bass.

Putnam, R. D. (2000). *Bowling alone: The collapse and revival of American community.* New York, NY: Simon & Schuster.

Rolheiser, R. (1999). *The holy longing: The search for a Christian spirituality.* New York, NY: Doubleday.

Rummery, G. (2008). A religious teaching congregation encounters the great religions. *Rivista Lasalliana, 75*(1), pp. 91–100. Rome, Italy: Brothers of the Christian Schools.

Salm, L. (2007). Lasallian association and the vow: Lasallian association; experiences and reflections. Retrieved from http://www.lasalle2.org/English/Resources/Publications/PDF/Association/Salm-Lasallian%20Association%20and%20the%20Vow.pdf

Sammon, S. D. (2002). *Religious life in America: A new day dawning.* New York, NY: Alba House.

Schneiders, S. M. (2000). *Finding the treasure: Locating Catholic religious life in a new ecclesial and cultural context.* New York, NY: Paulist Press.

Steinfels, M. O'B., Association of Catholic Colleges and Universities & University of St. Thomas. (1995). *Catholic higher education: Practice and promise, diverse expressions of Catholic identity.* Washington, DC: Association of Catholic Colleges and Universities.

The documents of Vatican II. (1996) Abbot, Walter M. & Gallagher, Joseph, (Eds). New York, NY: Guild Press. Retrieved from www.vatican.va/archive/hist_councils/ii_vatican.../index.htm.

Tönnies, F., & Loomis, C. P. (1957). *Community and society (Gemeinschaft und Gesellschaft).* East Lansing, MI: Michigan State University Press.

Weick, K. E. (1976). Educational organizations as loosely coupled systems. *Administrative Science Quarterly, 21*(1), 1–19.

Recommended Reading

Kramer, K.T. (2008). Blessed interruptions. *America, 199*(6), 28–30.

Notes

[1] "Mission" in this context signifies the university's statement of purpose and outcomes sought, as articulated in its catalog, on its Web site, or in other official documents.

[2] A "circular" is a letter sent to the Brothers and/or laypersons by the Brother Superior and the General Council on a topic such as association.

[3] The central premise of the social capital concept is that social networks have value. "Social capital" refers to the collective value of all "social networks" (whom people know) and the inclinations that arise from these networks to do things for each other ("norms of reciprocity"). The term "social capital" implies not just warm feelings, but a wide variety of quite specific benefits that flow from the trust, reciprocity, information, and cooperation associated with social networks. Social capital creates value for the people who are connected and—at least sometimes—for bystanders as well. For more information see Better Together: An initiative of the Saguaro seminar: Civic engagement in America. Retrieved from Harvard University's Kennedy School of Government Web site http://www.bettertogether.org/socialcapital.htm

[4] The studies were conducted by the Center for Applied Research in the Apostolate: *The associate-vowed relationship in the United States, part I* (2000) and *Partners in mission: A profile of associates and religious in the United States, part II* (2002). Available on the Web at nacar.org or from NACAR Associate Office 5900 Delhi Road, Mount St. Joseph, OH 45051, 253-256-2227 (253-25-NACAR).

[5] Putnam's graphic demonstration of the rapid decrease of membership in a broad cross section of voluntary associations during the 1960s provides a much-needed context for addressing the precipitous drop in membership among religious congregations.

[6] On the universality of religious life, see Schneiders, Religious life as a human phenomenon among the world's religious: Monastics, virgins, virtuosi, in *Finding the Treasure*, pp. 3–40.

[7] Sammon stresses two points: "In the first place, no matter its past or future form, apostolic religious life will always be marked by three distinct characteristics: ministry, community, and spirituality. Secondly, consecrated life, in any form whatsoever, must be worth the gift of one's life" (Sammon, 2002, p. xii).

[8] Schneiders relies on Raimundo Panikkar's archetype of the monk in her commentary on religious life.

[9] On this point see Part 3: Strategies for maintenance and renewal (pp. 177–214), in Benne, R. (2001). *Quality with soul: How six premier colleges and universities keep faith with their religious traditions.* Grand Rapids, MI: W. B. Eerdmans.

[10] See Walter M. Abbott, SJ, general editor, *The documents of Vatican II* (New York, NY: Guild Press, 1966). See also www.vatican.va/archive/hist_councils/ii_vatican.../index.htm.

ABOUT THE AUTHORS

John Richard Wilcox is professor emeritus of religious studies at Manhattan College, Bronx, New York. He holds a Ph.D. in Christian Ethics from Union Theological Seminary, NYC. Wilcox taught in the religious studies program at Manhattan College for twenty-nine years. He served as departmental chair from 1994 to 2002. From 2002 to 2010, he was the first vice president for mission at Manhattan and, most recently, director of the center for Lasallian studies. Wilcox has focused his attention on raising the consciousness level of the Manhattan community concerning the Catholic culture and religious heritage of the founding congregation (the De La Salle Christian Brothers). Through Lasallian luncheons, lectures, convocations, seminars, and recruitment for Lasallian education programs, he developed cadres of dedicated administrators, faculty, and staff committed to the future of Catholic higher education. He is the creator of the International Lasallian University Leadership Program held in Rome each year for Lasallian university educators worldwide. Presently, he is professorial lecturer at Manhattan College and engaged nationally in higher-education projects related to the Catholic culture and religious heritage of founding congregations. John may be contacted at john.wilcox@manhattan.edu.

Jennifer Anne Lindholm is UCLA's accreditation coordinator and special assistant to the vice provost for undergraduate education and holds a Ph.D. from UCLA. From 2001 to 2006, she served as associate director of the Cooperative Institutional Research

Program at UCLA's Higher Education Research Institute and director of the Institute's Triennial National Faculty Survey. Her scholarship focuses on the structural and cultural dimensions of academic work; the career development, work experiences, and professional behavior of college and university faculty; issues related to institutional change; and undergraduate students' personal development.

Jennifer may be contacted at JLindholm@college.ucla.edu.

Suzanne Dale Wilcox serves as spiritual director for individuals, groups, and retreats. She holds the doctorate in educational administration from Teachers College, Columbia University. Her career in higher education included serving as grants officer (facilitating and supporting faculty research and development) in the City University of New York. At Iona College, Suzanne was associate dean in the College of Arts and Science, taking on similar responsibilities in fostering faculty growth. At the University of Bridgeport, she was vice provost and then vice president for admissions and financial aid. Suzanne's training as a spiritual director was through the Shalem Institute for Spiritual Formation. She is a member of Spiritual Directors International and brings to the chapter on the spiritual journey an interest in the interior life and in the continuous growth of adults. Suzanne may be contacted at sdalewilcox@snet.net.

Made in the USA
Middletown, DE
23 May 2015